The Frankfurt Kabuff Critical Edition

THE FRANKFURT KABUFF

CRITICAL EDITION

BETH DRISCOLL

AND

CLAIRE SQUIRES

WILFRID LAURIER UNIVERSITY PRESS

KABUFF BOOKS

This book has been published with the help of a grant from the Canadian Federation for the Humanities and Social Sciences, through the Awards to Scholarly Publications Program, using funds provided by the Social Sciences and Humanities Research Council of Canada. Wilfrid Laurier University Press acknowledges the support of the Canada Council for the Arts for our publishing program. We acknowledge the financial support of the Government of Canada through the Canada Book Fund for our publishing activities. Funding provided by the Government of Ontario and the Ontario Arts Council. This work was supported by the Research Support Fund.

Library and Archives Canada Cataloguing in Publication

Title: The Frankfurt Kabuff critical edition / Beth Driscoll and Claire Squires [editors].
Names: Driscoll, Beth, editor, author. | Squires, Claire, editor, author. | Container of (work): Squiscoll, Blaire. Frankfurt Kabuff.
Description: Includes bibliographical references and index.
Identifiers: Canadiana (print) 20230198449 | Canadiana (ebook) 20230206174 | ISBN 9781771125987 (softcover) | ISBN 9781771125994 (EPUB) | ISBN 9781771126007 (PDF)
Subjects: LCSH: Squiscoll, Blaire. Frankfurt Kabuff. | LCSH: Driscoll, Beth—Criticism and interpretation. | LCSH: Squires, Claire—Criticism and interpretation. | LCSH: Publishers and publishing in literature. | LCSH: Australian fiction—21st century—History and criticism. | LCSH: English fiction—21st century—History and criticism. | LCGFT: Novellas. | LCGFT: Satirical literature. | LCGFT: Literary criticism.
Classification: LCC PR9619.4.S68 F73 2023 | DDC 823/.92—dc23

Cover and interior design by Michel Vrana.
Front cover image iStockphoto.com

Waterloo, Ontario, Canada
www.wlupress.wlu.ca

This book is printed on FSC® certified paper. It contains recycled materials and other controlled sources, is processed chlorine-free, and is manufactured using biogas energy.

Printed in Canada

Wilfrid Laurier University Press is located on the Haldimand Tract, part of the traditional territories of the Haudenosaunee, Anishnaabe, and Neutral Peoples. This land is part of the Dish with One Spoon Treaty between the Haudenosaunee and Anishnaabe Peoples and symbolises the agreement to share, to protect our resources, and not to engage in conflict. We are grateful to the Indigenous Peoples who continue to care for and remain interconnected with this land. Through the work we publish in partnership with our authors, we seek to honour our local and larger community relationships, and to engage with the diversity of collective knowledge integral to responsible scholarly and cultural exchange.

Table of Contents

Introduction: *The Frankfurt Kabuff* as Creative Critique
Beth Driscoll and Claire Squires / 1

The Annotated Text of *The Frankfurt Kabuff: A Beatrice Deft (Comic Erotic) Thriller*
Blaire Squiscoll / 25

Critical Essays

Genesis
Kim Wilkins / 97

Unplugging the Circuit: Historical Perspectives on Why Scholars Think Writing and Reading Books is the Easy Part
Leslie Howsam / 101

Rectangularity and *The Frankfurt Kabuff*
Ian Gadd / 107

Signature Cocktail: Negronis as Method in *The Frankfurt Kabuff*
Julie Rak / 113

The Frankfurt Kabuff and the Historical Sociology of the Detective Genre
Bridget Fowler / 119

Tinker, Tailor, Driscoll, Squires: Book Fairs and Liberal Bookism in *The Russia House* and *The Frankfurt Kabuff*
Mark Banks / 135

Romancing Book Culture
Sarah Brouillette / 148

Politics at Play in the Kabuff: The Buchmesse as a Political Space
Corinna Norrick-Rühl / 153

Charting a Path for Social Change, One Negroni at a Time: *The Frankfurt Kabuff*
Doris Ruth Eikhof / 161

A Frankfurt Memoir (inspired by *The Frankfurt Kabuff*)
Arpita Das / 169

OuFiPo: Hypothetical Film Criticism (or *Kabuff!* The Film Musical)
Elizabeth Ezra / 175

How to Take Over a Book Fair: A Bourdieusian Fiction
Roanna Gonsalves / 184

Tagging Beatrice: Fanfic as Reader Response
Danielle Fuller / 187

Kabuff or Wunderkammer?: Review of *The Frankfurt Kabuff*
Kelvin Smith / 195

Using *The Frankfurt Kabuff* in the Classroom
Alastair Horne / 197

CONTENTS

ASSEMBLAGES

Original Plot Diagram Drawn
at the Frankfurt Hauptbahnhof / 202

Paratextual Elements of *The Frankfurt Kabuff*
Print-on-Demand Edition / 203

"Dear Diary": An Account of the Production of the Print-on-Demand
Self-Published Edition of *The Frankfurt Kabuff* / 205

Advance Information (AI) Sheet for *The Frankfurt Kabuff* / 220

Publishers Weekly Report on Linksphilosophie Verlag List Launch / 221

Conference Abstract Proposal: "Tante Fran's Book Club:
Solidarity, Slogans and Knitting Needles" / 222

The Kabuff Joke Book / 225

Comic Strip Featuring Nunu and Otot / 228

Spotify Playlists / 229

"The Corona Kabuff" and Other Stories / 231

Map from *The Frankfurt Kabuff* / 241

Acknowledgements / 243
Bibliography / 245
Contributor Biographies / 261
Index / 265

Introduction: *The Frankfurt Kabuff* as Creative Critique

BETH DRISCOLL AND CLAIRE SQUIRES

IT MIGHT SEEM SURPRISING TO PUBLISH A SCHOLARLY edition with all the trimmings a mere four years after a (self-published) novella's original appearance. But *The Frankfurt Kabuff* is no ordinary novella. Despite its boldly emblazoned thriller features, the work is not an entirely straightforward work of popular fiction. *The Frankfurt Kabuff Critical Edition*—the volume you are reading right now—is also both slippery and genre-bending. In order to make sense of these challenges, this introduction to *The Frankfurt Kabuff Critical Edition* sets out the theoretical ideas which shaped the creation of the novella, and explains how, through an expansion of the possibilities of humanities and social sciences research into contemporary book culture's creative methods, the novella achieves its artistic and political ends. The apparatus of the scholarly edition, including this introduction, annotations to the text, a section of critical essays and various assemblages, frames *The Frankfurt Kabuff* for a broad audience, unlocking its potential to critique and reshape both the contemporary publishing industry and the academic field of book history and publishing studies (perhaps with the occasional mischievous obfuscation along the way).

This introduction begins that process by, first, contextualising *The Frankfurt Kabuff* within our program of research into contemporary publishing, aligned with our conceptual school, Ullapoolism. We then explain the novella's origins and development as a kind of autoethnography and indeed an autotheoretical creative work. This creative work aims to directly intervene in publishing studies and book history, and so we turn to analyse how writing and publishing *The Frankfurt Kabuff* can be understood as a "situation"—an interventionist research provocation. The next section of the introduction explores the role of satire in the work, and its connection to the novella's political aims. We bring these theoretical strands together in the idea of *The Frankfurt Kabuff*'s "interparatextuality." Finally, we outline the structure of the critical edition, including the role of the critical essays and the assemblages, showing how the theoretical aims of the novella are amplified and intensified through scholarly infrastructure.

The comic erotic thriller *The Frankfurt Kabuff* developed from our participation in a publishing trade fair, the Frankfurt Book Fair, or Frankfurter Buchmesse. We conducted fieldwork at Frankfurt from 2017 to 2019. This business-to-business trade fair has long been the pre-eminent forum for the global publishing industry, deeply storied as well as commercially influential. With origins in the fifteenth century, and a renewed role after the Second World War, the Buchmesse has grown to encompass a huge number of events, organisations, and objects. The 2019 Buchmesse (at which the print version of *The Frankfurt Kabuff* was launched) hosted around 7,500 exhibitors, over 300,000 visitors, 4,000 events and 10,000 journalists.[1] Plus a lot of books.

For scholarly readers, it is ironic that this temple of commerce and trade bears the same name as The Frankfurt School of Critical Theory, which decried the culture industries. During our research, we sometimes imagined Adorno, Horkheimer, et al. standing, mouths agape and eyes on stalks, as they contemplated the (to them) horror of hall after hall of books, an inarguable glut of product. Indeed, during our own research at Frankfurt we experienced similar sensations in response to commercial excess, and the protagonist of *The Frankfurt Kabuff* registers shock on her entrance to the fair: "Everywhere Beatrice looked, there were posters of forthcoming titles and rows of books. She had never seen so many."[2] Our research approach to Frankfurt has been to understand these reactions against the commercialisation of culture, but also to develop a post-critical response that accounts for cross-currents and anomalies. In so doing, we draw on the eccentricity and whim-chasing of "low theory". For Jack Halberstam, low theory is theoretical knowledge that "revels in the detours, twists, and turns through knowing and confusion, and that seeks not to explain but to involve."[3] Such an approach allowed us to move within and around the book fair fluidly, both intellectually and physically. We could join in the pleasures of the fair while resisting some boosterist, hyperbolic tendencies: notably, we resisted awe at the fair's magnitude.

We are not, in general, the types of researchers to be dazzled by size. As we conducted our research, we noted that the fair occupied two fewer halls in the Messe complex in 2019 than in 2015. In the pandemic-affected year of 2020, the fair's physical footprint shrank radically as it moved online (albeit with some events broadcast from locations in Frankfurt, including a favourite of ours, YokYok City-Kiosk). The years since then have seen a partly cautious, partly bullish return to on-site activity. Any shrinkage notwithstanding, the Buchmesse presents itself, and is thought of, as the key annual destination for international book business and the most important date on the global publishing calendar. So, while the fair is not as big as it used to be, it is still quite big, as well as being very complex and multilayered. A straightforward research project—one based only on interviews or a survey, for example, or a massing of numerical datapoints pinned down in time—would miss many of its nuances. We decided such normal research methods would not answer our questions about the nature and impact of this fair. Fortunately, we had some abnormal research methods at our disposal; ones which derive from our Ullapoolist approach.

Ullapoolism is the playful, activist conceptual school that we founded in 2016, and which provides the creative methodological inspiration and intellectual resources for our research. We named Ullapoolism for the site where we began our collaboration (the town of Ullapool in the Scottish Highlands). Ullapoolism embraces satire and the arts, and is driven by the need to reinvigorate scholarly critique so as to effect social and cultural change. Ullapoolism produces situated knowledge and creative critique.[4] Our Ullapoolist methods at Frankfurt were varied, incorporating, for example, the use of fortune-telling miracle fish, comically imprecise laser measurers, and very short but productive interviews.[5] All our methods relied upon our immersion in the fair, so that part of our approach was to reflexively explore the ethical possibilities and predicaments of autoethnographic research. We intended the central outcome of our research to be the scholarly monograph *The Frankfurt Book Fair and Bestseller Business*, in which we analyse the mechanisms by which the fair produces buzz, the physical structures and absences that enact the power relations of global publishing, and the fair's status as a carnival of sorts, marked by disruptive historical events and problematic socio-political dynamics.[6] Another of our outcomes, which was simultaneously a method, was a novella set at the Frankfurt Book Fair: *The Frankfurt Kabuff*.

As with all our playful, creative Ullapoolist projects, *The Frankfurt Kabuff* is a serious scholarly endeavour. This introduction aims to make the novella's contributions legible by explaining the thinking behind it and contextualising its role within research, art, and politics. While we created *The Frankfurt Kabuff* at lightning speed (in nine weeks, to be precise), it crystallised years of observation and critical thought. Furthermore, as an act of writing and publishing, the novella created the conditions for further development of our critical engagement with contemporary book cultures. This introduction, then, offers insight into the theoretical concepts that the novella advances, including autoethnography (and other "autos"); using the publication of a novella as a situation to rejuvenate book history and publishing studies; the political possibilities of art and satire; and interparatextuality. We begin with autoethnography and the use of the self in critical-creative work.

Autoethnography, Autotheory, and the Creative Work

Autoethnography, as a form of qualitative research based on systematic observation and participation, is central to Ullapoolism. Carolyn Ellis, Tony E. Adams, and Arthur P. Bochner define autoethnography as "an approach to research and writing that seeks to describe and systematically analyse (graphy) personal experience (auto) in order to understand cultural experience (ethno)."[7] Autoethnography relies on the active participation of researchers, so that their experiences become part of the object of study. For an Ullapoolist twist on this approach, we coined the term "NUNU OTOTS" to describe our authoethnographic position. The term is an acrostic of our slogan "No Insight Without Inside, No Inside Without Outside", which emphasises the need to move fluidly into and out of networks during the research process.[8]

One of the challenges of our autoethnography is something we call "The Predicament." This term refers to the ethical dilemmas that arise during fieldwork. In particular, The Predicament might arise during social events such as parties and receptions. As we have argued elsewhere, generally speaking "drunken carousing is not a recommended research method for obtaining accurate information"; however, "for researchers committed to observing and teasing out the nuanced, informal networks through which culture circulates, parties remain a key site of situatedness."[9] At Frankfurt, our research included autoethnographic attendance at parties to which we were invited, paused at en route to somewhere else, or gatecrashed, as well as at meetings, food trucks, and talks. Our fieldwork at Frankfurt had university ethics approval, which we followed closely (for example in gaining consent from interview participants). As autoethnographic researchers we observed and participated in various activities at the Buchmesse which nevertheless made us question the strict delineations of ethical research, both as formally approved and informally experienced.[10]

Our mode at parties, for example, was as participant-observers, but given the typical environment of such social gatherings our participation involved full bodily immersion: lipstick, party frocks, and the consumption of alcohol and canapés. Some of this activity confirmed the gendered and occasionally sleazy nature of the Buchmesse, which led us to create the "Sleaze-O-Meter," an old-fashioned tally counter which we clicked after each mansplain or leer we observed or experienced at the Buchmesse.[11] In order to investigate sleaze, our Predicament also involved experiments with a very mild version of what might be termed honeytrap methods. In 2017 and 2018, we wore friendly expressions as we listened to boring men, and we suffered some handsiness. In 2019, we experimented instead with instantly walking away from such men, a deeply satisfying action that is not always available to women working in publishing, or indeed to women in academic workplaces. The observation of and interaction with unethical behaviour was one of the challenges we faced in our autoethnographic research.

Immersion within research environments complicates the role of academic researchers, not least when they have—as we did—existing and developing networks and alliances, as well as a political sensibility when approaching and commenting upon research sites. Such complications made us question the validity of the distinction between researcher and researched. As we have previously argued, for Ullapoolists, researching within networks "is a key element of the situatedness of the academic who is not a disinterested observer but an active participant and sometime instigator of the situations of contemporary book cultures."[12] Our reflexive immersion at Frankfurt produced a host of impressions and experiences that saw us reaching, instinctively, towards fiction as a way to convey ethically nuanced, embodied situations.

Kay Inckle, in her work on body modification and young women, has argued for creative writing, or fictionalization, as an embodied methodology that accounts for the ethical issues that arise in ethnographic and autoethnographic research. She argues that embodied methodologies can "handle the complex and messy realities of corporeal experience," "reflect the multifaceted, contradictory, ambiguous nature of lived experience and the ways in which it defies easy categorization," and "integrate the equally complex ethical issues which pertain to such intimate knowledge."[13] Inckle's "strategy of fictionalization" enables research to be ethical but also embodied and critical.[14] One example of the ethical potential of fictionalization, she explains, is that creative writing can offer protection for the researcher by lending them a degree of confidentiality and safety equivalent to that offered by anonymisation to research participants.[15]

The sensory, embodied qualities captured through fiction writing are also alluded to by Ash Watson, who writes that "creative writing is a generative method for probing relationships between theoretical concepts and the complex, sensory experiences that researchers seek to investigate...Novels, short stories and other fictional forms allow a scope and nuance that is constructive for exploring social worlds."[16] Watson's approach encapsulates the impetus that led us to embark upon writing *The Frankfurt Kabuff.*

We began on the final day of the 2018 Frankfurter Buchmesse. Earlier that day, we had been taking in the atmosphere in the German Halls when our attention was arrested by a police officer standing at the back of Amazon's self-publishing stand. His uniform seemed not quite right. (It later turned out he was a hired model). Seated in front of him, a woman was reading aloud a story (a romance featuring a police officer) from her laptop. We took a few photos of the stand, the crowd, the police officer—why not call him Caspian—and moved on.

Back in our hotel room, we sat down to put together the abstract for a conference paper about book fairs.[17] In line with our observations of the additional security measures put in place at the Fair that year because of various threats of violence including those connected to far-right publishers, one of us wrote a sentence—"police patrol the aisles with guns and batons, and queues form at security bag checks"—which the other deemed "too exciting" for a conference paper.

After a little collaborative writing tussle, the sentence took us on another pathway. One of us remembered idly musing on the aeroplane from Australia that a portmanteau of our names would be Blaire Squiscoll. The exciting sentence about guns and batons seemed to match the name. Working at rapid-fire pace, and with the gleeful participation of Kim Wilkins (who discusses the genesis of the novella later in this critical edition), we established the scenario, the main characters, the title, and quickly designed a cover. We uploaded it to Wattpad, a self-publishing and writing platform designed for serial publication, and both Blaire Squiscoll and *The Frankfurt Kabuff* were born.[18] Over the next few days, we wrote and uploaded our first few chapters; Kim provided key input, including drawing a schematic outline for how to plot a novel in a notebook at the Frankfurt Hauptbahnhof before we boarded different trains away from the city (this document is included in the assemblages section). We then continued (with occasional guidance from Kim) penning the comic-erotic thriller, staying in touch over email, Messenger, and Google Docs, and publishing a new chapter on Wattpad every couple of days. Only a few weeks later, we put our virtual pens down. We had had our vision.[19]

The autoethnographic nature of the novella—as well as its creative inspiration and occasional moments of critical difficulty—is woven into its fabric. Most characters in *The Frankfurt Kabuff* share our initials (BD, CS, or KW). Real-life conversations are included, such as a discussion with a Frankfurt taxi driver about the novel he was writing. Heroine Beatrice Deft's dark hair and blue eyes are modelled on Kim; some of Deft's other mannerisms and behaviours may remind people of us. Other aspects are made up. Through its imagined and (sometimes very lightly) fictionalised versions of Buchmesse stands, events, and parties, *The Frankfurt Kabuff* allowed us to examine geopolitical and gender dynamics at the fair in ways a traditional scholarly monograph might shy away from (e.g., sex scenes). Each link between our experience of the fair and the novella was a bridge that helped us process our observations—capturing them, working them through, playing with their possibilities. Writing the novella enabled us to incorporate aspects of participant observation *and* imagination in a manner beyond that which more standard approaches to academic writing typically provide.

Our combination of personal experience (through autoethnography) and theory (our engagement with publishing studies and book cultures) within *The Frankfurt Kabuff* recalls the critical term autotheory. As Lauren Fournier defines it, autotheory blends autobiography and theory—a mode she associates with feminist works such as Chris Kraus's *I Love Dick* and Maggie Nelson's *The Argonauts*.[20] Fournier considers autotheory a post-1960s extension of the longstanding feminist commitment to revealing the "illusory separations between art and life, theory and practice, work and the self, research and motivation."[21] Fournier's expanded definition notes that:

> Along with other terms—such as creative criticism, conceptual criticism, theoretical fiction, biofiction, fictocriticism, critical memoir, queer phenomenology, queer feminist affect theory, philosophical novels and novels in essay form,

> essayistic films, performance philosophy, and performative autoethnography—autotheory points to modes of working that integrate the personal and the conceptual, the theoretical and the autobiographical, the creative and the critical, in ways attuned to interdisciplinary, feminist histories.[22]

While Fournier's definition might not entirely encompass *The Frankfurt Kabuff* and its critical edition, her formulations are nonetheless a useful articulation of our work; with the caveat that we also work substantially with humour (an element of autotheory underplayed in some leading examples, but present in our favourite works in the genre, such as Barbara Browning's *The Gift*), as we explore later in this introduction.[23]

The Frankfurt Kabuff fuses disparate genres—satire, erotica, and theory—within the overarching form of the thriller. We chose the thriller structure not just because it happened to fit our initial sentence about police, guns, and batons, but also because of its intrinsic drama and intensification of socio-political issues, and its corresponding potential for affectionate parody that does not diminish critique. *The Frankfurt Kabuff*'s thriller plot addresses gender inequity, political controversies, interaction between print and digital formats, and other key issues facing the industry. The thriller genre allowed us to incorporate both real and imagined scenes that struck us as dramatic (a publisher's party held in a strip club, for example). And it allowed us to characterise neo-Nazi publishers as the baddies, develop a romantic subplot with a broad-shouldered, sensitive German police officer, and establish a noble theme—the "continuing international exchange of translation rights, cultures and ideas"—as the quest for heroine Beatrice Deft.[24]

Much of the thrilling action takes place in book fair cupboards, or Kabuffs. What, though, is a Kabuff, and how does it provide shape to our autoethnographic approach? A crucial scene comes in Chapter Sieben, as Beatrice is invited to peruse a scale model of the Buchmesse:

> She could see a small stand marked Linksphilosophie Verlag, and right opposite, a stand marked White Storm. And at the back of that tiny cardboard stand, a tiny cardboard cupboard.
>
> "I see you have noticed the Kabuff," the Vice President said.
>
> "The what?"

> "The Kabuff. A Kabuff is a cupboard, a cobwebby cupboard where things are hidden. Where unpleasant surprises may lurk. Have you not read Heinrich Mann?"[25]

The Vice President's comment provides a not very veiled warning, as he simultaneously chides Beatrice for what he assumes are her predominantly Anglophone reading practices, threatens the stand of her new publisher friend Kurt Weidenfeld, and also—not especially adroitly—explains in dialogue what a Kabuff is. Kabuff is German for a shadowy, closeted space. It is an apt name for the cupboard in which publishers store their paraphernalia (handbags, bottles of mineral water, spare stock) during the Buchmesse, and which forms a striking contrast to the bright public-facing image of the fair. It is the location for secretive activity, the shadowy unconscious of the fair, and a metonym for the work being done by *The Frankfurt Kabuff* itself. This aspect of Kabuffs, and the fair more broadly, is something we turned attention to in *The Frankfurt Book Fair and Bestseller Business*, but *The Frankfurt Kabuff* adds an autofictive layering.[26]

More broadly, the importation of real-life places and events into the novella allowed us to interlace ideas with a new focus. For example, much of the discursive rhetoric of the Frankfurt Book Fair emphasises the value of freedom of speech. Given that the fair's highly contested decision to allow far-right publishers to exhibit led to violence in 2017, this discomforted us, alongside other attendees of the fair.[27] However, it wasn't until we wrote the villain of *The Frankfurt Kabuff* as the fair's Vice President for Intellectual Freedom that our critique of this rhetorical positioning was fully realised. Writing *The Frankfurt Kabuff* allowed this problem to emerge explicitly, amongst all the noise of Frankfurt. The novella was a tool for the gathering, processing, and refining of our autoethnographic research observations.

Creative writing is thus central to the research we undertook at the Frankfurt Book Fair, both as one of our array of research methods and as an output—*The Frankfurt Kabuff*, as well as this critical edition. The edition, indeed, includes forms of exegesis, including this introduction and the accompanying critical essays which appear later in the book. As such, our work has allegiance to forms of practice-led research, or research-creation, both in its creative forms and its explanatory accompaniments. "Practice-led research" is generally used to describe the work of practitioners of the creative arts in academic settings, while "research-creation" is defined (by the Social Sciences and Humanities Research Council of Canada) as "an approach to research that combines creative and academic research practices."[28] Both terms are most usually applied to the research outputs of artists working in a university context. Where our work differs from such approaches is that our creative work—*The Frankfurt Kabuff*—arises from and is primarily intended as a strategic intervention in the disciplines of book history and publishing studies. We use creative methods to make particular critiques of both industry and academia, while nonetheless providing a fast-paced fictional read. Our approach—as the next section outlines—is the novella-as-situation.

Novella as Situation: An Expanded Mode for Publishing Studies and Book History

As our discussions of autotheory prefigure, our autoethnographic creativity extends beyond incorporating observations of the fair to also include theoretical reflections. While we are first and foremost researchers of twenty-first-century publishing industry and book cultures, we situate ourselves within the longer chronological overview of book history. That is to say that we are attentive to the production, circulation, and reception of books across time periods, and share and learn from historians' interest in the physical, networked, and interpersonal ways in which these processes occur. Indeed, *The Frankfurt Kabuff* takes these processes as a central theme, making it a scholarly work within the fields of book history and publishing studies, as well as a contribution to broader post-critical theorisations and actualisations of cultural spheres in the contemporary period. It offers metacommentary: for example, in a flashback scene when our protagonist Beatrice challenges Callum, her chapbook publisher boyfriend, who has turned to dodgy dealings in the chicken shop because his publishing company has not received the grant he applied for. Callum bitterly attributes this rejection to the push for more diversity in publishing and claims, himself, to "only see excellence"—a fallacious line of thought frequently used to uphold the systemic status quo. The ensuing argument between Beatrice and Callum makes reference to key conceptual frames from book history and the sociology of literature. The depiction of a relationship falling apart is intensified and satirised by Beatrice's dig at Robert Darnton's communications circuit of the book and Pierre Bourdieu's theory of symbolic capital, two models that are frequently cited in book historical scholarship. As the critical essays in this volume show, this scene has proved popular with scholars, who welcome this sarcastic nudge against overreliance on a limited number of (white, male) theorists.[29]

Our interest in book history not only infuses the text of *The Frankfurt Kabuff* but also extends into its publishing process. After all, what better way to understand the Frankfurt Book Fair, contemporary publishing, and book culture than by publishing a book and then tracking, in real time, the current dynamics of independent, mainstream, traditional, and digital publishing systems? As we uploaded the novella chapter by chapter to Wattpad, we experienced the agility of digital serial publication. We received reader comments and votes as well as social media engagement, thereby encountering a community of knowledge production and exchange. Then, in 2019, we created a print edition of the novella using print-on-demand services, hosted live and virtual launches, and distributed marketing collateral outlining the novella's key selling points (see assemblages). Our experiences confirmed that digital publishing platforms and technologies have made the journey from author to self-publisher radically easier, but the process still has its difficulties. These difficulties include the very real physical challenges of distribution, as books make their way from digital sites through print-on-demand to—perhaps—bookstores (see the assemblage "Dear Diary," page 205, for more detail). The performative act of publishing *The Frankfurt Kabuff* highlights material affordances and constraints across different forms: chapters with comments on Wattpad, ebook, print book.

With this combination of modes—creative, critical, autoethnographic, material—*The Frankfurt Kabuff* is rendered into a particular kind of work: a novella that is also a *situation* in the terms and methods of the Situationist International. *The Frankfurt Kabuff* shows that a work of fiction can be a situation that provokes and interacts with all the elements of book culture—including authors, readers, publishers, and book fairs.

As with many elements of the conceptual school of Ullapoolism, *The Frankfurt Kabuff* is inspired by the situationists, who drew their lineage through the avant-garde movements of Dada, the Surrealists, and the Lettrists.[30] To the situationists' artistic and self-publishing practices they brought Marxist critique of the dystopian "society of the spectacle."[31] Their method was the construction of situations, defined in the first issue of their journal as "moment[s] of life, concretely and deliberately constructed by the collective organisation of a unitary environment and a game of events."[32] To construct situations, the situationists made use of two modes in particular. One is the *dérive*, an "active drift" through space. The other is the *détournement*, which involves rewriting images and texts in a parodic style. The purpose of the détournement is aesthetic and political, the act of turning capitalism against itself. Situationist détournements included altered words in comic strips, mashed-up films, and vandalised paintings; this approach went on to inspire movements such as punk and culture jamming.

One of the most playful situationists was Michèle Bernstein, author of much of the situationists' journal, and for a time married to Guy Debord, the movement's most well-known figure. Bernstein wrote two détourned novels, both based on Laclos's 1782 classic *Les Liaisons Dangereuses*. In her preface to the second, *The Night*, she explains the financial impetus behind her aesthetic exercises. She and her husband were "skint"; Bernstein notes dryly that she "was a member of the lumpensecratariat, working for tuppence ha'penny at a humdrum publishing house. Guy Debord, naturally, wasn't working."[33] The fictions Bernstein wrote, Nicholas Thoburn argues, were in part loosely autobiographical novels that détourned the situationist life; they were instances of "self-critique of the [male] heroism of the SI and its theory."[34] They were also designed to be widely read bestsellers. As Greil Marcus elaborates, Bernstein's background in publishing meant that "she knew craft and story; she knew cliché, and how to extend clichés until they both held their shape and spoke new languages. So she contrived a book out of every fragment of popular fiction [...] a prefabricated bestseller."[35] This description of Bernstein's work, and its play with genre convention, relates to Fournier's extended definition of autotheory to include "works that exceed existing genre categories and disciplinary bounds, that flourish in the liminal spaces between categories, that reveal the entanglement of research and creation, and that fuse seemingly disparate modes to fresh effects."[36] Wrapped in the package of a thriller, *The Frankfurt Kabuff*, like Bernstein's novels, is intentionally replete with cliché, but as with autotheory it also transcends boundaries, providing critique of prevalent modes for approaching the literary economy and new ways to write criticism.

Art, Satire, and the Political Force of Fictocriticism

The Frankfurt Kabuff is not only research but, we argue, art. In conceptual art, creativity is found not only in the outcome but in the process. This aspect of the novella links our work back to practice-led research, although we instead choose "fictocriticism" from Fournier's expanded list of autotheory synonyms, and add a Ullapoolist, humorous twist. *The Frankfurt Kabuff* is a playful practice as much as it is a work of fiction. Puckish elements of its authorial production included the back-and-forth collaborative process, the gleeful use of genre tropes, writing jokes to amuse each other, our lightly satirical handling of political and theoretical themes, and the inclusion of an erotic romance plot. The latter has occasioned some of those (men) interested in our collaborative processes to ask how we wrote the sex scenes. Our stock evasion to this question is, "on Google Docs." At these moments, our collaborative fictocriticism recalls, and draws on, the work of mischievous partnerships and collective performances in academia and elsewhere, from artists Gilbert and George, to feminist geographers J K Gibson-Graham (who combined their names), and anonymous art activists the Guerrilla Girls.

As with our performative responses to predictable questions, *The Frankfurt Kabuff* offers a focus on Frankfurt's people and places and on writing and publishing itself that is intentionally sideways, drawing on low theory. As an extremely self-referential piece—self-referential to the point of mise-en-abyme—we recognised it might not have a mass readership, but we were determined it would have the activist and reconfiguring potential of conceptual high art.

The fact that *The Frankfurt Kabuff* is conceptual high art doesn't mean it isn't also political. We do not align ourselves with those who advocate "art for art's sake."[37] Rather, our purpose is to drive social and cultural change. Ruha Benjamin writes of such an imperative in relation to the "racial fictions" she created as a response to the Black Lives Matter protests:

> Novel fictions that reimagine and rework all that is taken for granted about the current structure of the social world—alternatives to capitalism, racism, and patriarchy—are urgently needed. Fictions, in this sense, are not falsehoods but refashionings through which analysts experiment with different scenarios, trajectories, and reversals, elaborating new values and testing different possibilities for creating more just and equitable societies.[38]

Benjamin's account of the activist potential of research-led fiction complements feminist understandings of the value of this qualitative research method for exposing existing inequities (as well as imagining alternative futures). Patricia Leavy, for example, sees feminist possibilities in academic fiction writing, which can lead to consciousness-raising through depicting "hard-to-get-at dimensions of social life."[39] Experimental works, however, may appeal to a small audience, potentially limiting their political efficacy. Fournier considers the difficulties that autotheory may encounter in its attempts to critique institutional power, not least of which is theory's "niche appeal." She pointedly asks, "What place does philosophizing and theorizing have—if we are being honest with ourselves—in today's publics, including artistic and academic ones, and how might we approach this question intersectionally?"[40] We recognise the barriers that academia's specialised concerns impose on readers, and certainly *The Frankfurt Kabuff* had a niche distribution. However, we do not see *The Frankfurt Kabuff* as divorced from the urgent political questions that affect society. We hold that fiction is—or rather, it can be—a form of direct action. In the case of *The Frankfurt Kabuff*, the action is directed at the publishing industry and the broader creative economy of which it is part, as well as those who comment upon it, including our academic peers. When we drew from our autoethnographic observations of the fair in writing the novella, we did not do so solely for entertainment. Rather, our aim was to critique. We critique the misuse of freedom-of-speech rhetoric to give entry to and even support far-right political movements. We ridicule the boringness of debates about print-vs.-digital book formats.[41] We satirise the ridiculousness of pitching according to previous bestsellers, a practice that shows the financial conservatism and closemindedness of the industry. We decry the exclusion of women and other marginalised people. We expose an alignment of literary snobbishness with exclusionary industry practices. The novella's recoil from the reissue of *Mein Kampf* and its characterisation of neo-Nazis as villains indicate the moral import and political heft of the publishing industry—and its potential to abuse such values. Our intersectional response was to create a story that exposes these institutional and systemic wrongs, and, within this critical edition, to further our arguments and interventions.

There is an invigorated potential for progressive, committed political interventions in the mechanisms of contemporary genre fiction, self-publishing, and digital platforms. As *The Frankfurt Kabuff* amply demonstrates, these mechanisms can facilitate pointed commentary about cultural inclusion and exclusion, uneven power relations, censorship, and intellectual freedom. An additional layer of political activism, then, is found in the modes by which we published *The Frankfurt Kabuff*. Our publishing methods, explored further in the "Dear Diary" assemblage on page 205, navigated the routes determined by digital capitalism: Wattpad, Amazon, Ingram. As such, *The Frankfurt Kabuff* invited us to reflect on the neoliberalism of the publishing industry, and its manifestations in both conglomerate publishing companies and the techno-capitalist systems of the 2010s and early 2020s, something which the various parts of *The Frankfurt Kabuff Critical Edition* intensifies and makes more evident.[42] Our experience working with and among the platforms confirms their availability for playfulism, autonomy, and critique. As with other forms of capitalism, we can work with digital systems even as we work against their most harmful effects.

At the same time, we recognise that in addition to the restrictions of a potentially small audience, the effectiveness of *The Frankfurt Kabuff*'s political critique is somewhat compromised, or at least affected, by its literary form. The thriller genre and its textual conventions mean that *The Frankfurt Kabuff* replicates some conservative logics—logics which are inherent to much genre fiction, and are sustained by readerly demand. The retro feel of the novella, which includes uncritical references to smoking, alcohol (particularly Negronis), and an international jet-setting lifestyle, shores up a glamourised model of publishing that does nothing to advance its environmental sustainability. We have willingly participated in this model during our time as autoethnographic researchers at the Buchmesse. This critique is made by Kelvin Smith in his review of *The Frankfurt Kabuff*, which concludes:

> There will be further adventures, but they had better hurry, because this old world of international publishing will soon be brought to a juddering halt, not, as this story suggests, by the threat of right-wing terrorism, but by the surveillance state it has created, the security apparatus it spawned, and—in this time of climate breakdown—the impossibility of sustaining all that smoking, drinking, meat-eating and carbon-fuelled travel that are at the core of the international book fair circuit.[43]

These limits to our political project are revealing to us, as well as creating intriguing predicaments for readers who may also relish conservative tropes while desiring progressive change—a critical point which has been explored in scholarship of genre fiction.[44] As a situation, *The Frankfurt Kabuff* enacts a political struggle and advances critical arguments about the structure and practices of publishing, and by extension, other cultural sectors, but it also risks reinforcing those structures and practices through the play with stereotype and satire.

It is therefore apposite to consider the role of humour in *The Frankfurt Kabuff*, and indeed in this critical edition. Humour is an integral (and non-negotiable) element of Ullapoolism and its interventions in academia and the publishing industry, and we align ourselves specifically within a literary tradition of satire. One of our favourite websites, Wikipedia, has an entry on satire that defines it as (more or less) a fruit bowl: "The word satire comes from the Latin word *satur* and the subsequent phrase *lanx satura*. Satur meant 'full' but the juxtaposition with *lanx* shifted the meaning to 'miscellany or medley': the expression *lanx satura* literally means 'a full dish of various kinds of fruits.'"[45] Satire is thus rhetorically complex, with split voices—an apt description of *The Frankfurt Kabuff* with its multiple levels, including its pseudonymous and combined authorship. Within and through rhetorical complexity, satire pursues its ethical objectives. We see our work in the tradition of Juvenalian satire, aimed at reform, rather than the gentle funniness of Horatian satire or the mental gymnastics of Menippean satire. Like Orwell's *Animal Farm*, *The Frankfurt Kabuff* embraces a playful genre (for Squiscoll, the erotic thriller; for Orwell, the farmyard tale) to pursue political engagement through ridicule. Our satire thus operates within a tradition of politically committed, interventionist writing. We use humour to make serious and scholarly points; absurdity, exaggeration, and a knowing play on stereotypes expose inequities and closemindedness in the contemporary publishing industry. However, we recognise that the impact of humour can be interrogated. Mockery can cause discomfort; the sudden surprise of laughter, or finding something funny, requires us to ask why we had that response. We want to encourage this self-reflection and, ultimately, transformation, which is why humour is so important to us. Key to this self-awareness is understanding that we use mockery here to attack systemic and oppressive hierarchies and the normative behaviour that sustains them, rather than to punch down or to attack those with less power.

Interparatextuality

How, then, might the totality of *The Frankfurt Kabuff* be viewed, in its various guises as research, as art, as satire, and as political project? We conclude the conceptual work of this introduction by offering the novel term "interparatext" as a way to encapsulate the novella's relationship with the Frankfurt Book Fair and the contemporary publishing industry more broadly. Our neologism develops from Gérard Genette's "paratext", a frequently utilised concept in book history and studies of the material book, which can be summarised as the physical and broader environmental surrounds of the book (e.g., its cover, its copyright page, related marketing materials).[46] In describing the intervention made by *The Frankfurt Kabuff*, we propose that paratext can be productively combined with Julia Kristeva's term "intertext," a book that is referenced in another book.[47]

To illustrate how the concept of interparatext operates, imagine a scholar who is interested in the (imaginary) bookshelves of the (pseudonymous) Blaire Squiscoll.[48] Such bookshelves would reveal the intertextual materials that contributed to Squiscoll's intellectual and narrative formation. However, given the ontological status of Squiscoll, the only way to imagine the bookshelves—other than to examine our own—would be to glean references to other texts found within *The Frankfurt Kabuff*. Yet, these references are a medley, ranging from Bourdieu and Darnton to Angela Carter, Michelle Obama, and Heinrich Mann. *The Frankfurt Kabuff*'s idiosyncratic mash-up of intertextual references hints at the novella's status as not solely fiction, but also a low theory research method—another way of knowing, of finding, an epistemological way into the publishing industry.

The Frankfurt Kabuff's biggest intertext is the Frankfurt Book Fair itself. But can an event, even one that focuses on books, really be thought of as a "text"? After all, the fair might more commonly be described, as we did at the beginning of this introduction, as the leading international forum for the exchange of rights and a showcase for books and publishing. Yet in this role the Buchmesse operates as an Ur-text-and-paratext, standing in for the multiple cross-cutting dimensions of contemporary book cultures. The Buchmesse is a paratextual intertext—an *interparatext*—to *The Frankfurt Kabuff* and, indeed, vice versa. As autoethnographic researchers, and as Squiscoll, we have developed and continue to develop this interparatextuality, including through the manifold components of the critical edition that you are currently reading.

The Structure of
The Frankfurt Kabuff Critical Edition

With the themes, genres and theoretical and political purposes of this critical edition established, it is time to turn to its structure, a matter that requires a little explanation since this is a work of many layers and considerable formal complexity. After the relative normality of this introduction, the critical edition presents the entire novella of *The Frankfurt Kabuff*, which has been extensively annotated, as is the norm for scholarly editions, in order to elucidate, occasionally at some length, its sometimes compressed and allusive argument. The annotated novella is followed by a series of reflective critical essays by scholars and publishing industry practitioners from around the world, and a number of assemblages that creatively complement the novella.

The critical essays in this volume show the deeply collaborative nature of this intervention in the disciplines of publishing studies and book history. They vary in length, form, and approach, and include the earliest critical review of *The Frankfurt Kabuff*, meditations on the way in which it furthers conceptual thinking, examinations of its genre allegiances, and creative and pedagogical engagements with its text and contexts.

Wilkins's opening essay documents her close involvement with the creation of *The Frankfurt Kabuff*, her creative writing teaching that "the trick is knowing where the beginning ends, because that's where the middle begins, and so on," and Blaire Squiscoll's wayward handling of this writing advice. Wilkins's "Genesis" is followed by three essays that focus on *The Frankfurt Kabuff*'s relationship to cross-disciplinary conceptual modes and methods. First, Leslie Howsam argues that the novella functions as a critique of the interdiscipline of the history of the book, aligning with a reordering which she perceives to be taking place in this field of study. Ian Gadd takes a bibliographical approach by considering the novella through its material but invisible "rectangularity," a shape that pervades "cigarette packets, suitcases, tote bags, bills, business cards, envelopes, newspapers, windows, boxes, flags, stands, posters, greeting cards, doors, walls, mobile phones, computer screens, iPads, notebooks, trapdoors, red carpets, papers, laptops, clipboards, pages, e-readers, and above all else, books." In "Signature Cocktail: Negronis as Method in *The Frankfurt Kabuff*," Julie Rak brings playfully Derridean and methodological scrutiny to Beatrice Deft's drink of choice, a discussion that is anything but dry.

The signature cocktail is a genre trope, and the next three essays address the novella as genre fiction from three different angles. First, Bridget Fowler considers *The Frankfurt Kabuff* within the historical sociology of the detective genre, noting the fissures or cracks which the novella reveals in the structures governing everyday life. Mark Banks offers a comparative analysis of *The Frankfurt Kabuff* and an earlier thriller, John le Carré's *The Russia House,* both set at international book fairs, and both illuminating aspects of sociological "bookism." Sarah Brouillette explores how *The Frankfurt Kabuff* is an act of "Romancing Book Culture," in all its twenty-first-century affordances of digital self-publishing platforms and romance writing.

The next set of essays focus on aspects of politics at the Frankfurt Book Fair and in the novella. Corinna Norrick-Rühl's "Politics at Play in the Kabuff: The Buchmesse as a Political Space" focuses on the "complex space" of the Fair and its political positioning, arguing that the "fair can and should no longer pretend to be neutral." Doris Ruth Eikhof examines the characters, action, cocktails, and outfits of *The Frankfurt Kabuff* as indicators of a variety of approaches towards social change. Then, Arpita Das gives an autoethnographic account of attending the Buchmesse as a "short South Asian woman," with all the political implications of that perspective.

Creative responses to *The Frankfurt Kabuff* animate the subsequent three essays. Elizabeth Ezra imagines the novella as a musical, inventing a new conceptual school ("OuFiPo") along the way. Roanna Gonsalves writes a Bourdieusian fiction, surreally riffing on *The Frankfurt Kabuff,* in which fish attempt to take over the Buchmesse. Danielle Fuller then reflects upon the fan fiction of "Janielle Frak," which itself responds to and extends the worlds of Blaire Squiscoll. This section of the critical edition draws towards its conclusion with the first full critical response to *The Frankfurt Kabuff* by Kelvin Smith, originally published on his website of fictional accounts of publishing in 2019. Finally, Alastair Horne offers some pedagogical notes that can be used alongside *The Frankfurt Kabuff* in the classroom.

The collection of assemblages amplify the novella. These objects are of considerable variety. Some make this critical edition usable in the classroom, alongside Alastair Horne's teaching guide. Others include creative and sometimes hypothetical paratexts, such as marketing collateral for *The Frankfurt Kabuff,* that play with the conventions of publishing. Still others offer contextual detail, such as the plotting diagram drawn by Kim Wilkins. A comic strip provides both entertainment and a visualization of the principle of NUNU OTOT. The lengthiest assemblage, "Dear Diary," is a radically transparent account of the nuts and bolts of digital publishing that illuminates the novella's role as situation. The assemblages thus work together with the critical essays, the annotated text, and the introduction to comprise *The Frankfurt Kabuff Critical Edition*, enabling it to present the fullest realisation of the novella's affordances.

The Frankfurt Kabuff Critical Edition is part of a large autoethnographic project that layers different forms of writing, criticism and publishing to better understand the dynamics of contemporary publishing and book cultures. The novella itself, as a specific formation at the centre of this layered concoction, is a highly focused reflection on this industry and cultural sector. *The Frankfurt Kabuff* is what happens when autoethnographic methodology and critical theory fuse with fictional accounts. It demonstrates the potential for ethical reflection, mischievous critique, and activism in contemporary book culture through the creation and publication of works of fiction. As we write elsewhere, "The unusualness of our research, the way it veers away from conventional scholarly modes and formats, is part of its point."[49] Creative critique can open up sideways movements, new possibilities that have the potential to regenerate academia and intervene in culture. Writing and publishing (and reading) *The Frankfurt Kabuff Critical Edition* is interparatextual research, creativity, and politics.

Notes

1 "Frankfurter Buchmesse Ends with Significant Increase in Visitors," Frankfurter Buchmesse, accessed March 31, 2021, https://www.buchmesse.de/en/press/press-releases/2019-10-21-frankfurter-buchmesse-ends-significant-increase-visitors.

2 Pages 45–46 of this edition.

3 Jack Halberstam, *The Queer Art of Failure* (Durham: Duke University Press, 2011). Our acknowledgement that the Frankfurt School comprises more than cardboard theory cut-outs is influenced by Toby Bennett's autoethnographic review of *The Frankfurt Book Fair and Bestseller Business*: Toby Bennett, "A Post-Critical Theory of Cultural Production? A Review of The Frankfurt Book Fair and Bestseller Business," *Journal of Cultural Analysis and Social Change* 7, no. 1 (July 2022): 6, https://doi.org/10.20897/jcasc/12257.

4 For more on Ullapoolism, see https://ullapoolism.wordpress.com/ and Beth Driscoll and Claire Squires, "The Epistemology of Ullapoolism: Making Mischief from within Contemporary Book Cultures," *Angelaki* 25, no. 5 (September 2020): 137–55, https://doi.org/10.1080/0969725X.2020.1807147.

5 A full table of the research methods is available in Beth Driscoll and Claire Squires, *The Frankfurt Book Fair and Bestseller Business* (Cambridge: Cambridge University Press, 2020), 9.

6 See Driscoll and Squires, *The Frankfurt Book Fair and Bestseller Business.*

7 Carolyn Ellis, Tony E. Adams, and Arthur P. Bochner, "Autoethnography: An Overview," *Historical Social Research / Historische Sozialforschung* 36, no. 4 (138) (2011): 273–90.

8 For more explanation, see Beth Driscoll and Claire Squires, "Experiments with Book Festival People (Real and Imaginary)," *Mémoires Du Livre / Studies in Book Culture* 11, no. 2 (June 2020), https://doi.org/10.7202/1070271ar.

9 Driscoll and Squires, "The Epistemology of Ullapoolism," 149.

10 We note ongoing debate about university ethics processes, including Shamser Sinha and Les Back's suggestion that "anxiety within universities regarding the moral dimension of academic research, we argue, is producing 'ethical hypochondria' and unthinking conservatism." Shamser Sinha and Les Back, "Making Methods Sociable: Dialogue, Ethics and Authorship in Qualitative Research," *Qualitative Research* 14, no. 4 (August 2014): 473–87, https://doi.org/10.1177/1468794113490717.

11 See Claire Squires and Beth Driscoll, "The Sleaze-O-Meter: Sexual Harassment in the Publishing Industry," *Interscript*, March 8, 2018, https://www.interscriptjournal.com/online-magazine/sleaze-o-meter.

12 Driscoll and Squires, "The Epistemology of Ullapoolism," 148.

13 Kay Inckle, "Telling Tales? Using Ethnographic Fictions to Speak Embodied 'Truth,'" *Qualitative Research* 10, no. 1 (February 2010): 27, https://doi.org/10.1177/1468794109348681.

14 Inckle, 38.

15 Inckle, 44.

16 Ash Watson, "Writing Sociological Fiction," *Qualitative Research* 22, no. 3 (January 2021): 337–52, https://doi.org/10.1177/1468794120985677.

17 The conference was SHARP (Society for the History of Authorship, Reading and Publishing) 2019, held at Amherst, Massachusetts on July 15–19, 2019.

18 Blaire Squiscoll, *The Frankfurt Kabuff* (Wattpad, 2018), https://www.wattpad.com/myworks/164522893-the-frankfurt-kabuff.

19 "It was done; it was finished. Yes, she thought, laying down her brush in extreme fatigue, I have had my vision. THE END." Virginia Woolf, *To the Lighthouse* (1927; repr., London: Penguin Books, 1992), 226.

20 Lauren Fournier, *Autotheory as Feminist Practice in Art, Writing, and Criticism* (Cambridge, Mass: The MIT Press, 2021); Chris Kraus, *I Love Dick* (1997; repr., Cambridge, Mass: Semiotext, 2006); Maggie Nelson, *The Argonauts* (Minneapolis: Graywolf Press, 2015).

21 Fournier, *Autotheory as Feminist Practice*, 2–3.

22 Fournier, 7.

23 Barbara Browning, *The Gift* (Minneapolis: Coffee House Press, 2017).

24 Page 92 of this edition.

25 Pages 51–52 of this edition.

26 For more on Kabuffs, see Corinna Norrick-Rühl's essay on page 153 and various footnotes to the novella.

27 "Frankfurt Book Fair: Violence Follows Calls for 'Active Debate,'" *Deutsche Welle*, October 14, 2017, https://www.dw.com/en/frankfurt-book-fair-violence-follows-calls-for-active-debate/a-40955476.

28 Hazel Smith and Roger T. Dean, eds., *Practice-Led Research, Research-Led Practice in the Creative Arts* (Edinburgh: Edinburgh University Press, 2009), 1; Natalie Loveless, *How to Make Art at the End of the World: A Manifesto for Research-Creation* (Durham: Duke University Press, 2019), 5–6. SSHRC's definition of "research-creation" is available at https://www.sshrc-crsh.gc.ca/funding-financement/programs-programmes/definitions-eng.aspx#a22. Similarly, the UK's Arts and Humanities Research Council (AHRC)'s Research Funding Guide provides a gloss for "creative output", detailing that it "can be produced, or practice undertaken, as an integral part of a research process [...] The Council would expect, however, this practice to be accompanied by some form of documentation of the research process, as well as some form of textual analysis or explanation to support its position and as a record of your critical reflection." (see https://www.ukri.org/wp-content/uploads/2021/08/AHRC-010223-ResearchFundingGuide.pdf).

29 Page 201 of this edition.

30 Driscoll and Squires, "The Epistemology of Ullapoolism."

31 Guy Debord, *The Society of the Spectacle*, trans. Ken Knabb (Berkeley: Bureau of Public Secrets, 2014).

32 Ken Knabb, *Situationist International Anthology*, Revised and Expanded edition (Berkeley: Bureau of Public Secrets, 2006).

33 Michèle Bernstein, *The Night*, trans. Clodagh Kinsella (London: Book Works, 2013), 9.

34 Nicholas Thoburn, *Anti-Book: On the Art and Politics of Radical Publishing* (Minneapolis: University of Minnesota Press, 2016).

35 Greil Marcus, *Lipstick Traces: A Secret History of the Twentieth Century, Twentieth Anniversary*, 2nd edition (Cambridge, Mass: Belknap Press, 2009). Bernstein is quizzed on the genre conventions of her fiction in a television interview, but typically refuses to commit to a clear response; see https://www.youtube.com/watch?v=PlIc_1cjCdg.

36 Fournier, *Autotheory as Feminist Practice*, 2.

37 The development of a belief in artistic autonomy, which was especially pronounced in the nineteenth century as a precursor to modernism, is described by Pierre Bourdieu in *The Field of Cultural Production: Essays on Art and Literature*, trans. Richard Nice (Cambridge: Polity, 1993) and as described earlier in this Introduction satirised through the character of Beatrice's boyfriend Callum in *The Frankfurt Kabuff.*

38 Ruha Benjamin, "Racial Fictions, Biological Facts: Expanding the Sociological Imagination through Speculative Methods," *Catalyst: Feminism, Theory, Technoscience* 2, no. 2 (June 2016): 1–28, https://doi.org/10.28968/cftt.v2i2.28798.

39 Patricia Leavy, "Fiction and the Feminist Academic Novel," *Qualitative Inquiry* 18, no. 6 (July 2012): 516–22, https://doi.org/10.1177/1077800412442813.

40 Fournier, *Autotheory as Feminist Practice*, 3–4.

41 For more on this, see Beth Driscoll and Claire Squires, "'Oh Look, a Ferry'; or The Smell of Paper Books," *The Lifted Brow*, October 24, 2018, https://www.theliftedbrow

.com/liftedbrow/2018/10/24 oh-look-a-ferry-or-the-smell-of-paper-books-by-beth-driscoll-and-claire-squires.

42 Scholars who have described these systems, including some of their negative social effects, include Melanie Ramdarshan Bold, "The Return of the Social Author: Negotiating Authority and Influence on Wattpad," *Convergence: The International Journal of Research into New Media Technologies* 24, no. 2 (April 2018): 117–36, https://doi.org/10.1177/1354856516654459; Safiya Umoja Noble, *Algorithms of Oppression: How Search Engines Reinforce Racism* (New York: New York University Press, 2018); Claire Parnell, "Mapping the Entertainment Ecosystem of Wattpad: Platforms, Publishing and Adaptation," *Convergence* 27, no. 2 (April 2021): 524–38, https://doi.org/10.1177/1354856520970141; and Sarah Brouillette, "Wattpad's Fictions of Care," *Post45*, July 13, 2022, https://post45.org/2022/07/wattpads-fictions-of-care/.

43 Kelvin Smith, "Kabuff or Wunderkammer?" *The Point of Publishing* (blog), July 5, 2019, https://pointofpublishing.com/2019/07/05/kabuff-or-wunderkammer/. On his website, Kelvin Smith publishes short reviews of books featuring fictional publishers, as well as fictional publishers in film; see https://pointofpublishing.com/books/. His review is republished in this critical edition on page 195. For an examination of the respective accounts of book fairs in *The Frankfurt Kabuff* and John le Carré's *The Russia House* (1989), see Mark Banks's essay on page 135.

44 See Kim Wilkins, Beth Driscoll, and Lisa Fletcher, *Genre Worlds: Popular Fiction and Twenty-First Century Book Culture* (Amherst: University of Massachusetts Press, 2022).

45 "Satire," in Wikipedia, February 14, 2023, https://en.wikipedia.org/w/index.php?title=Satire&oldid=1139352738.

46 Gérard Genette, *Paratexts: Thresholds of Interpretation* trans. Jane E. Lewin (Cambridge: Cambridge University Press, 1997).

47 Julia Kristeva, "Word, Dialogue and Novel," in *The Kristeva Reader*, ed. Toril Moi (Oxford: Basil Blackwell, 1986), 37.

48 We developed this question via the performative conference paper: Beth Driscoll and Claire Squires, "Blaire Squiscoll's Bookshelves: An Ullapoolist Intertextuality" (Bookshelves in the Age of the COVID-19 Pandemic: An Online Conference, The Open University, UK, 2020).

49 Beth Driscoll and Claire Squires, "Serious Fun: Gaming the Book Festival," *Mémoires Du Livre / Studies in Book Culture* 9, no. 2 (May 2018): 1–37, https://doi.org/10.7202/1046988ar

The Frankfurt Kabuff

A Beatrice Deft (Comic Erotic) Thriller

BLAIRE SQUISCOLL

with annotations by the author(s)

CHAPTER EINS

BEATRICE SIPPED HER NEGRONI[1] AND TOOK A LONG DRAG of her cigarette,[2] leaving a bright red lipstick stain on the filter. Frankfurt was unseasonably warm,[3] with hot sunlight beating through the autumn leaves.[4] Bodies blurred past, but she paid them no heed. Beatrice wasn't here for anyone but herself. The chicken shop incident had wrung her dry.

---

1. The origin of the Negroni is contested, although regularly traced to 1919, a round hundred years before the print publication of *The Frankfurt Kabuff*. The ingredients are also round: one part gin, one part sweet vermouth, one part Campari, served over ice with orange peel. Delicious. Note textual variant: "negroni" was written in lower-case in the original, and has been capitalised throughout.
2. Smoking is bad for you but it is a trope of genre fiction.
3. Frankfurt, like every other city and region in the world, has contributed to and undergone climate change. The City of Frankfurt has developed a "Masterplan 100% Climate Protection" which is available at https://frankfurt.de/-/media/frankfurtde/frankfurt-themen/klima-und-energie/pdf/energiereferat-79a/masterplan-climate-protection---summarised-version.ashx#:~:text=Since%20the%20beginning%20of%20 2013,95%20%25%20reduction%20of%20carbon%20emissions.
4. It is not yet clear from this point in the narrative, but this seemingly idyllic city scene and the season—autumn—contributes to Beatrice's sense of alienation, configured in the subsequent three sentences. Squiscoll's heroine has travelled several thousand miles, and two seasons, from her native Australia.

In the distance she heard sirens, the European nee-nah[5] that she had found so amusing on her first trip here... how many years ago now? Too many to count; how had she become so jaded at the age of only thirty-two, and a Scorpio at that.[6]

The solicitous young waiter stopped at the end of her table. His chiseled jaw moved as he spoke, his words English but his accent distinctly Teutonic.[7] "May I bring you anuzza drink, madam?" His bright blue eyes sparkled down at her, the hint of a flirtatious smile played at the corners of his lips.

She assessed him coolly. Once, before the chicken shop, she wouldn't have hesitated to twinkle back at him, make a flirtatious joke even. But some spark inside her had gone out, and remained unlit for months now. His smile faded suddenly and she wondered if a shadow had passed across her face. She tried a smile of her own, but it felt more like a baring of teeth.

"Madam?" he asked again.

"Just the bill," she said abruptly. "And where can I buy more cigarettes and red lipstick?"

She wondered why he had given her a second glance. Her enormous blue eyes were hidden behind sunglasses, and all her lipstick had come off while chain smoking. Her luggage had gone missing and she was still in the clingy tunic and leggings she had slept in on the long flight from Australia. The Negroni was her first meal of the day.

The waiter smiled. "If you give me your room number, I will charge it to your account. And the shops are zat way." He indicated with a shrug of his well-developed shoulder.

---

5. The range of sounds of emergency vehicles from other parts of the world includes the Australian (wee-oh-wee-oh-wee-oh), the American (oooooaaaaeeeeeeooooaaaeeeooo), and the Indian (oweeoweeoweeoweeowee). Pascale Casanova has written of the "World Republic of Letters," trans. M.B. Debevoise (Cambridge: Harvard University Press, 2004), a hierarchical space in which the centres of Paris, London, and New York exert much greater power than peripheral or minor literary cultures. Casanova's analysis did not extend to depictions of siren noises, however; as with so many other granular features of writing, the ways in which these are transcribed reveal the intended audience. Here, Squiscoll estranges the "normality" of the European siren sound through focalising Deft's postcolonial subjectivity (and allowing Deft's amusement and then jadedness to wryly invert traditional power relations between the European centre and Australia).
6. For further details on the attributes of the Scorpio, see https://twitter.com/poetastrologers.
7. Textual variant: the 2019 edition has "teutonic."

"Five-oh-seven," she said. Then she jabbed her cigarette at the crowded gathering she could see across the road. "What is going on over there?"

"Die Buchmesse, Madam. The Frankfurt Book Fair. Do you like books?"[8]

She shrugged. "I did. Once." She pushed back her chair and pulled her bag over her shoulder, and went upstairs to her room. She didn't notice the quiet elderly man at the next table, who had carefully noted her room number.

8. The waiter's small talk ends here with a loaded question. Whether or not one "likes books" is a question that speaks to identity formation (see Jessica Pressman, *Bookishness* (New York: Columbia University Press, 2020) and the considerable body of research on historical and contemporary readers). Furthermore, while the publishing industry is a subset of larger media and entertainment industries, its members often see themselves as "book people," a carry-over of older ideas of the symbolic and cultural heft of books. Really, the waiter is asking Deft whether she is an insider or an outsider in relation to the Frankfurter Buchmesse, a question that will go on to drive the dynamics of the plot.

CHAPTER ZWEI

Klopf klopf![1]

Beatrice jerked awake, her body working more quickly than her mind. She felt the touch of 100% Egyptian cotton on her skin, then the sound of another loud knock. Frankfurt, she thought. Autumn. But how long had she been asleep?

---

1. The onomatopoeic word "klopf" is initially ambiguous. While the ambiguity is swiftly resolved (it is a knock on the door), the word also recalls the sound made by horses' hooves. There is a famous horse of Frankfurt, Jenny, a white Arabian mare who roamed the city streets on her own every day for over fifteen years, and was beloved by locals. However, she did not work as a hotel porter, being over twenty years old and therefore retired at the time when this novella is set. (For more information, including videos, see https://www.youtube.com/watch?v=9zDNxJY6DZo, https://www.haaretz.com/world-news/.premium.MAGAZINE-my-name-is-jenny-the-mare-and-i-m-out-1.9281885, and the documentary "The Walk" https://www.walkwithjenny.de/). Incidentally, "klopf" is also one letter away from a famous US publishing company (Knopf), which was established by Alfred A. Knopf Sr. and Blanche Knopf shortly before the Negroni. However, Knopf's logo, designed by Blanche in 1925, is, disappointingly, a borzoi dog rather than a horse. Knopf has undergone the typical round of publishing merger and acquisitions, being bought by Random House in 1960, and now being part of the Penguin Random House group (see https://en.wikipedia.org/wiki/Alfred_A._Knopf). Pleasingly, one of Knopf's current editors—and authors!—is called Jenny (Jackson), and has authored a book called *Pineapple Street.* It is noted that since the initial formulation of this footnote, Jenny the Horse has sadly passed on, but hopefully continues her daily walks on rainbow-hued streets.

She jumped up, pulling the sheets around her as she opened the door a crack. A scent of musky cologne hit her as her jetlagged eyes appraised brilliantined stubble.

"Madam," said the porter, gesturing by his hip. Beatrice lowered her gaze to a black suitcase. Hers.

"Ja, it has arrived." He gestured his dimpled chin over her shoulder, into the room. "Do you want me to bring it in for you?"

She dragged her hand through her jet black hair, lifting her eyes back up to meet his. Only the sheet stood between her and the porter. Then she remembered throwing clothes into the suitcase in her Melbourne apartment, swearing to herself she would never look upon the sinisterly bright facade of that chicken shop again.[2]

"No… not now," she breathed, taking the handle of the bag and dragging it into the room, closing the door behind her.

She leaned back heavily against the door, casting her eye around the room. The empty cigarette packet stared back, its rumpled cellophane taunting her. She closed her eyes for a second, then swooped down with/in[3] one agile movement to unzip her luggage. She grabbed her toiletry bag and strode towards the shower.

Ten seconds later[4] Beatrice emerged, refreshed. She spilled clothes out of the suitcase, strewing them across the luxurious carpet, a sea of black on the ocean of russet-green. A shapeless yet stylish black dress topped the pile.[5] She threw it on, laced up her black leather boots to the thigh with red ribbons,[6] and headed out into the fading evening light.

* * *

2. The repeated hints of trauma associated with the chicken shop in the first two chapters of the novella were a focus of comments and questions from beta readers of the serialised version of the novella on Wattpad, directly influencing the writing process. Note textual variant: the original has "sinsterly."
3. Textual variant: the 2019 edition has "within."
4. Coming from Australia, Beatrice is aware of the devastating effects of drought and is water-wise, conserving this precious resource through her short showers. She is also a generally efficient person.
5. Typical Melbourne fashion.
6. Not typical Melbourne fashion.

The smell of piss hit her first. One street had led to another until she found herself in a cluttered laneway. Men in stained sleeping bags called out to her. Beatrice hated all forms of economic inequality.[7]

"Hey, Australian lady," a rough voice hailed her. "Got any cigarettes?"

She was flush with cigarettes; stocking up had been her reason for this long walk in the first place. She strode over, boots clinking on cobbles and dodging construction paraphernalia. She fished in her Allen & Unwin tote bag, and withdrew a Camel, which he took gratefully.

He pointed at the bag. "You here for the publisher party?"[8]

She shrugged. "I suppose I could. Where is it?"

He pointed with his Camel at the Red Russian pole-dancing club. "Down there. Thanks for the cigarette."

"No problem."

A dark-haired Frankfurter at the door gave her a quick glance and ushered her in. She found herself walking along a crimson corridor, surrounded by erotic art.[9] She followed it to a steep staircase, into a womb-like space below. In the tiny dark room, Primal Scream's "Loaded" blasted from tinny speakers.[10] Beatrice was unexpectedly charmed. Everywhere she looked,

---

7. Beatrice's moral compass is partially shaped by her upbringing, which was informed by her mother's involvement in the May 68 protests in Paris, as were those of several other characters within the evolving character sphere of Blaire Squiscoll (see Chapter Sechs, page 44, note 3).

8. The rough sleeper knows Beatrice is Australian because he recognises Allen & Unwin as the name of one of Australia's largest publishers (currently publishing over 250 titles a year). Allen & Unwin was founded in 1914 (shortly before the Negroni) when Stanley Unwin (who went on to publish J.R.R. Tolkien's *The Lord of the Rings*, among other books) bought a controlling stake in the British firm George Allen and Co. The firm opened an Australian subsidiary in 1976. Following a takeover of the parent company by HarperCollins, the Australian office was bought out by local management in 1990, creating the independent company Allen & Unwin Australia Pty Ltd. For more, see Angela Crocombe, "Allen and Unwin: A Short History," *Publishing Studies*, no. 5 (Spring 1997): 42–46, https://search.informit.org/doi/10.3316/ielapa.8111425426.

9. This setting is based on the 2018 C—— Party, held at The Black Russian on Elbestrasse, a lounge and dance bar in Frankfurt's red-light district near the Hauptbanhopf. Video footage captured by Blaire Squiscoll gives a brief taste of the event's vibe; see https://www.youtube.com/watch?v=CT6vaiG9oBg.

10. There exists a Spotify playlist that partially recreates the eye-watering music choices of this publisher party, which ran the full gamut from Kanye West's "Gold Digger" to the Ray Charles song it samples (see assemblages, page 229). Primal Scream's "Loaded" was played at the C—— Party in 2017 and 2018 (there was no C—— Party in 2019). It

suited men and chicly dressed women smiled, talked, and bobbed along to the music. Genuine enthusiasm animated their gestures and expressions.[11] Once, she had been this optimistic. She wondered if she could be again.

As she moved towards the bar, she noted with a frown that a tall, dark-haired man with well-developed biceps, a thick baton, and the word POLIZEI emblazoned across his jacket, glowered from the corner of the room.[12] Why would they need a police officer here? Everybody seemed so nice.

While Beatrice waited for her Negroni,[13] drumming her dark red fingernails on the bar, she found herself pressed against two older men in blue suits,[14] as they shouted to be heard over the music.

At first she could only hear snatches of their conversation, words that didn't seem to belong in this happy, carefree space. "Threat of violence" "mitigate against the danger" "guns" "bombs".[15]

Even if she knew this wasn't her problem, she was intrigued enough to lean closer.

Then, in an oddly long gap between songs,[16] one of their voices reached her ears as clear as a bell.

"Something terrible is going to happen at the book fair tomorrow."

---

is noted that as recently as 2019, C—— publisher J—— B—— was overheard in the foyer of the Hessischer Hof introducing himself to a woman as a "former DJ."

11. Many publishing people are very nice. See also the last line of the next paragraph.
12. Beatrice's overt reaction to sighting the police officer at the publisher party is one of puzzlement, yet at the same time her eyes clearly have taken in his shapely form.
13. Textual variant: another instance where the 2019 edition has "negroni."
14. The ubiquitous uniform of male publishing professionals at the Frankfurter Buchmesse. One night, a small press owner from the north of England confessed his relief at changing into casual clothes to drink apfelwein and eat schnitzel at a bar, saying "I've been dressed like a Tory all day."
15. The idea that publishing is a space apart from politics is a furphy.
16. A feature of the C—— Party DJ-ing style.

CHAPTER DREI

BEATRICE'S LUNGS HEAVED IN THE NIGHT-TIME AIR. Was there no escape from danger, even thousands of miles and two seasons away from Australia?

A soft step sounded in the laneway behind her. She span round, instinctively tightening her knuckles.[1]

It was the tall policeman from the party. Her breath pumped around her breast as she took in flawless tanned skin, straight nose, full lips.

"Are you alright?" His voice was deep, concerned. Warm brown eyes fixed on hers. "I saw you running out of the club."

"I… two men were discussing an attack, bombs, at the book fair… I needed air."

The man shifted his weight. "Ach so. Everyone is talking about this book. It is the book of the fair, I hear.[2] Are you a publisher?"

---

1. Beatrice's reaction is, unfortunately, that of women worldwide in locations known and unknown, day-time and night-time, light and dark.
2. In this interchange, the police officer demonstrates—alongside his physical attributes—his facility for discussing literature, and its wider industry contexts, including the generation of "buzz" at the fair for the "book of the fair." What is less clear is what this title actually was. Perhaps Andreas Malm's *How to Blow Up a Pipeline: Learning to Fight in a World on Fire*, first published by Verso Books in 2021 and therefore plausibly the subject of trade fair rights meetings around 2019, when the book appears to be set.

Beatrice looked down at the cobbles before replying. "Why were you at the party? Is there a security issue?"[3]

"Nein, nein. One of the Ambassadors wanted to come. He loves books. And parties."

"And Ferrero Rocher?"[4] she riposted.

The policeman smiled, showing a set of perfect white teeth. "Something like that. Listen, my shift has finished. Can I walk you to your hotel? It's late, and this area…"

"Officer… what's your name?"

"Polizeiobermeister Schorle.[5] But call me Caspian. I am off duty now."

"Caspian…" She rolled the letters round her mouth like a long cooling drink after a hot day. "Sure, why not. If you're heading in my direction."

* * *

Beatrice threw off her dress and climbed onto the bed, clutching the small business card that Caspian had thrust into her hand. When they'd parted at the hotel entrance, she'd thought for a moment about inviting him in for a nightcap. She'd felt something kindling inside of her.[6]

Instead, she'd asked for his number. She laughed as she remembered him bashfully pointing to his shapely uniformed shoulder. 6969.[7] Who says numbers aren't sexy, she thought. Three stars, as well.

---

3. Despite the already mounting physical attraction between Beatrice and the police officer, the former is not distracted from her urgent need to understand the discussion of bombs at the fair.
4. Ferrero Rocher are, according to the advertising for the exquisite chocolate, "a sign of good taste," which links the worlds of chocolate manufacture, diplomacy, and books. Ferrero Rocher are served at all ambassadorial receptions, and—while at university—Beatrice appeared as a bit player in one of the advertisements, available at https://www.youtube.com/watch?v=4P-nZZkQqTc. Ferrero Rocher are further known as a potent symbol of "the good life" for immigrants to America; see https://www.thrillist.com/eat/nation/ferrero-rocher-chocolates-status-symbol-immigrants.
5. Schorle is German for juice.
6. "Kindling" is a glancing reference to the e-reader developed by Amazon. For more details on the early days of the Kindle, see Simon Peter Rowberry, *Four Shades of Gray* (Cambridge, Mass: MIT Press, 2022).
7. Police officer numbers are randomly, but sometimes perfectly, assigned.

She scrutinised the card he'd given her: a red boot, a shop name and a Frankfurt address. As they parted, he'd told her that if she needed him, to go to this shop. "My aunt—Tante Fran—she will help," he said earnestly.

Shaking her head, a wry smile playing on her lips, she sank back into the feather pillows. For the first time in months she let her body relax.

As she reached over to turn off the bedside light, she noticed an envelope propped up by the telephone. She grabbed it, feeling its weight and texture. 300 gsm minimum.[8]

An elaborate cursive script read *B.D., Room 507*. Startled, she sat up, and tore open the envelope:

> *Sehr geehrte Frau Deft:*
> *Never have we met, but many years ago I knew your mother. When you receive this, whatever time of the day or night, please call me. I need your help. I am in Room 233.*
> *K.W.*

Beatrice's heart accelerated. Her hand moved towards the phone. She thought about last time someone needed her help, and pulled her fingers back sharply. But he'd known her dear, late mother; he might have memories of her.

* * *

Down in the hotel bar, the Bösendorfer[9] tinkled and low conversations hummed. The light was dim, but she spotted an elderly, bearded man in a sharp blue suit, nursing a Campari and soda[10] and gazing at her intently. She strode over and thrust out her hand.

8. The term gsm stands for grams per square metre. No matter the size of a sheet of paper, its weight is always measured using a square metre. Measurement and weighing are important in apprehending the materiality of book culture.
9. Bösendorfer is a renowned Austrian brand of pianos established in 1828. In a parallel with the mergers and acquisitions that have characterised recent decades in the publishing industry, Bösendorfer was acquired by the multinational Yamaha company in 2008.
10. Kurt demonstrates his continental sophistication by drinking the bitter Italian liqueur, and also an affinity with Beatrice, given Campari is a key constituent of the Negroni.

"Are you Kurt Weidenfeld?"[11]

"Sit, sit," he said. "Ah, you are ferry[12] image of your mother."

Beatrice smiled. She had been told this before, and it never failed to delight her.

A cloud moved across his face. "I could always count on your mother to care for those in danger."

Beatrice's heart twisted. Her mother had pushed a young boy's pram out of the way of an oncoming bus, only to feel its full force herself. It had been Beatrice's tenth birthday. "Caring can be dangerous," she said, snapping her fingers for the waiter.

His tone became stern. "So can not caring, mein Liebchen."

She sighed. "You'd best explain yourself."

"I am a publisher of left-wing philosophy. For the past month I have been receiving threats from The White Storm, a network of newspapers and zines[13] dedicated to reviving the worst ideas and policies of the twentieth century."

Beatrice gulped. "Nazis?"[14] The waiter arrived with her Negroni. Clearly she already had a reputation.

Kurt waited for them to be alone again, then spoke, "They have warned me, and others like me, to stay away from Frankfurt. They want it all to

---

11. How does she know his name? Confusing. Note that the use of an actual publisher's name, Weidenfeld, is a coincidence or at least subconscious on Blaire Squiscoll's part.
12. Ferries are important in the iconography of Ullapoolism. See Beth Driscoll and Claire Squires, "'Oh Look, a Ferry'; or The Smell of Paper Books," *The Lifted Brow*, October 24, 2018, https://www.theliftedbrow.com/liftedbrow/2018/10/24/oh-look-a-ferry-or-the-smell-of-paper-books-by-beth-driscoll-and-claire-squires, aka OLAF. Here it is a play on words that participates in the genre trope of egregiously mangling the transliteration of accents. This aspect also was part of the fabric of OLAF, as Squires's (French) mother understood her daughter to be asking for "fairy" pyjamas rather than "ferry," which would have been an odd request for someone in their mid-forties.
13. Zines are generally thought to be the preserve of left of centre, counter-cultural communities. However, there is nothing inherently progressive about a format, and such media can be used for evil as well as (political) good. For scholarship on zines, see Janice Radway, "Zines, Half-Lives, and Afterlives: On the Temporalities of Social and Political Change," *PMLA* 126, no. 1 (2011): 140–50. For more on zines in the work of Blaire Squiscoll, see *The COP26 Kabuff* as referred to in the assemblages.
14. Beatrice immediately cuts through the metaphorical iconography of the media grouping to understand her interlocutor's point: that "The White Storm" is a Nazi, or neo-Nazi, organisation.

themselves. They say, if we cannot have die Buchmesse as our exclusive platform, then they will destroy it."[15]

Beatrice interjected. "But Frankfurt Book Fair is about the exchange of ideas!"[16]

"I know, Liebchen. But there are those who would seek to control it. If I turn up tomorrow, I am in danger. My small press requires international rights sales to survive. While I am in meetings, can you be my eyes and ears?"

She hesitated. Last time she had got involved in somebody else's problems, it had all gone horribly wrong. Her eyes misted over as she remembered…

15. So much for freedom of speech.

16. Beatrice's idealistic interjection demonstrates her own affinity with books, and also the prominent discourse surrounding the Frankfurter Buchmesse, particularly in its post-Second World War ideological leanings. Driscoll and Squires interrogate this aspect of the Buchmesse in chapter 3 of *The Frankfurt Book Fair and Bestseller Business* (Cambridge: Cambridge University Press, 2020).

CHAPTER VIER

COLD DRIZZLE[1] *FALLS THROUGH THE GUM TREES AND settles around my shoulders like a shawl. Crickets chirrup and a possum scampers across the electricity wires.*[2] *I turn the key in the lock of our Federation-style townhouse.*[3]

"Callum?" I call.

"Back here." I hear in his voice that he's in good spirits.

---

1. The change in weather from the previous Frankfurt scenes, alongside the change in font (from roman to italic type) indicate a change in register, which is quickly confirmed by the switch in style (to a more literary tone) and point of view (to Beatrice's first-person). Melbourne is well-known for its rainy climate: as the joke goes, in Melbourne you can have four seasons in one day as long as each season contains intermittent rain.
2. In this extended depiction of the flora and fauna of Melbourne, the author demonstrates insider knowledge of the biodiversity of the urban Australian environment.
3. Federation homes were built in Australia at the turn of the nineteenth and twentieth centuries, their name coming from the Federation of Australia on 1 January 1901 (see https://intrimmouldings.com.au/blog/why-federation-homes-are-fabulous/), i.e. roughly the same period as the Negroni. Such homes typically feature extensive decorative woodwork and complex roof forms. In Australia, Federation homes are associated with affluence and townhouses with young couples and families, so this dwelling would place Beatrice and Callum firmly in the social demographic formerly known as "yuppies" (young urban professionals or young upwardly mobile professionals) were it not for the fact that Federation townhouses do not really exist in Melbourne or anywhere else.

I find him in our cupboard-sized kitchen.[4] *The red wine is open. He hasn't waited for me.*[5]

"The meeting went well then?"

He rounds the table and kisses me distractedly. "Allen & Unwin have agreed to distribute us. Florencia Intelligensia books will be in all reputable bookstores!"[6]

"Congratulations." His dream come true.

"Here's a tote bag[7] *they gave me. You can have it. You're always carrying around those old books you love so much."*

"They're called classics, Callum, and they are changing my students' lives."[8]

"It's just high school," Callum says. "They'll stop reading when they graduate, just like the other sheeple in this godforsaken Melbourne suburb."

I bite my lip. We've been over this ground before.

I place the bag from Kev's Hot Chicken on the table. "I got us dinner." He hands me a glass of wine. "A real celebration then."

"Amina served me. I'm so proud of her. Her family came here with nothing as refugees from Sudan, and now she's topping my English class as well as

---

4. This mention of the cupboard-sized kitchen is both an early foreshadowing of the centrality of the Kabuff to the erotic thriller plot of *The Frankfurt Kabuff*, and an indicator of the domestic choices which Beatrice and Callum have made.
5. In Beatrice's opening first-person observations, there already appears to be some tension in her relationship with Callum.
6. Allen & Unwin, referenced in Chapter Zwei, page 32, note 8, are not only one of Australia's biggest independent publishers but also provide distribution services to smaller Australian publishers and a number of well-known international publishers, including Bloomsbury, first publisher of the Harry Potter novels. Distribution is one of the most significant challenges facing the publishing industry as a whole, and small independent publishers in particular. Distribution is even more difficult in countries with relatively low populations and large geographical areas, such as Australia and Canada. For more on the challenges of distribution, see Kylee Bristow, "Distribution—the Fatal Flaw?," *Publishing Studies*, no. 4 (March 1997): 36–44.
7. The fieldwork for *The Frankfurt Book Fair and Bestseller Business* (Cambridge: Cambridge University Press, 2020) included the creation of custom tote bags; see https://ullapoolism.wordpress.com/2017/10/26/frank-furt-school/. For a concerted discussion of tote bags in the publishing industry, see Alexandra Dane, "Cultural Capital as Performance: Tote Bags and Contemporary Literary Festivals," *Mémoires Du Livre / Studies in Book Culture* 11, no. 2 (June 2020): 1–29, https://doi.org/10.7202/1070270ar.
8. The discussion about whether books change people's lives—and indeed whether books are good for you—has been well rehearsed in academic scholarship and the general media.

holding down a part-time job. She seemed a bit tired, though. I hope nothing is troubling her."

"You worry too much about other people, Bea."

"But she's our next-door neighbour."

He doesn't respond, tearing into juicy flesh with one hand, while the other adjusts his man bun.[9]

Callum changes the topic and we chat over dinner, mostly about his supply-chain logistics.[10] *The wine disappears quickly. While he is getting a second bottle from our wine rack, I hear the slam of a car door and raised voices.*

"What is that?" I say, rising from my chair.

"Leave it, Bea," Callum says.

I walk outside to the paved courtyard, where the last few bougainvillea flowers cling sadly to the dripping vine. I can see a sliver of the street. Two white men, broad across the shoulders, loom over Amina, whose slight body is flexed in a posture of defiance.

I strain to hear, but nothing comes to me clearly. Then one of the men—I recognise him as Kev—shakes his fist and shouts at Amina over the deepening rain. "You need to forget what you saw!"

9. Man buns have a long history stretching back millennia (see https://www.fashionbeans.com/article/man-bun-guide/), but Callum's particular iteration is late 2010s hipster.

10. Supply-chain logistics *might* be perceived as the dullest part of the publishing industry, but they are, of course, crucially important (as the worldwide supply chain issues during COVID-19 demonstrated). They are investigated very thoroughly (and entertainingly) by Matthew Kirshenbaum in "Bibliologistics: The Nature of Books Now, or A Memorable Fancy," *Post45*, April 8, 2020, https://post45.org/2020/04/bibliologistics-the-nature-of-books-now-or-a-memorable-fancy/.

CHAPTER FÜNF

THE SUN BEAT DOWN ON FRANKFURT. BEATRICE PACED the streets, the skyscrapers of the banking district overshadowing her, reminding her of Melbourne.[1] She wanted to forget what she'd seen… but she couldn't. She'd come to Germany to escape, but Herr Weidenfeld wanted her eyes and ears.

She turned into the cobbles of the New Old Town. Tourists were queuing for ice creams. Her head throbbed. She'd brought the wrong clothes for this unseasonably warm weather.

"New shoes," she whispered to herself, pulling the business card that Caspian had given her out of the thick fabric of her dress pocket.[2]

---

1. Apparently, "as the home of the European Central Bank (ECB), Frankfurt is the financial capital of the Eurozone. The bank makes monetary policy decisions for an economic area that is home to around 330 million people and anchors the euro into the global financial system" (see https://www.gcb.de/case-stories/kompetenzfelder/frankfurt-the-financial-centre-of-the-continent.html). Melbourne too has skyscrapers, but in a rare error that betrays Squiscoll's position in relation to the Melbourne–Sydney rivalry, it is Sydney and not Melbourne that is the banking capital of Australia.
2. All feminist dresses require pockets. For discussion of this see, for example, Chelsea G. Summers, "The Politics of Pockets," *Vox*, September 19, 2016, https://www.vox.com/2016/9/19/12865560/politics-of-pockets-suffragettes-women, which notes "Take away pockets happily hidden under garments, and you limit women's ability to navigate public spaces, to carry seditious (or merely amorous) writing, or to travel unaccompanied."

The shop front that Google Maps had directed her to hadn't been decorated in decades, red paint flaking from its woodwork.[3] But the modest window display had some surprisingly stylish footwear. A bell tinkled as she pushed the door open.

She trailed her fingers across the shelves, picking out some heels. She slipped her right foot in, revelling in the caress of its insole against her skin. This was a heel that meant business.

"Zat is the Schuh for you," a soft female voice sounded.

Beatrice jumped, looking to the shadows at the back of the shop. "Is that..." she hesitated, "Tante Fran?"

"Ja," replied the women. "And you must be Beatrice, am I correct? I will get you the left shoe."

Tante Fran emerged from the cupboard, holding the matching heel. Beatrice could see in her face Caspian's full lips and deep eyes.

"Thank you. I'll take them."

Tante Fran put both shoes into a cardboard box and a bright red bag.

"Caspian told me you are interested in ze structural inequalities of society," Tante Fran said as Beatrice held out her credit card. "Though not how beautiful you are. Would you like to join our reading group while you are visiting? We meet every Wednesday. We're on Marcuse's *Eros and Civilisation*. Or on Fridays we paint slogans..."[4]

Beatrice clasped her shoes to her chest, unsure how to reply.

The tinkling of the bell broke the heavy silence of the shop. "Caspian, Neffe!" called Tante Fran.

Beatrice span round. Caspian's broad silhouette was framed in the door. Deep in her pelvis, she felt the sensation that had evaded her for months.

---

3. Tante Fran's shoe shop is an autoethnographic insertion, based on Rudolf Molzberger Schuh Krolla, a shoe shop located on the corner of Münchener Straße and Weserstraße. This excellent shoe shop sold stylish, comfortable, and affordable footwear until its demise in 2019. This made it an appropriate complement to the dominant industry rhetoric surrounding the Frankfurt Book Fair, which is that participants need comfortable shoes (see Driscoll and Squires, *The Frankfurt Book Fair and Bestseller Business*, chapter 2).
4. Book clubs have long been a forum for women's self-education and activism. See Elizabeth Long, *Book Clubs: Women and the Uses of Reading in Everyday Life* (Chicago: University of Chicago Press, 2003); Elizabeth McHenry, *Forgotten Readers: Recovering the Lost History of African American Literary Societies* (Durham: Duke University Press, 2002). For emerging scholarship on Tante Fran's Book Club, see the assemblages section, page 222.

CHAPTER SECHS

CASPIAN'S EYES MET BEATRICE'S FOR A MOMENT OF smouldering intensity. A charge passed between him and her, but then he abruptly turned away to address Tante Fran, although his use of heavily accented English indicated he wanted to include Beatrice.

"I had to come and find you. White Storm is gathering at die Buchmesse!"

Tante Fran's face took on a resolute expression. "I will phone the book club immediately!"[1]

Caspian turned to Beatrice. "I'm sorry. You tried to warn me at the party. I was wrong to dismiss you."[2]

"White Storm?" Beatrice said. "An old friend of my mother's, Kurt Weidenfeld, told me he had been receiving threats from them."

"Kurt Weidenfeld! The famous publisher of left-wing philosophy?" Tante Fran exclaimed. Her voice softened. "Kurt and I have known each other for many years."[3]

---

1. Using the telephone as a communications method (rather than carrier pigeon, pneumatic, or WhatsApp) situates Tante Fran within a particular demographic.
2. Here, Caspian demonstrates his credentials by proffering a full apology and acknowledging that Beatrice was right and he was wrong.
3. For the back story of how Tante Fran and Kurt Weidenfeld met, please see Blaire Squiscoll, *Tante Fran's May 1968 Book Club* (Wattpad, 2019), https://www.wattpad.com/story/202577230-tante-fran%27s-may-%2768-book-club.

"He asked me to be his eyes and ears in meetings, but I didn't want to get involved."

"But we must involve ourselves in the lives of others who need our help," Caspian said firmly. "That is what it is to be truly human."

Beatrice felt warmth rise in her breast; he shared her values.

Then Caspian said, "Come."

A few moments later, they were hailing a cab to the book fair. In the back of the cab, she could feel the heat from his body radiating towards her. His muscular arms were tightly crossed, making his shoulders bulge against his dark blue uniform. She wondered what kind of books he read.

"You are going to the book fair?" said the cab driver. "I have an idea for a book I've always wanted to write since I arrived here from Turkey."[4]

Beatrice had a twinge; she had no commissioning power as she didn't work for a publisher, but she wanted to know this man's story. She was interested in every human being. "I have little influence in the publishing world," she said, "but go on."

"It's David Nicholls's *One Day* meets Harry Potter. Two young wizards meet on the same day, July 31st, every year, for 20 years. It will appeal to young adults around the world!"[5]

Beatrice was impressed with the commercial potential of this idea, which could reach readers across class, race, and gender divides. "You have a talent," she said. "May I pass your pitch on to my friend, Kurt Weidenfeld?"

"The famed philosophical left-wing publisher? Of course!"

They pulled up outside the Messe. Red and white flags fluttered in the sunshine, small stall holders were selling secondhand books, German sausages, beer, and pretzels. Caspian took her through a special side entrance, nodding to a police officer who turned her lips up in a smile in return, and said something to him in German. Inside Hall Four, row upon row of publishers stalls greeted her gaze. Some of the stands were very small, but others were colossal, like fortresses.[6] Everywhere Beatrice looked, there

4. This exchange is inspired by an encounter between a researcher in Frankfurt and her taxi driver.

5. A satire of pitching in the publishing industry and the creative industries more generally, mashing up two very dissimilar genres. Such an approach sees its acme in titles such as Jane Austen and Seth Grahame-Smith, *Pride and Prejudice and Zombies* (Philadelphia: Quirk Books, 2009).

6. Driscoll and Squires write about size in the publishing industry in chapter 2 of *The Frankfurt Book Fair and Bestseller Business*, "Big, Small, Nowhere at All", as well as the

were posters of forthcoming titles and rows of books. She had never seen so many. Men in blue suits milled around.[7] Several police officers patrolled the corridors, their guns and batons conspicuous.

Caspian laid a firm hand on her upper arm. She was surprised by the heat on her skin. "I must go to meet with my commander," he said. "You'll find Kurt in row B." He fixed her in his magnetic gaze. "Be careful."

"I will," Beatrice said, and hurried off to find Kurt's stand. Towards the end of row B, she discovered him wedged between other small, left-wing publishers and, surprisingly, a greeting card manufacturer.[8] The Linksphilosophie Verlag sign was pinned to the wall behind his desk, where he sat in a meeting with a doe-eyed young woman, selling his rights.

When he saw Beatrice, he leapt to his feet. "Mein Liebchen!" he exclaimed. "I thought you would not come."

"I was persuaded," she said meaningfully. "But first, could you direct me to the ladies room?" It had been a long cab ride.

"Behind the Google Play stand," he said, gesturing, then sat down to return to his meeting.

Beatrice strode towards the stand. As she walked past Google Play,[9] she saw a plain white wall with a gap in it, and assumed this must be the way to the toilet. She stepped through and was shocked to find that the gloss and colour of the Hall had disappeared. This space was different. Vast, bare concrete floor and rudimentary plywood greeted her eyes. Were there not

---

efforts made by some publishers to render their stands impenetrable. They comment that "in the English-speaking international hall we immediately noticed the stands that took up immense space, from Penguin Random House's almost aisle-length stand, to the similarly large HarperCollins, and to the colloquially named 'Fortress Hachette' (a nickname that recognises its size as well as the impermeable crenellated panels of its custom stand design)." Driscoll and Squires, *The Frankfurt Book Fair*, 39.

7. More blue suits.
8. Driscoll and Squires note in passing the existence of a dedicated area for "NON-BOOK", or "book-adjacent products" at the Buchmesse, Driscoll and Squires, *The Frankfurt Book Fair and Bestseller Business*, 58.
9. At Frankfurt, the Google Play stand represents a portal to another world, figured by its atypical appearance (austerely white, no books). As Driscoll and Squires, comment, "In 2018 we took a trip to the toilets in Hall 6.2 and discovered a world behind the scenes of the Buchmesse. Once past the Google Play stand, we opened a door and entered a hauntingly empty space lined by the reverse of publishers' stands on one side and the entrance to the toilets on the other." Driscoll and Squires, *The Frankfurt Book Fair and Bestseller Business*, 49.

enough publishers to fill the hall? What was happening to the industry?[10] Her steps echoed as she found her way to the toilets, still thinking.

She pulled open a door, but it wasn't a washroom. It was a cupboard, the size of a small store room, with coats, bags, and trays of mineral water. Shelving lined the back wall, and held cardboard boxes and odd shapes wrapped in canvas. Before she had a moment to realise she was in the wrong place, a woman's voice called shrilly in German. She turned to see a tall, strapping, blonde woman glaring at her. The woman, seeing Beatrice was uncomprehending, marched over and slammed the cupboard door.

She switched to English. "Don't go in there and don't come back here again. You'll be sorry if you do."

---

10. Beatrice's questions about the seeming retraction of the industry accord with those of Driscoll and Squires, in which they describe how, "In Hall 6, the vast empty space between the stands and the toilets is, perhaps, the repressed unconscious of the Fair, the space where the secrets of industry failure hide behind confident pronouncements of growth growth growth and the bold face of business as usual. The sudden transition from bustling Hall floor to dead zone made us contemplate industry retraction, the global economy, and the various costs—including those of environmental sustainability—of such large events. This hidden space offers both a reprieve from the bustle of the Fair, and an encounter with its shrinking footprint and wasteful underside: loose cables, discarded chairs, paper rubbish." See Beth Driscoll and Claire Squires, "Megativity and Miniaturization at the Frankfurt Book Fair," *Post45*, April 8, 2020, https://post45.org/2020/04/megativity-and-miniaturization-at-the-frankfurt-book-fair/.

CHAPTER SIEBEN

BEATRICE BACKED AWAY, HER HEELS CATCHING ON THE rough concrete. The blonde stood, arms crossed, legs akimbo, blocking the cupboard door.

The woman's unblinking eyes locked on Beatrice's, and the two women stood still for a second. Tumbleweeds crossed the empty floor.

Beatrice felt a vibration at her hip, and dropped her gaze as she took her phone from her dress pocket to scrutinise the screen. "CASPIAN message," it read.[1] She felt a tightening in her body as she swiped:

> **KW asks me to inform you that the location of his next meeting has been altered. Meet him at the Executive Club.[2] There are good women's facilities, he says.**

---

1. This clumsy description of smartphone features and practices is the first in what becomes a series of repeated jokes that gently satirise the publishing world as frequently behind the times, technologically speaking. The awkward references to technology also satirise techno-thrillers, which date very quickly.
2. The Executive Club is modelled on the real-life Business Club, which was first established as a part of the Buchmesse in 2014 (https://www.booksandpublishing.com.au/articles/2014/04/08/30063/frankfurt-book-fair-launches-business-club-ticket/). The 2018 brochure for the Business Club describes it as "The lounge for business at Frankfurter Buchmesse" and sets out its offer: "The BUSINESS CLUB COMPANY HUBS give companies who do not have an own stand or those who need additional meeting space

Beatrice's fingers hovered over the reply box, contemplating what to reply.[3] The phone thrilled again in her hand.

Cx

A rush swept through her. Without pondering the consequences, she thumbed:

Bx

She lifted her eyes from the intimate glow of the screen.[4]

The woman was gone. The door of the cupboard had melted into the plywood facade.

* * *

---

an exclusive opportunity for their business at Frankfurter Buchmesse"; for the price of just over 8,000 euros companies can use its facilities (https://www.buchmesse.de/files/media/pdf/exhibit-business-club-company-hub-frankfurt-book-fair.pdf). A feature of the Business Club is its Ambassadors program, which offers free access in exchange for promoting the Club (https://publishingperspectives.com/2015/07/frankfurt-book-fair-business-club-is-seeking-ambassadors/). One attendee at the 2018 Bushmesse said, in the irony-laden tone of a teen and from a position of superiority (having a prominent custom stand), that the fair should "stop trying to make the Business Club happen." The Business Club conveys an air of both privilege and uncoolness (very appropriate for the book trade). The air of privilege derives from the decor (see page 50, note 6), the presence of staff (predominantly young women at reception, the cloakroom, and the cafe), and the people-watching opportunities. The uncool factor derives from the fact that it is more generic and less fancy in appearance than the custom publisher stands in the main hall, and its overt attempts to advertise itself.

3. "Reply box" is another joke. No one in real life calls it that. The repetition of "reply" at the end of the sentence draws additional attention to the point about labouredness.
4. Screens can be intimate too, contra the discourse of bookish booklovers. See, for discussion, Beth Driscoll and DeNel Rehberg Sedo, "Faraway, So Close: Seeing the Intimacy in Goodreads Reviews," *Qualitative Inquiry* 25, no. 3 (March 2019): 248–59, https://doi.org/10.1177/1077800418801375; Cristina Miguel, "Visual Intimacy on Social Media: From Selfies to the Co-Construction of Intimacies Through Shared Pictures," *Social Media + Society* 2, no. 2 (April 2016): 1–10, https://doi.org/10.1177/2056305116641705.

Beatrice slicked lipstick over her mouth, ran her fingers through her hair, and met her own eyes in the Executive Club mirror, smiling at her appearance. The young woman guarding the entrance to the Club had frowned as she had searched on an iPad for Kurt's meeting.

"Ja, I have it. He is meeting with ze boss." Her eyebrows lifted, but her expression became no more friendly. "Let me take you," the woman said, gesturing into the dimly lit interior of the Club. "The toilets are that way if you need them."[5]

Beatrice emerged from the toilets, and the young woman weaved her through low tables surrounded by grey upholstered club chairs. Fringing separated out areas at the sides of the Club.[6] Men and the occasional woman talked in hushed tones, their monochrome outfits barely discernible against the grey and black.

They approached a table in one corner. Beatrice saw Kurt first, his frame—so debonair in the bar of hotel—crumpling towards a grey-haired man with his back to her. She noted the expensive cut of the grey-haired man's blue suit. A young woman was sitting passively between the two men, her hands clutching a notebook and pen, her blonde hair neatly tied into a ponytail. An empty chair sat opposite her.

Kurt noticed Beatrice's approach, and got to his feet with some effort, putting his hand gently to her elbow.

"Beatrice, Liebchen, thank you for coming… Let me introduce you…"

She looked down to the imposing face of the man with whom Kurt was meeting. He met her gaze impassively, and for a moment she thought he was going to refuse to take the hand which she had proffered to him. Then he clasped her hand in both of his, and she felt him pull her down into the

5. Toilets are very important at the Frankfurt Book Fair. They offer a moment of respite for those on their feet all day, as well as an additional site for networking and the exchange of gossip, aka informal buzz. They constitute an interstitial non-meeting space, as well as a reminder of the embodiedness of publishing industry professionals.
6. The Frankfurt Book Fair Business Club has had consistent decor through the years accompanied by black and gold monogrammed branding. A 2014 video (https://www.youtube.com/watch?v=pwbc_LZmmno) produced by the fair shows leather club lounges, black shaded tall lamps, timber tables (note the disturbing Eurocentric and gender politics of this video and by implication of the Business Club in 2014; things have improved only marginally in a 2016 promotional video https://www.youtube.com/watch?v=J2mvd9kJEro); the 2015 video mentions a (pale grey) "loungey atmosphere" to encourage collaboration (https://www.youtube.com/watch?v=aKSZP-mb1TE).

fourth chair.[7] The young woman opposite her did not lift her eyes from her notebook.

Kurt glanced between them. "Beatrice," he said, his voice low, "we are discussing the issue of White Storm."

The young woman wrote something down in her notebook.

"A drink, perhaps?" said the man. "I hear you take Negronis." He waved over the waitress from the bar.

"Just a tea," Beatrice said. She would need her wits around her for this conversation.

"As the Vice President of the Buchmesse, I am committed to freedom of speech." The Vice President's piercing blue eyes bored into her. "The robust exchange of ideas is our raison d'etre. But Herr Weidenfeld wants me to censor the fair."

The young woman reached forward and moved some pieces on the table. Beatrice realised it was a scale model of Hall 3.[8]

"White Storm poses more than an ideological threat!" Kurt exclaimed. "The safety of exhibitors and visitors is at risk!"[9]

The VP's impassive face remained so.

"What needs to happen before you will take this seriously?" Kurt's appeal was impassioned, but also weak, as if he knew he would not be listened to.

Beatrice bent down and looked closely at the model. She could see a small stand marked Linksphilosophie Verlag, and right opposite, a stand

---

7. Ah, the politics of the handshake (in pre-COVID times). To say nothing of the gender politics in this room.

8. Building a cardboard model of the Frankfurt Book Fair was a method used by Driscoll and Squires, *The Frankfurt Book Fair and Bestseller Business*. Squiscoll here presents a fictional model of a cardboard model.

9. Violence associated with far-right publishers at the 2017 Frankfurt Book Fair was reported in Deutsche Welle, "Violence after 'active debate' at book fair," *DW.COM*, October 14, 2017, https://p.dw.com/p/2lqOC. The spectre of violence was also in the spotlight at the 2021 fair, when four authors withdrew from appearances at the Buchmesse due to the presence of far-right publishers. Author Jasmina Kuhnke was scheduled to speak at a stage adjacent to the stand occupied by Philip Stein, a publisher and far-right activist who has previously called for Kuhnke to be deported. Vanessa Guinan-Bank and Maite Fernández Simon report that "Kuhnke said she was pushing for safety, not censorship," "Authors Pull out of Frankfurt Book Fair over Presence of Far-Right Groups," *Washington Post*, October 20, 2021, https://www.washingtonpost.com/world/2021/10/20/frankfurt-book-fair-far-right/.

marked White Storm. And, at the back of that tiny cardboard stand, a tiny cardboard cupboard.

"I see you have noticed the Kabuff," the Vice President said.

"The what?"

"The Kabuff. A Kabuff is a cupboard, a cobwebby cupboard where things are hidden. Where unpleasant surprises may lurk. Have you not read Heinrich Mann?"[10]

Beatrice felt a chill run through her. Was she being threatened? How much did he know?

"I didn't catch your name, Herr Vice President," she said coolly.

He handed her an embossed, heavy white card. Kristoff Wiel, Vice President for Intellectual Freedom, Frankfurt Buchmesse. She tucked it into her purse.

"ACHTUNG!!!" It was Caspian! Standing at the entrance of the Executive Club, firmly gripping his lengthy baton. For a moment the room stood still as she appraised Caspian in action.

"Everybody needs to clear the room NOW. SCHNELL!"

No sooner were the words out of his mouth than a loud noise, like a gunshot, cracked through the air. A shocked silence gripped the room, before people started rushing for the exit. Half a dozen men and women in white shirts and caps were running through the main entrance. One of Caspian's fellow officers came in just behind them, his face swollen and his nose bleeding.

The young woman grabbed Beatrice's arms. "We must go. But find me later if you can. I have information for you." She slipped a business card into Beatrice's palm before melting into the crowd.[11] Beatrice looked around wildly, her heart pumping. Where was Caspian? Where was Kristoff? More punches were being thrown in the melee. Beatrice pocketed the card, took Kurt's arm, and pushed him towards the exit.

10. Heinrich Mann (1871–1950) was a German novelist. He criticised fascism on several occasions and was forced to flee Germany in 1933.

11. The weight of this business card is not noted in the text, either qualitatively or quantitatively. Is this omission an authorial error? Or is it a nod to the hectic atmosphere in the Executive Club during this scene, which disrupts normal attentiveness to materiality?

CHAPTER ACHT

BEATRICE SLUMPED AGAINST THE EXTERIOR WALL OF the Executive Club, the gold lettering of its signage mirroring back her still-sharp hairstyle. She wished she'd ordered that Negroni after all. Herr Weidenfeld was talking to a group of older women they had met in the Agora—Tante Fran's book club, she supposed—and Beatrice was alone. Alone, shaken, and desperate for answers. How did it all join together? The threats against the left-wing publisher, the Kabuff and the blonde woman who guarded it, the small-scale model of the fair, Herr Vice President and the blonde woman with the notebook, the White Storm violence. Beatrice shuffled the business cards in her wallet. She was getting quite a collection.[1] Her touch lingered on Caspian's card, tracing the embossed curves of his name and email address.[2]

"You are craving a cigarette, perhaps?" The deep, startling voice interrupted her musings. No, Beatrice thought, she didn't crave cigarettes

1. Observations from the Frankfurter Buchmesse demonstrate that the old-fashioned business card was still, in 2019, a crucial means of B2B interchange.
2. It is not entirely clear whether police officers normally have business cards, and thus whether the erotics of Caspian's business card derive from his (relatively) high office, to being issued them specifically for the Buchmesse, or to being custom-made by him, demonstrating his attentiveness to the varied modes of communication of various industrial sectors and affection for print objects.

anymore. Odd. She looked up and into the eyes that had cast such a spell on her.

"You never did tell me what books you like to read, Caspian."

"Biographies, mostly."[3]

Her breath hitched. Reading about those who had overcome obstacles to lead great and meaningful lives inspired her, too.

"You were impressive in there."

Caspian held her gaze for a few beats, then looked away in frustration. "It is not enough. They are toying with us. This was a distraction while they plan something else."

Before she knew it, she had reached out and taken his hand in hers. For a moment they stood there together against the exterior wall of the Executive Club, drawing mute comfort from each other's physical presence even while they worried about the future. Suddenly Beatrice snapped to attention.

"The Kabuff!" she cried. "There must be more to what is happening in that mysterious cupboard."

She put her hand up to Caspian's cheek. "I have to go and have another look. Keep messaging me, OK?"

Caspian's face dipped towards hers, his mouth electrifyingly close as he whispered, "I will." Then the contact was broken, and Beatrice strode off towards Hall 3.

* * *

As she turned down aisle B, Beatrice noticed Kurt was back at the Linksphilosophie[4] Verlag stand, talking animatedly with his rights director.[5]

---

3. In preferring non-fiction to fiction, Caspian demonstrates himself to be a typical male reader. Another such, albeit one who also believes ebooks to be "terrible", is Ian Bogost, in his article "Ebooks Are an Abomination," *The Atlantic*, September 15, 2021, https://www.theatlantic.com/books/archive/2021/09/why-are-ebooks-so-terrible/620068/.
4. Textual variant: the 2019 edition has "Links Philosophie".
5. The international exchange of (copy)rights and licences is the underpinning business of the Frankfurter Buchmesse. Rights directors therefore play an essential role, despite sometimes seeming less glamorous than editors. Their networks also demonstrate multilingual and multicultural reach.

Kurt noticed Beatrice, and raised his hand to her. She lifted her finger to her lips, motioning him to silence. He nodded, swiftly, and went back to his conversation. The rights director was frowning at Kurt's gesticulations, and looking anxiously across the aisle at the austere stand opposite them. White Storm.

The stand was fronted by a man as broad as he was tall, his shiny blue suit and tie mirroring his gristly, misshapen face. He scowled at each passerby, who looked away and hurried onwards without meeting his eye.[6] Behind him were none of the colourful displays of books featuring on the other stands in the aisle. Instead, there was a pile of newspapers, their typeface reminiscent of the 1930s.[7] The back of the stand was covered with a black and white printed design of a crowd holding their right arms aloft, palms down.[8]

Beatrice shivered. The image should be relegated to a high school history class, she thought.

Suddenly the printed crowd moved forward, and Beatrice wondered if jet lag had finally caught up with her. But then, she realised a door had opened in the back drop, shifting a portion of the picture of the crowd towards her. Behind the door, she glimpsed something. The Kabuff!

She stepped back quickly into the protection of the next-door stand, as a tall blonde emerged and closed the door quickly behind her. It was the strapping woman who had warned her away earlier from the cupboard in the concrete area. Beatrice watched as she locked the door, nodded to the man on the front of the stand, and handed him a small key before she marched off in the direction of the toilets.

Beatrice took a sharp intake of breath. She knew she had to get into the Kabuff.

She took out her phone and texted Kurt:

> **I am going to investigate White Storm's Kabuff.**
> **Ask Adriana to distract the oaf on the stand.**

---

6. Despite this publisher's seemingly similar sartorial choices to other male publishers, his unfriendly demeanour marks out his difference.
7. Fraktur, the typeface typically used by neo-Nazi groups in the twenty-first century, was actually banned by the Nazis, due to Hitler's dislike of it. Indeed, in 1941, it was decreed that roman type should be used as standard throughout Germany. See https://99percentinvisible.org/episode/fraktur/. Newspapers using a similar typeface to Fraktur were present at the Frankfurt Buchmesse in the 2010s.
8. An image referring to Nazi rallies and the infamous salute.

Kurt picked up his phone, then looked over to her, consternation on his face. She nodded, emphatically, and Kurt reluctantly whispered in the rights director's ear, who got up, smoothed her skirt, and crossed the aisle, shooting Beatrice a conspiratorial glance.[9]

* * *

Beatrice waited five minutes, until she saw Adriana had managed to make the stand minder laugh, though it looked more like a contorted grimace.[10] She dodged into the stand, and remembering the technique from a novel, twisted her hand into the minder's pocket, extracted the key without him noticing.[11] She smiled to herself, thinking at last she had something to thank Dickens for,[12] unlocked the door, and let herself into the Kabuff.

As she silently pulled the door behind her, darkness closed in. She used her hands to see, feeling coats, bags, bottles, and cardboard boxes. She moved forwards a step, and stubbed her toe. She swore under her breath, hoping her new shoe wasn't damaged, then remembered Tante Fran. With resolve, she switched on her phone's flashlight, and saw a trapdoor on the Kabuff floor.

* * *

The space underneath the Kabuff was dusty and cobwebby. Beatrice realised she must be in the ceiling space between floors. Shining her flashlight around her, she saw markings on the wooden uprights of the stands. Raised arms, pointing in one direction. She calculated, and realised they were heading in the direction of the concrete area she'd discovered earlier.

Half bent over, Beatrice followed the arms, keeping her flashlight low, coughing occasionally from the dust. She passed an area with many electrical cables descending from the ceiling. "Must be Google Play," she thought.

---

9. An indicator of female solidarity.

10. For more on the challenging aspects of gendered interchanges and abusive behaviours at the Frankfurter Buchmesse, see Claire Squires and Beth Driscoll, "The Sleaze-O-Meter: Sexual Harassment in the Publishing Industry," *Interscript*, March 8, 2018, https://www.interscriptjournal.com/online-magazine/sleaze-o-meter.

11. As indicated in the subsequent sentence, this trick is reminiscent of the pickpocketing of characters in Charles Dickens's *Oliver Twist*.

12. Beatrice does not like all classics indiscriminately.

The raised arms led her beyond the cabling. She started to hear muffled voices, and switched off the flashlight as she continued to creep towards them.

The noise of voices intensified, coming now from directly above her. She lifted her hand up, and felt the shape of a trapdoor, similar to the one she had lowered herself down into from White Storm's Kabuff.

"Am Morgen! Wir schlagen zu!" one voice, the loudest, called.[13] The others cheered.

Beatrice felt the dust of the secret passageway close her throat. She pinched her nose, but she couldn't hold it in any longer. A huge sneeze filled the empty space around her, just as the voices above her quietened.

Her arm was suddenly wrenched upwards, and bright light blinded her temporarily. When her eyes focused, she saw first twelve steel-capped boots, blue jeans, white shirts, then six faces looming over her, their heads topped by caps bearing White Storm's insignia.

Her defiance drained away. It was too late to escape.

13. Translation (by Google Translate): "In the morning! We strike!"

CHAPTER NEUN

A CONCRETE FLOOR, GRITTY UNDER MY FINGERTIPS. A PAIR OF steel-capped boots. And in my mind, still, the image of Amina, slight and defiant in the grey evening light. I peer under the door from my vantage point in the chicken shop store room, shivering in the refrigerated air.

"It's time to move." Kev's voice is guttural. "Have you got the stash?"

Heavy steps cross the floor, and someone drops a black duffel bag in front of the boots.

"It's all in there, thanks to our literary friend and his associates." A snort. "So much for the tolerant left."[1]

I go rigid with shock. Callum is involved in this? Something inside me crumples. All that advice about not getting involved—it was to save his own skin. And all those nights out with the literati, selling chapbooks of poetry and glasses of red wine—a money laundering scheme?[2] *I'm roiling with a sense of betrayal, before the next words send me into a spiral of fear.*

1. "So much for the tolerant left" is a meme, explained by the website Know Your Meme as a quote that has long been associated with conservatives who use it to expose leftist hypocrisy, and which has in more recent years been reappropriated by leftists on Twitter who use it to mock conservatives and (re)assert the importance of not tolerating oppressive or violent practices. https://knowyourmeme.com/memes/so-much-for-the-tolerant-left.
2. The idea that a poetry night with the literati would generate enough cash to launder is another of this novella's jokes.

"And Amina?"

"He's taken care of her too. Told her his girlfriend had assigned her some extra homework. Angela Carter or some bloody thing. Amina won't notice nothing on her shift tonight, with her head stuck in a book.[3] *Your slimy politician mate can come back here with the goods."*

"Right then. Let's go."

Thank God, I think. It's a risk, being here. And I need to get moving—to warn Amina, to confront Callum, to think about where I stand now.

"Wait a minute. I have to get the chooks on. I'll just grab them from the store room. Flick on the spit, willya?"

The boots come closer, heavy step by heavy step. I'm panicking now. My eyes flick around the store room, looking around for hiding spots. There are sacks of pre-cut chips and loaves of white bread piled in a corner, but nothing substantial enough to cover me. The freezer section with the chickens, right at the back of the room, is the only possibility, but it's too dangerous. There must be another way.

Suddenly, a cockroach scurries across the floor in front of me. Then another, then another. Acting quickly, I catch a dozen of them in my hand, then push them out the gap under the door.

"Jesus!" That guttural voice is barking now, frightened. "What the?!"

Kev's mate's voice cuts in. "We don't have time for your namby-pamby cucaracha fears, or for pest extermination, or for the chickens. Leave the cooking for Amina. We've gotta roll, or the Ice Queen is not going to be happy."[4]

The front door of the chicken shop creaks open, then closes behind them. I breathe out, relieved not to have been found, stunned and heartbroken by what I've heard. I rest my cheek on the concrete floor. Under the gap in the door, far in the distance, I see a piece of aluminium foil on the ground.

And reflected upon the foil is an image. The flame of the spit, flickering.[5]

---

3. Books—even books by Angela Carter—can be part of evil plans. Reading produces distraction from events around the reader, which is useful for evildoers.
4. This is an obviously, hilariously bad pastiche of how people might think criminals talk.
5. A self-consciously literary use of imagery that resonates with the reference to Angela Carter and Beatrice's then-interest in literary fiction. As a satirical literary cliché, it contrasts with the satirical thriller clichés in this flashback scene.

CHAPTER ZEHN

THE VOICES ABOVE HER WERE SPEAKING IN A FAST GERMAN. Beatrice was too dazed to understand. Her eyes searched the Kabuff, looking for anything that might help her. Slabs of mineral water, teetering precariously. A rack with coats. Those misshapen, wrapped parcels were still there at the back.[1] Squinting, Beatrice thought perhaps she could see some wires poking out from their sides. She shuddered and turned her head. A few metres away Beatrice could see stacks and stacks of books; hundreds of copies of the same book, the words MY STRUGGLE stamped on the spine.

Perhaps, she thought, it was one of the volumes of Karl Ove Knausgaard's memoir, which had appropriated that title from one of history's darkest texts.[2] Beatrice felt a familiar flush of annoyance with the amorality of

1. Thus far, this Kabuff has very typical contents of a Buchmesse publisher cupboard, as observed by Driscoll and Squires during guided tours undertaken during Frankfurt fieldwork.
2. Karl Ove Knausgaard was one of the featured authors when Norway was the Frankfurt Guest of Honour in 2019, although it was not clear whether he arrived on the special Literature Train observed by Penny and Polly (journalists) in Driscoll and Squires, *The Frankfurt Book Fair and Bestseller Business*, 32. For more on the Guest of Honour programme at Frankfurt, see Corinna Norrick-Rühl, "'Die Buchwelt Zu Gast in Frankfurt': Understanding the Impact of the Guest of Honour Presentation at Frankfurt Book Fair on the German Literary Marketplace," *Mémoires Du Livre / Studies in Book Culture* 11, no. 2 (Spring 2020): 1–34, https://doi.org/10.7202/1070263ar and Luise Hertwig, "State-Funded Support of International Trade in Rights and

some contemporary literary fiction. And yet, while she hated to think that Knausgaard's reflections on consciousness and middle-class life in Norway might have been weaponised by White Storm, the alternative was worse…

Beatrice felt herself hauled upwards, her arms wrenching from from[3] their sockets. One of the white caps tied rope roughly around her hands and emptied her pockets, before shoving her towards a corner of the Kabuff. Beatrice stumbled, falling against the books. As she feared, the book was not Knausgaard's, but the first new edition of *My Struggle* which had been allowed in Germany since the Second World War. Even with its careful paratextual apparatus, she feared the worst from this incendiary volume.[4]

"You vill stay here, until ze Ice Queen comes to deal with you," barked one of the caps at her. "She vill not be happy at your incursion."[5]

Eleven eyes and one eyepatch glared at her, each one piercing blue.[6] Then they turned away from her, exiting via the Kabuff door. She heard the lock turn in the door.

Darkness.

* * *

Beatrice was slumped against the copies of *My Struggle*.[7] She had twisted and turned her hands for what felt like hours, rubbing her wrists raw as she tried to extract them from the tight noose that held them captive. She thumped the back of her head against the books in desperation, her mind

---

Licenses. Translation Funding Programs of Guests of Honour Argentina and France at the 2010 and 2017 Frankfurt Book Fair," *Mémoires Du Livre / Studies in Book Culture* 11, no. 2 (Spring 2020): 1–38, https://doi.org/doi:10.7202/1070264ar.

3. The repetition "from from" is an error from the 2019 edition, which is retained in this text to indicate the very rough wrenching feeling undergone by Beatrice.
4. The publication of *Mein Kampf* in post-war Germany was prevented by the state of Bavaria, which held the rights. However, when the text came out of copyright in 2016 it was republished as an annotated edition; the only touching point between that text and this one. See https://www.theguardian.com/world/2017/jan/03/first-mein-kampf-reprint-germany-since-war-sixth-print-run-hitler.
5. This is an obviously, hilariously bad pastiche of how people might think German neo-Nazis talk.
6. As the copyeditor for this critical edition pointed out, "This sounds like the eyepatch is also blue"—an astute observation which highlights the not always entirely perfect grammar that goes along with a high-speed creative venture.
7. An uncomfortable position, it goes without saying.

jumping between the present darkness of the Kabuff and the past flickering of the chicken shop flame.

* * *

She had no idea what time it was. The white caps had said they would strike in the morning. Had a night passed already?

She renewed her efforts to release her hands. She had to get out, and stop White Storm.

* * *

Tears streamed down Beatrice's face. She had fled Melbourne, the Chicken Shop, for this? She hung her head, her breast heaving with the pain.

A grating noise. In the darkness, she looked to the Kabuff door. But no light came in.

By her feet, she felt a rush of air. The trapdoor!

A light shone into the Kabuff, blinding her. Instinctively, she tried to raise her hand to shield her eyes. She twisted her head away.

"Beatrice!" a deep voice sounded in the small space.

She opened her eyes. She could see. Between her splayed legs, she saw a head. Thick brown hair, deep brown eyes.

"Caspian!"

* * *

He took her wrists, gently rubbing the marks from the rope which now lay, discarded, on the floor of the Kabuff.[8] A low light played around the enclosed space, the torch on the floor beside them.[9]

"How..." Beatrice stuttered, "How did you find me?"

"Linksphilosophie Verlag," he replied, his eye reaching deep into hers. "Adriana told me. I followed the signs." He ran his hands up both her arms, his eyes never leaving hers.

---

8. Readers may note the rather old-fashioned trope of the male love interest saving the female protagonist from jeopardy, thus denying her agency and independence. However, this analysis is rejected because she was in a lot of danger and anyway Caspian is quite hot.
9. Caspian demonstrates he understands the value of mood lighting, an aspect explored by Prof Dr. Theobald Jürgen Marx-Voss von Adorno in an unpublished conference paper, and used to posit that he is bisexual.

She felt a sensation running deep into her core. She leaned towards him. Her heart beat loud in the silence of the Kabuff.

* * *

Her lips on his created a fire she hadn't felt for years. His hands were on her thighs, lifting her dress over her head. She pulled her liberated hands above her head, feeling the soft air around her body. Her hands scrabbled on his bullet-proof vest, struggling to find a way in. He laughed, low, and lifted the heavy garment over his head. She ripped the shirt open, and ran her hands down his naked chest.

She breathed heavy, as she reached towards his belt.

"Polizeiobermeister Schorle...." she gasped.

He pulled her knickers down her legs, his hands stroking her thighs with a firmness that arched her naked back.

"Beatrice..." he growled into her neck, pushing towards her then pausing a moment. "The plot thickens...?"[10]

"We must be quick, Caspian. White Storm..."

"Ja," Caspian replied, before his mouth came towards her again, their tongues leaping together as Beatrice pulled him into her, her legs crossing tight around his back, her shoes keeping time with their rapidly accelerating rhythm.[11] She lost herself deep in his physicality.

They cried out simultaneously, and held each other for a long moment, their breaths slowly coming back to the pace of the room around them.

The books. The canvas-covered parcels. The wires.

Beatrice pressed herself into his full lips one more time. As she pulled herself away, she let out one last gasp, pushed away Caspian's hot body, and reached for her dress.

"Come," she said. "We have a Buchmesse to save."

10. Attentive romance fiction readers will notice that contra the emerging norms of that genre in the twenty-first century, although there is a clear signalling of seeking and giving consent in this interchange, Squiscoll has not explicitly written dialogue in which Beatrice and Caspian discuss safe sex. This footnote confirms that they did indeed have this discussion, and that any good Kabuff is well-stocked in prophylactics.

11. Although not present in this scene, Tante Fran gives her blessing to this happy—if rapid—union via the presence of shoes from her shop.

CHAPTER ELF

BEATRICE STRODE THROUGH HALL 3, CASPIAN BY HER side. She reached into the pocket of her somewhat crumpled dress and started rifling through the business card stash.

"Vat are you looking for?"[1]

"That young woman from the Executive Club. She said she had information for me. It might help us defeat White Storm." Her hand stopped on a white card. Lotte Frankel: International Rights Agent, Translator, and Executive Assistant to the Vice President for Intellectual Freedom. Beatrice looked up.

"Give me your phone, Caspian. There's a call I need to make."

Her fingers pressed the screen with confidence, despite the adrenaline coursing through her body.

"Lotte. It's Beatrice Deft. You said you had information for me?"

Beatrice could barely make out the whispered voice at the other end of the metaphorical line.[2]

---

1. The inconsistent Germanification of Caspian's dialogue is a feature of the novella.
2. A recognition of the material history of the telephonic system, which was originally based on copper and aluminium "lines" or loops that transmitted voice signals, but now works on signals beamed through the air. Despite this shift, the language of "lines" remains part of common speech. Media archaeologists note that older media technologies often persist in idioms or symbols (such as the floppy disk symbol for saving). See https://en.wikipedia.org/wiki/Telephone_line and scholarly work including

"I cannot say much. I am surrounded by them. But your friend is in danger. This morning, when he is awarded the Peace Prize, they will strike.[3] It is not just the White Storm flunkeys, either. This goes all the way to the top. Well, the Vice Top."[4]

Beatrice was delighted to hear that Kurt's publishing career was being recognised by this honour, but given the circumstances, she asked only a single question.

"When?"

"You have ten minutes to save him."

Beatrice flung the phone at Caspian and increased her pace.[5] This was going to be tight.

* * *

One minute later, they emerged into an Agora thronged with people: paparazzi, smartly dressed publishers, and glamorous public intellectuals. A red carpet was rolled out and up to a bulbous white pavilion formed from interlocking plywood curves and tightly stretched canvas.[6]

"What's happening?" Beatrice heard a voice say to her left.

"I don't know, but the canapés are great!"[7]

Matthew Kirschenbaum, "'Poor Black Squares': Afterimages of the Floppy Disk," in *The Routledge Companion to Media Technology and Obsolescence*, ed. Mark J.P. Wolf (Abingdon: Routledge, 2019), 296–310.

3. Since 1950 the Frankfurter Buchmesse has awarded the Friedenspreis des Deutschen Buchhandels, or Peace Prize of the German Book Trade. Traditionally announced at the Paulskirche during the fair, the prize contributes to the Buchmesse's image as a bastion of cosmopolitanism and an ethical standard-bearer for the industry. See https://www.friedenspreis-des-deutschen-buchhandels.de.
4. The novella plays with the double meaning of "vice". On the one hand, it means one level down from the Top, as the text indicates. It also pleasingly means immorality, crime, or wickedness.
5. There's a lot of rapidity and quick movement in thrillers.
6. The novella here contributes to a material history of stand construction at publishing industry trade fairs.
7. Canapés are great; however, it is important to consider their role as signifiers of climate and social justice issues in the global book business. For more on this, go back in time and attend the conference paper, Beth Driscoll and Claire Squires, "'CANAP-YAY or CANAP-NAY?' The Canapé as Environmental Signifier in the Global Book Business," 2021.

Gatecrashers, she thought. They were at every publishing party.[8]

"Technically we, too, are gatecrashers," said Caspian as he shouldered a path through the milling intelligentsia and cultural entrepreneurs, moving towards the pavilion. Beatrice chose not to reply. Her eyes were busy scanning the crowd. It wasn't until they were inside the venue, however, that she saw Herr Weidenfeld.

Seated on the stage.

Spotlit.

* * *

Beatrice took a seat at the end of a row three from the front, and swiftly applied some lipstick.[9] Excited anticipation sounded around the Agora. On the other side, Caspian had taken up position. He was almost hidden behind the television cameras, but she could see him speaking on his phone, his eyes glancing towards the back as more police officers arrived at the back of the hall. On the front row, Tante Fran and the book club were smiling up at the stage. Herr Weidenfeld surveyed the room, a look of self-consciousness on his face. Beatrice caught his eye, and a smile broke out on his face.

Trumpets sounded.[10] The crowd hushed. The lights, apart from a light on a lectern, and the spotlight on Herr Weidenfeld, dimmed.

The Vice President for Intellectual Freedom marched onto the stage. Lotte followed, looking nervously towards the crowd.

Beatrice leaned forwards in her seat.

The Vice President stopped at the lectern, tapped the microphone twice, took a paper out from the breast pocket of his blue suit. He cleared his throat.

"Meine Damen und Herren," he boomed.[11] "Ladies, gentlemen. I am the Vice President for Intellectual Freedom, and on behalf of the administration, I welcome you to this, the key event of the Frankfurt Buchmesse. Every year, we award the Peace Prize, which goes to a key figure in the world of literature and books, who has over a sustained period of time contributed

8. Indeed. Driscoll and Squires have gatecrashed several (as research method).

9. Not as a time travel device, in this instance.

10. Unlikely to occur at the real Frankfurter Buchmesse, but you never know.

11. A very non-inclusive opening that does not acknowledge the spectrum and fluidity of gender.

to the peace, humanity and understanding among all peoples and nations of the world."

The Vice President paused. He shot a cold look at Herr Weidenfeld.[12]

"Past winners include Victor Gollancz, Astrid Lindgren and Jürgen Habermas; publisher, writer, intellectual."[13]

The Vice President glared across the public sphere of the Agora.

"Tonight..." he continued. Beatrice saw Lotte whisper in his ear. A look of disgust travelled rapidly across his face.

"This morning...we break with tradition." He picked up his paper, and looked at it as if in disbelief. "This morning, we are gathered to commemorate the life and work of Herr Kurt Weidenfeld, publisher of Links/phil/oso/phie Verlag, a left-wing publisher known even by Turkish taxi drivers." He spat out the final three words.

Beatrice saw a quizzical expression on Kurt's spotlit face. A hum started in the Agora, as the audience turned to one another, confirming what they had heard. She glanced over to where Caspian had been standing. The cameras were shrouded in darkness.

The crowd fell silent again. Beatrice clenched her knuckles, shifting to the edge of her seat, her muscles primed for action.

"So this morning," announced the Vice President, "we are here to provide the ultimate accolade to Herr Weidenfeld."

He raised his right arm to the air, palm downwards. The gesture on White Storm's Kabuff door.

"Hail Victory!" he screamed.

In the stunned silence that followed, Beatrice saw Tante Fran's hands flutter down into her lap—had she been knitting?—as the members of the book club exchanged glances with one another. Then, a sound of murmuring and coughing swelled from the edges of the pavilion. Chairs scraped on the floor. People stood up. White smoke billowed up from the ground.

"Smoke grenades!" yelled Beatrice, as the air thickened around her.

She leaped to her feet, running for the stage steps.

Above her, Herr Weidenfeld was already a hazy silhouette. Time slowed down. Beatrice noticed four things happen, one after the other.

---

12. The use of "shot" here is heavy-handed foreshadowing as per the conventions of the thriller genre.

13. It was intended that a very intelligent disquisition on Habermas be inserted into this footnote, but Wikipedia was down on the day of writing.

A shot rang out.

Herr Weidenfeld slumped.

Caspian and six officers rushed onto the stage.

And, quietly exiting the pavilion via a secret door, was a figure that looked very much like the Vice President. As a gust of fresh air blew in, Beatrice caught one glimpse of a mass of white-capped bodies outside, before the smoke closed around her once again.

CHAPTER ZWÖLF

I RUN BACK HOME, AND FIND CALLUM SITTING AT THE KITCHEN table with his MacBook Air, leaning back on two legs of the chair, a cigarette in the ashtray. Smoke curls around the kitchen, delicate wisps rising and dispersing in the cool air. My heart is still twisting as I take in every detail of this, the life I thought I knew. It all seems the same. Well, almost all. There's an envelope for me under the ashtray, postmarked from Germany.[1]

I take his cigarette, and draw on it deeply. He shoots me a confused glance, and switches off the podcast he is listening to.[2]

"We have to talk, Callum."

He doesn't deny his involvement with Kev's plan when I confront him.

"I've been telling you for years how hard making a living as a poetry publisher is, but what should you know with your steady teacher's salary." His face is contorted, as he spits the words out.[3]

---

1. Who can it be from…?
2. Podcasts are apparently very popular nowadays, but not for people who have Buchmesses to save. NB podcasts usually don't have switches.
3. Callum has, in fact, been relying on Beatrice's salary since they moved in together, an economic aspect of their relationship of which she is not resentful, but is nonetheless very aware.

"Writing and reading books is the easy part," he lectures. "The difficult part of the circuit of the book is publishing it."[4]

"Yes, Darnton's communication circuit," I sigh. I can't believe we're going over this again. "And you're also a hero struggling for symbolic capital."[5]

Callum looks up sharply. He can tell something's shifted between us; I've criticised Darnton before, but I've never been sarcastic about Bourdieu. There's a moment when genuine theoretical conversation seems possible, but then his facial muscles shift again, he ignores my words, and just looks at me beseechingly.

"Now we've got that distribution deal with Allen & Unwin, this will be the last time I work with Kev. Bea, I did it for us. So we can leave this outer suburban neighbourhood and move to North Fitzroy. When I got that funding knockback from the Australia Council because our list wasn't hitting 'equalities targets' I couldn't think of any other way. But you know how good our books are, Bea… I only see excellence."[6]

I stare at him, as he tucks a long strand of hair into his Alice band.[7] *I take another drag of the cigarette, the nicotine hitting my system, my heart rate rising.*

BOOM!

An enormous noise ricochets around the neighbourhood, breaking the tense silence between Callum and me.

For once, it's not just me rushing out into the street. Callum is by my side. "It's the chicken shop," he says, with a thin note of panic in his voice. "I just got an internet message from the lookout guy. I need to retrieve my stuff."[8]

Our feet hit the footpath in tandem, a bittersweet echo of the intimacy we once shared.[9] *We hurtle around the corner towards the clutch of shops that is the*

---

4. This iconic, and contentious, statement also functions as the strapline of *The Frankfurt Kabuff* in its 2019 publication.
5. This retort from Beatrice, referencing Robert Darnton and Pierre Bourdieu, two key theorists in the history of the book, has already become the most commented upon passage in the novella.
6. Squiscoll here satirically voices the words of many a publisher who does not see the systemic and institutional barriers presented by the creative industries to those from under-represented and minoritised backgrounds. For one example of such prejudiced thinking, see the discussion by Claire Squires of the debacle surrounding the *Scottish Review of Books* in 2019, https://bellacaledonia.org.uk/2019/06/04/patchy-and-negligible/.
7. To be honest, it's very unclear why Beatrice is even with Callum.
8. Callum is clearly not very adroit in the use of modern technologies.
9. This image is intentionally over-explained.

heart of our neighbourhood. The burger shop. The frozen yoghurt shop. The kebab shop. And right at the end—blackened and pouring out smoke—the chicken shop.

BOOM!

A second explosion rings out and Callum and I reel backwards. But it's just a momentary check. Callum's eyes are steely and he is faster than me. He ducks into the shop.

I arrive at the front door of the chicken shop a few seconds later. I can hear Callum shouting deep in the interior, but the sound fades to a ringing in my ears as I take in the scene. The heartbreaking scene.

Amina's body is crumpled behind the counter. I glimpse Angela Carter's feminist reworking of Bluebeard just beside her and feel a stab in my heart —of course Callum knew that I would recommend this book, of course he knew Amina would love it so much that it would absorb her, blind her to the danger in the chicken shop. When even the best books could be turned to evil purposes, what use were they?[10]

Flames, red orange and pale pale blue, leaping from the fryer. Thick smoke. I realise I have only seconds to act.

"Help, Bea!" comes Callum's voice from the back of the shop, "I need help to carry the goods! We need these for our future."[11]

But my future is clear, and it doesn't include Callum. I bend down and scoop up Amina and run through the chicken shop door, out into the street.

* * *

Sirens are wailing,[12] *and the neighbours are out on the street in force. Amina sits in the back of the ambulance, wrapped in a blanket. She's going to be fine. She's already discovered that the young paramedic woman treating her is an Angela Carter fan, who has promised to lend her more books. I haven't seen Callum yet. The news reporter recording a TV segment out the front of the shop is talking about a corrupt politician, bribes, a drug ring, rival bikie gangs, and more. But I'm done here.*

---

10. Such questions have repeatedly been asked through time, and—at least at the beginning of *The Frankfurt Kabuff*—remained unanswered in Beatrice's traumatised mind.

11. It is extremely unclear what these "goods" actually are, or indeed how the money laundering aspect of Callum and Kev's dirty dealings operated.

12. This wailing is the standard Australian emergency vehicle sound. See Chapter Zwei, page 28, note 5, for European sounds.

I turn to the elderly couple standing nearby. "Either of you got a smoke?"[13]

The woman passes me one, and I stride towards the chicken shop. I bend down and light the cigarette on the still glowing coals by the door, under the fluttering remnants of the lunchtime specials poster.[14]

The chicken shop will haunt me, I know that. But I will keep moving.

13. An understandable reaction.
14. The history of printed ephemera such as this lunchtime specials poster is also folded into the capacious interdiscipline, the history of the book.

CHAPTER DREIZEHN

BEATRICE MOVED TOWARDS THE STAGE, THE SIRENS AND the chicken shop still in her mind. She fought through the smoke, rushing towards the chair where Herr Weidenfeld had been seated seconds before the gunshot had sounded in the pavilion. She reached for his body, but felt instead a sticky liquid on her fingertips.

Blood.

She got to her knees, crawling across the floor. She scrabbled for Herr Weidenfeld, her eyes smarting from the smoke which still swirled around the stage. She felt the heaviness of a prostrate body.

"Herr Weidenfeld..." she called, her voice cracking as her hands touched the soft wool of his blue suit.

The body convulsed. A cough. "Herr Weidenfeld?"

"Mein Liebchen," Herr Weidenfeld croaked. "Is it you?"

"Yes," Beatrice replied, her heart rising. "They shot you...?"

Herr Weidenfeld coughed again. "A flesh wound, mein Liebchen." He pulled a stash of papers from inside his jacket.

"A taxi driver gave this to me on my way into the Buchmesse this morning. I know it is old-fashioned, Liebchen, but I prefer to read on paper." A bullet had wormed its way through the pages.[1]

---

1. An absolutely key moment in the novella. It literalises the popular view that print books have value that digital books do not; here, the value of being able to save a life

Beatrice smiled at the publisher. "We should get you to an ambulance."

A siren sounded outside the pavilion. As the air cleared, she saw Caspian leading the paramedics towards the stage, his phone glued to his ear as they ran.

Beatrice got to her feet, making way for the paramedics who knelt down and got to work. Tante Fran and the book club stood around them, looking down anxiously to Herr Weidenfeld.

Beatrice's eyes met Caspian's, and for a second she was back in the Kabuff.

"Beatrice," he said, urgently, his voice low. "There is not a moment to spare. This action, it is a literal smokescreen.[2] There are bombs all around the Buchmesse. We must hurry."

Beatrice span on her heel, ready to rush towards the hall.

"Wait," Tante Fran said. "Before you go."

She reached into her tote bag and pulled out a knitting needle.

"Take this with you. It may be important."

Beatrice nodded, then twisted her black hair into a simple bun and stuck the needle through it.

"Also, I advise you to start your search at the stairwell at the base of Hall 4. There is a network of tunnels there, which connects everything. The networking of Frankfurt is not just about parties and meetings, but also about infrastructure."[3]

Caspian interjected. "I'll join the SWAT team in the halls while you investigate the stairwell. Take my secondary work phone with you. Now, let's move."

---

by stopping a bullet. Accounts of books stopping bullets are highly emotive and indeed become the stuff of legend. This has particularly been the case when the book in question is a Bible, for obvious religious reasons. In WWII, special editions of Bibles were sold that had a metal cover and were designed to be worn in a chest pocket; these were advertised as potential lifesavers (both symbolic and actual; see https://americanhistory.si.edu/collections/search/object/nmah_687121). The American rock band Green Day even has a 2005 live album called *Bullet in a Bible*.

2. A literally correct use of the word "literal."

3. The novella here makes a further contribution to a material history of publishing trade fairs. One of the necessary but daunting tasks for new attendees to the Frankfurter Buchmesse is familiarisation with a map of the Messe. Devoid of comforting bookish signifiers, such maps lay bare the size and complexity of the infrastructure (entrances, tunnels, bridges) that undergirds and shapes the action of the Fair. A map of the Messe is available at https://www.sitemap.messefrankfurtlocations.com/.

* * *

Beatrice opened the heavy door at the base of Hall 4. She gripped the stainless steel handrail tightly, hearing a loud noise reverberate around the concrete floor and walls of the stairwell.

BANG!

Should she go up or down? Instinct told her the Kabuff network would be underground, but all bets were off in the labyrinth of the Messe. Google Maps would be no help to her here. She wasn't even sure she had reception.

BANG!

Beatrice peered down the twisting flights of stairs, and glimpsed something—a shoulder? A cap? It was enough. She sprinted down the stairs, grateful once again for the sturdy but elegant shoes from Tante Fran's shop.

Seven flights further down, and a corridor opened up. Electrical wires dangled from the ceiling and cardboard boxes were stacked haphazardly. It was dark here. Beatrice could never remember which screen buttons to press to activate the torch on her own phone let alone Caspian's, but it didn't matter—her eyes adjusted quickly. She stepped softly through the corridor, keeping to the edges.

BANG!

As a third bang ricocheted off the corridor walls, Beatrice paused and sucked in her breath. She was closer now. There was a bend in the corridor up ahead. Beatrice thought of Herr Weidenfeld, of Caspian, of Tante Fran. It was time to confront the evil despoiling the heart of the publishing industry and culture more broadly.

She strode forward. "Herr Vice President, I presume."

The tall, blue-suited figure at the other end of the corridor turned around.

"Ja, you haff found me, Beatrice Deft. Willkommen to the Vorbunker. Those polizei swarming through the halls will not be able to foil our plan. Every uber race has its superman, and even though I am a vice president, today I ascend to become the plenipotentiary, the chancellor, the noble leader who will bring our plan to fruition. No one will ever turn down my writing again!"[4] He held out his hand. On it was a small, wired device with a large red button.

---

4. Not all rejected authors become neo-Nazis. Indeed, some of them turn to publishing on Wattpad and have fulfilling authorial lives advancing the causes of equity and inclusion.

"When I press this button, a chain of bombs will detonate. They have been carefully arranged so that the stands of every organising body of every book fair around the world, from Hall 2 to Hall 6, will explode."[5]

He was becoming more and more animated, spittle flying from his mouth and his arms gesticulating as if giving a conference talk.[6] Beatrice eyed the device nervously.

"There will be NO MORE exchange of ideas! There will be no more translations! No more co-published editions!"[7]

BANG!

The metallic sound rang again through the echoing corridor.

"It is time. My white-capped people are communicating with me through the pipe system that connects Kabuffs with hot water for tea and coffee.[8] Four bangs, and all is ready. You cannot stop me now, Beatrice Deft."

Beatrice didn't know if this was true or not, but thought she should at least try. She lunged forward swiftly, pulling the knitting needle out of her bun. Her hair settled back into its sharp cut as she held the needle at the Vice President for Intellectual Freedom's neck.

"Drop the device, Herr Kristoff Wiel. I mean it."

"One knitting needle will not stop me, Frau."

"It is not...just...one."

The voices came from behind Beatrice. A group of formidable women was standing there: the book clubbers, slogan-painters, knitters and shoe salespeople. The readers.[9]

Tante Fran stepped forward and spoke again, addressing the Vice President with a steely glint in her eye.

"It is time for you to leave this Buchmesse. You have done enough harm."

Reaching forward, she swatted the device out of his hand. Another woman came forward and dismantled it expertly. She looked up and addressed Beatrice.

---

5. The status of Hall 1 is uncertain.
6. There's one at every conference.
7. A brutal encapsulation of the Vice President's evil mission.
8. Non-book forms of communication can be just as important as books.
9. The strapline of this novella may well be "writing and reading books is the easy part," but the triumphal arrival of Tante Fran's Book Club demonstrates that readers have agency and, working collaboratively, can enact change.

"Alles Gut. I have worked in digital publishing services. I know how to make technology stop."[10]

Meanwhile, two other women had restrained Herr Wiel with wool, and were marching him along the corridor.

"Direct action, sideways thinking, Schwester," said Tante Fran, nodding at their retreating backs.[11] She enveloped Beatrice in a hug, and Beatrice felt the warmth of feminist solidarity swell inside her breast. The dust and noise of the Kabuff network settled around her. The infrastructure of the Buchmesse was sound, for now.

---

10. This is a joke.

11. An Ullapoolist slogan. For more of these, and accompanying photographs of the slogans in action, see Beth Driscoll and Claire Squires, "THE ULLAPOOLISM MANIFESTO," *ASAP/J*, November 1, 2021, https://asapjournal.com/the-ullapoolism-manifesto-beth-driscoll-and-claire-squires/.

CHAPTER VIERZEHN

BEATRICE, TANTE FRAN AND THE REST OF THE BOOK club swept into the Executive Club, their shoes in sisterly synchronicity. The gathered publishers and staff started to applaud, and at the centre of the Club, Lotte stood to greet them.

"Tante Fran, I should have known you and your colleagues would be involved," said Lotte, holding out her hands to the women, who gathered around her. "I've just heard from Polizeiobermeister Schorle. His team has apprehended all the White Storm operatives."

On the badge hanging from her lanyard, Beatrice noticed Lotte's title had changed. "LOTTE FRANKEL, International Rights Agent, Translator, and Vice President for Intellectual Freedom and Inclusion."[1]

"And yes, now Kristoff Wiel is in custody, I've been promoted," Lotte concluded.

Beatrice's eyes flicked down to Lotte's matte-black, embossed heels. This was a woman who knew where to buy her footwear.

---

1. With this change of title to Kristoff Wiel's Vice Presidency, Squiscoll here notes that "Intellectual Freedom" must be counterbalanced with inclusion, and that freedom of speech should not be absolute if it excludes or further oppresses certain minoritised or under-represented groupings.

"Beatrice, I want to thank you. Join me over here, please—I have more information for you." Lotte gestured towards one of the booths at the side of the Club. "Tante Fran?"

Tante Fran shook her head and patted her tote bag. "We have book club this afternoon. Luxemburg's *The Accumulation of Capital*." She addressed Beatrice. "We have a Goodreads page if you want to join us virtually. And… I'm glad our letter reached you. It is hard to tell with the postal service nowadays."

"The letter…?" Beatrice had a flashback to her Melbourne table, the ashtray, the day of the chicken shop incident.[2]

"Ja. We had heard of the good work you had been doing with getting high school students to read, so we invited you to the Buchmesse. Thank you for coming."

Beatrice smiled wryly. She had never had a chance to open that letter, but something about the postmark had driven her to impulsively book a flight to Frankfurt when staying in Melbourne had been unbearable. What was the Turkish word? Kismet. She gave Tante Fran a last hug, then settled into the black pleather seats of the booth.[3]

Lotte had procured two black coffees from the Executive Club bar. Without further preamble, she launched into conversation.

"Beatrice, Genossin.[4] You know, perhaps, that the publishing industry is changing in the twenty-first century. No longer do roles sit in well-defined categories, such as editing, sales, marketing, and production. Increasingly we have need for people with… diverse skills. Skills such as yours."[5]

For a second, Beatrice was confused. She knew digital technology was transforming the profession of publishing, but she wasn't a big user of social media, nor was she familiar with XML.

"What skills do you mean? I don't even have a wordpress dot com site."

2. In this moment, the two parts of the novella come together, using the device of a delivered but unread letter.

3. It is evident that the interior design of the Executive Club will need to be altered as part of Lotte's new brief.

4. "Genossin" is German for a female comrade.

5. In this statement, Lotte refers to the rather tedious conversation about skill sets in the publishing industry occasioned by the rise of digital technologies but, as the text reveals, the skills she refers to are more political than technological.

"I am not talking about digital skills," Lotte said sternly. "I am talking about your capacity to chart a moral path between the freedom to publish and the need to support marginalised voices."[6]

Beatrice thought aloud, hesitating. "Lotte, I never saw myself as the publishing industry's saviour. I've seen the damage books can do."

She took a deep breath, and smoothed the fabric of her shapeless yet stylish dress over her thighs. "But yes, I care about people, and yes, I have started to love books again. Danger does not faze me. And I am a Scorpio. Count me in."[7]

Lotte's eyes glowed. "You know what this means?" she smiled. "You are now a publishing consultant." She handed Beatrice a business card. In thick black letters it read:

BEATRICE DEFT
International Publishing Consultant

6. Lotte references the growing momentum to redress the lack of diversity and inclusion in book culture and the publishing industry. Scholarship and reports on this issue include Radhiah Chowdhury, "It's Hard to Be What You Can't See: Diversity Within Australian Publishing" (Australian Publishers Association Beatrice Davis Fellowship Report, 2020), https://web.archive.org/web/20210715215113/https://www.publishers.asn.au/documents/item/799; Laura B. McGrath, "Comping White," *Los Angeles Review of Books*, January 21, 2019, https://lareviewofbooks.org/article/comping-white/; Anamik Saha and Sandra van Lente, "Rethinking 'Diversity' in Publishing" (London: Goldsmiths Press, 2020), https://research.gold.ac.uk/id/eprint/28692/1/Rethinking_diversity_in_publishing_full_booklet_v2.pdf; Claire Squires, "Publishing's Diversity Deficit," *CAMEo Cuts* 2 (June 2017): 1–12; Susannah Bowen and Beth Driscoll, "The Australian Publishing Industry Workforce Survey on Diversity and Inclusion" (Australian Publishers Association, 2022), https://publishers.asn.au/Web/Member-Resources/ResearchReports/Workforce_Survey_2022.
7. For more on Scorpios, including the fact that if they were a city they would be Rio de Janeiro, see "The Astro Poets: A Field Guide to Scorpios," *Literary Hub*, October 29, 2019, https://lithub.com/the-astro-poets-a-field-guide-to-scorpios/.

"Like other consultants, you'll no doubt develop a portfolio of clients. But I would like to make you a proposition. I speak on behalf of a network of book fair champions around the globe. We need someone who can troubleshoot when political extremists threaten all we hold dear. And we are hearing disturbing rumours. There is work to be done in Latin America, in China, in Sweden. Will you be our eyes and ears?"

Beatrice nodded, her words "yes, subject to appropriate financial remuneration" almost drowned out by the sudden sound of power tools.[8]

She turned and saw the central screened booth of the Executive Club being cut down, and workmen[9] starting to hack away at the raised platform.

"Ja," said Lotte. "There will be change round here. We're going for an atmosphere which is closer to the ... how do you say it in your country ... vibe of the thing?[10] More inclusive. Less fringing."

Beatrice laughed. Australian culture had spread throughout the world. Maybe the next Nobel Laureate in Literature (if it was ever awarded again) was even tending chicken shop in a dusty Australian town.[11]

---

8. Beatrice models freelance behaviour here: ask for a fee.
9. Possibly some workwomen and non-binary people too. Squiscoll was concerned with the forward momentum of the plot and the publishing industry and made an error in terms of gender equalities in all professions. But then who doesn't like a man who is handy with a drill?
10. "The vibe of the thing" is a catchphrase from the iconic Australia film *The Castle* (1997).
11. Beatrice is referring to a *New York Times* article on Australian author Gerald Murnane (Mark Binelli, "Is the Next Nobel Laureate in Literature Tending Bar in a Dusty Australian Town?," *The New York Times*, March 27, 2018, sec. Magazine, https://www.nytimes.com/2018/03/27/magazine/gerald-murnane-next-nobel-laureate-literature-australia.html), and to the 2018 suspension of the Nobel Prize in Literature, following its #MeToo moment as the Academy was embroiled in sexual abuse. The prize was, in fact, awarded again but immediately plunged itself into further challenge. The committee announced two awards in 2019: the 2019 Nobel Prize for Literature went to Olga Tokarczuk, and the delayed 2018 Nobel Prize for Literature went to Peter Handke, a genocide denier: see Ed Vulliamy, "Peter Handke's Nobel Prize Dishonours the Victims of Genocide," *The Guardian*, October 12, 2019, sec. Opinion, https://www.theguardian.com/commentisfree/2019/oct/12/a-nobel-prize-that-dishonours-the-victims-of-genocide-peter-handke. For more on Gerald Murnane and his surprising similarities to Janelle Monáe, please complete the Monáe or Murnane quiz: https://ullapoolism.wordpress.com/2018/04/25/yet-another-very-mysterious-project/.

Just as her mind wandered back to the Melbourne suburbs, more cheering began in the Executive Club. Caspian strode in, trailing a slight limp. As he approached, she saw a bruise on his cheek, and her heart jumped a beat.[12]

"Caspian… what happened? Are you alright?"

"Oh nothing. A storm in a teacup. They're all in prison now, and the Buchmesse has been cleared of all the bombs."

Lotte shook Caspian's hand. "Thank you, Polizeiobermeister Schorle," she said gravely.

The celebratory mood of the Executive Club left Beatrice, as she remembered what had happened over the past few days, and how much worse it could have been. Books, bombs, injured bodies…

"How is Herr Weidenfeld?" she asked, anxiously, looking between Caspian and Lotte.

"He's resting, but he will be ok," Lotte replied. "It's just a flesh wound. He'll join us at the Literaturhaus this evening. We're going to make his award there. You'll come too?"

A weight lifted from Beatrice. She turned to Caspian, who looked at his watch.

"Time to party?" he asked, a crooked smile on his face. The heat of his body radiated towards Beatrice.[13]

She nodded at Lotte, and returned Caspian's smile. Her body remembered the Kabuff. "To the Literaturhaus!"

12. All straight women love a slightly physically and emotionally damaged hero. Don't they?

13. All straight women love going to a hot party with a slightly physically and emotionally damaged hero. Don't they?

CHAPTER FÜNFZEHN

THE BRIGHTLY LIT FACADE OF THE LITERATURHAUS spilled its illumination across the street and onto the river below.[1] Beatrice was feeling jubilant, refreshed by a brief shower and a short nap and wearing shiny red heels that had been delivered to her room in the Hessischer Hof "with the compliments of the book club." With Caspian by her side, Beatrice approached the Literaturhaus, a smile playing on her lips and her heart leaping in time with the deep bass beat pumping out from between its vast pillars. As they mounted the steps, she felt the hair on Caspian's arm brush against hers. She let out a delicious shiver in the still-warm evening Frankfurt air.

1. A Literaturhaus is a centre for bookish activity, such as author talks, writing workshops, reading and discussion groups, and book launches. There are fourteen Literaturhauses in German cities. Frankfurt's Literaturhaus was founded in 1989 and moved to its present location, the former city library, on the banks of the river in 2005. It hosts around 100 annual events including the Frankfurt Poetics Lectures. The building also includes the Goldmund restaurant. One room is dedicated to the Frankfurt cabaret artist and writer Matthias Beltz (1945–2002) and features much of his furniture (see https://de.wikipedia.org/wiki/Literaturhaus_Frankfurt). On October 12, 2013, user Yasmine H on the social website Foursquare wrote of the Frankfurt Literaturhaus: "Whomever said you couldn't party in a library obviously hasn't been here" (https://foursquare.com/v/literaturhaus-frankfurt/4b05885of964a52008be22e3).

They pressed through the chatting crowd on the steps, a merry babel of languages from all around the world surrounding them over the robot sounds of Kraftwerk's "Trans-Europe Express."[2] Beatrice recognised some of the faces from the Buchmesse as they reached a clipboard-bearing attendant by the door. He scrutinised them both briefly, before his face broke into a flirtatious smile as he addressed Caspian.

"Guten Abend, Polizeihauptmeister Schorle!" the attendant said, winking. "Willkommen. And you must be Beatrice Deft? Please come in." He gestured towards a grand hallway, where people were already dancing to the beats and more attendants stood with trays laden with sparkling wine and ingeniously designed canapés. Beatrice felt her body start to move to the rhythm of the music. Above their heads were hundreds of glass balls with water suspended in them, a conjunction of water and bookishness that thrilled Beatrice with its riskiness while also reminding her of how much she liked reading on ferries, and in the bath.[3]

Caspian took Beatrice's hand and led her inside, picking her a glass of sparkling wine as they passed a tray, before helping himself to another. She shouted over the noise into his ear, "Hauptmeister, hey? You got promoted?"

"Ja. I have four stars now. But my number is still the same," he grinned, lopsidedly.

Beatrice laughed, remembering his bashfulness after the first party. "I'm delighted to hear it," she replied, entwining her fingers further with his, reliving the feel of his body on hers in the Kabuff. "Congratulations!" she lifted her glass, her eyes pouring into his. "Great champagne!"

"We call it Sekt, Deft," replied Caspian seriously, then took a long draught through his full lips. "Mmmm," he breathed, as their bodies both started moving to the beat of Kelis's "Milchshake."[4]

---

2. Kraftwerk is a German group founded by Ralf Hütter and Florian Schneider and widely considered innovative. "Trans-Europe Express" (aka "Trans Europa Express") is a hypnotic electronic tune from 1977 which was a number one hit in France. The music video features the band in long coats on a train trip. The song was sampled by Afrika Bambaata in "Planet Rock."
3. The connection between water and bookishness (with particular emphasis on ferries) is elaborated upon by Driscoll and Squires in OLAF ("'Oh Look, a Ferry'; or The Smell of Paper Books"), as previously discussed in Chapter Zwei, page 37, note 12.
4. The song "Milkshake" (not Milchshake) by Kelis was a worldwide hit in 2003. This song choice positions publishing parties as approximately fifteen years out of date in their contemporary music choices, or alternatively a decade/Jürgen or so early in their classic music choices. The word milkshake is generally agreed to be a suggestive sexual

Beatrice saw publishers and related industry professionals all around her, dancing, smiling, air kissing and still talking about books, occasionally stopping to exchange business cards. She thought back to her first Frankfurt party, her feeling of estrangement while others enjoyed themselves. But now she knew there was no threat to the Buchmesse, and after several months her body had reawakened with Caspian's. She might even, she thought, pick a new book to start reading tomorrow. As Caspian swung her expertly in and out of hold, she closed her eyes with pleasurable anticipation at the thought of several hours in a bookshop, imagining running her fingers across their spines just as she was now touching the sculptural muscle of Caspian's back.

A microphone crackle sounded over the music. "Is there anybody here from the BOOK FAIR?!" the DJ called out, whipping the crowd into a frenzy as each person lifted their arms high into the air, waving in her direction. Nelly's "Hot In Herre"[5] blared at full volume as Beatrice, Caspian and the rest of the publishing industry shook off the pressures of the week, and the vexed question of the fate of books more generally.

---

euphemism, although in an interview Kelis instead emphasised the feminist aspects of the song by asserting that a milkshake is "the thing that makes women special. It's what gives us our confidence and what makes us exciting" (see https://uproxx.com/music/5-songs-you-didnt-know-pharrell-wrote/). Kelis has also shared an actual milkshake recipe that includes Baileys, ginger beer and chocolate ice cream (see https://metro.co.uk/2017/09/08/kelis-finally-explains-whats-in-her-milkshake-that-brings-all-the-boys-to-the-yard-6912740/). In 2022, "Milkshake" was sampled by Beyoncé, but due to the extremely dubious and unfeminist writer credit and copyright holding of the song (by Pharrell Williams), Kelis commented at length on Instagram about the music business and its population of "bully's and secrets and gangsters in this industry that smile and get away with it until someone says enough is enough" (see https://www.instagram.com/p/CgklOQiDTXf/?hl=en). Solidarity to Kelis.

5. Rapper Nelly's 2002 hit is indeed called "Hot in Herre"—this is not a play on words in the text, even though the word "Herre" is (happily) a German word translated into English as "gentleman". The spelling "herre" can be interpreted in a number of ways. Songfacts suggests the additional r indicates that it is "really hot" (the r is for extra heat) and also is a reference to Nelly's midwestern accent, by suggesting elongated pronunciation of the word "here" (see https://www.songfacts.com/facts/nelly/hot-in-herre#:~:text=The%20extra%20%22R%22%20in%20%22,because%20it%20was%20really%20dirty). Like "Milkshake," referenced in footnote 4 of this chapter, this song was produced by The Neptunes. However, a news item from 2016 suggests that Nelly holds rights to his songs, due to his call-out for Spotify plays to pay a huge and looming tax bill (see https://www.npr.org/2016/09/15/494127919/fans-stream-hot-in-herre-on-repeat-to-save-nelly-from-tax-debt).

Beatrice was warm, too warm now, and her long, shapeless but stylish black wrap suddenly felt superfluous. "Do you know if there's a cloakroom here?" she shouted into Caspian's ear, her lips brushing against his tender lobe. He raised a thick brown eyebrow, his warm brown eye underneath it twinkling. "Ja. Of course."

Placing his hand in the small of her back, Caspian guided Beatrice towards the rear of the hallway, where an ornate carved marble staircase wound into the shadowy depths. "So what's the best biography you've read lately?" she asked as they headed towards the top of the staircase.

Caspian's face drew together in thought. "Malala Yousafzai's, perhaps. Though I confess that is a memoir, not biography. The buzz I have heard at the Buchmesse about Michelle Obama's forthcoming memoir makes me suspect I will like that also."[6]

They had reached the bottom of the stairs. To the right, a group of women laughed as they exited an oddly futuristic bathroom, with walls that changed from translucent to opaque and back again. To the left, there was a counter, and behind it, racks of coats. Beatrice strode up to the desk. "Hello? Hello?"

It seemed to be deserted. Beatrice was suddenly extremely hot, flushed in fact. She shrugged out of her wrap, and felt the capable hands of a hot cop on her shoulders. "Let me help you," his deep voice whispered in her ear as he took her wrap. She whirled around and stared up into Caspian's face. "I'll show you how you can help me," she said, nodding her head towards the coat racks at the back of the cloakroom.

In just a few moments they were behind and underneath the coats, limbs tangled and breathing ragged. Beatrice leaned back against a pile of wool and velvet, and Caspian slid his hands up her thighs, parting her legs wide. He shot her a questioning look as she nodded, then gasped in anticipation as his hands eased her knickers off, then slid further up her body, reaching for her breasts. His head replaced his hands between her legs, and she felt the pressure of his tongue begin to circle her. She plunged her hands into his thick brown hair, encouraging his mouth as he explored and licked and circled. A tremor started in her, radiating out from where Caspian's

6. Both books were published by large multinational publishers (Hachette and Penguin Random House respectively). One might have expected Caspian to support small and independent presses (although not ones like Callum's), in addition to his support for women authors of colour.

tongue was repeatedly caressing her to her thighs and stomach and beyond. A huge warmth swept through her body and she cried out in abandon.

Beatrice brought Caspian's head back up to hers, and kissed his glistening lips deeply, after tremors still coursing through her body.

She sighed. Now that was stress relief. From high above them, a sound she recognised came floating down: Janelle Monáe, I Got the Schorle.[7]

"I love this song!" Beatrice leapt up, her gauze skirt floating back into place. She ran up the stairs two at a time, her red shoes clicking jauntily on the marble. Caspian laughed behind her. In the grand hallway, the dancing had become looser, more wild and joyful. The crowd exhaled when the song finished and a peaceful hush descended.

Tap, tap. Someone was checking a microphone. Beatrice's head swivelled towards the stage, where Lotte Frankel was standing next to the DJ and holding the handheld mic in her hand. To Lotte's right was Adriana, her black hair swept to the side and eyes dramatically made up. Adriana looked over to Beatrice and Caspian, still flushed from their exertions, and gave a quick conspiratorial wink. Beatrice smiled, remembering how Adriana had helped her get into that first Frankfurt Kabuff. So much had happened since then. Beatrice and her friends had saved the Buchmesse, stopped a neo-Nazi resurgence, and fought off a villain with knitting needles. And somehow, in the process, Beatrice had shaken off the legacy of the chicken shop and rediscovered her interest in both books and physical pleasure. What more was there for anyone to say?

Lotte, the new Vice President, pulled the microphone close to her lips and began.

"Meinen Damen, Herren, und all non-binary friends. We have a leetle unfinished Buchmesse business that must be concluded."

The crowd inhaled. Beatrice noticed people looking nervously at the cupboards dotted around the hallway.

Lotte raised her hands, wincing when the microphone screeched with the sound of feedback and lowering it again quickly. "Do not be alarmed! I am talking, of course, of the awarding of Herr Weidenfeld's Peace Prize."

The quality of attention in the room softened and the crowd parted, creating an aisle down the centre. Kurt, who had been standing quietly

7. Janelle Monáe's song is in fact titled "I Got the Juice." Schorle means juice in German. This is a play on words because Caspian's surname is Schorle, as previously explained in Chapter Drei, page 35, note 5.

against the wall, walked towards the stage: a little frail, but unbowed. The glass balls of water clinked gently overhead. Lotte embraced Kurt before placing a gold medallion around his neck.

Someone behind the DJ started clapping slowly but strongly, and soon everyone had joined in, whooping and cheering for the publisher—this independent, passionate supporter of left wing philosophy, with an open submissions policy and an even-handed embrace of both paper and digital formats—the embodiment of hope for the future of publishing.[8]

Herr Weidenfeld took the microphone from Lotte, and the room hushed again, as he touched the medal at his neck.

"Frau Frankel," he bowed towards Lotte graciously. "I thank you and the Buchmesse from the bottom of my heart. Often my work has felt difficult and lonely, and in the last year dangerous as well." He nodded over towards where Beatrice and Caspian were standing.

He continued. "This is an accolade that I never expected, but I am profoundly grateful for its recognition of what I have been working for my whole life. I said a moment ago that my work has often been lonely, but there have always been comrades to support and nourish my work." He smiled over to another corner of the room, and Beatrice saw Tante Fran beaming back.

"But now, with this award, I feel it is time for me to pass on my work to the next generation." He gestured towards Adriana, who stepped forwards from Lotte's side. "I have been assisted recently by Adriana, who started working with me only a few months after she found safety in our land thanks to the open borders our country offers to those seeking asylum. She has taught me much over the past few years, insight into experiences of which horror I could only imagine, and yet confirmed my belief that cultural interchange is the best way for us to understand each other and continue to work towards a better world. Adriana will from now take over as Publisher at Linksphilosophie Verlag." He took her hand, and raised it in the air as the crowd broke into further cheers. He passed her the microphone.

"Thank you, Kurt, and thank you to this country and this book community, from the bottom of my heart," said Adriana, her voice strong but with a slight quaver that betrayed her emotion. "I will not speak at length as I know we stand between you and more canapés. But I am delighted that Kurt has accepted my invitation to continue as Editor-at-Large at

8. What a vision.

Linksphilosophie Verlag, and I hope in my leadership I will honour his great contribution to literature, and life."

Adriana turned to Herr Weidenfeld, and kissed him on both cheeks before indicating to the DJ to spin more discs. "99 Luftballons" pulsed from the speakers as red streamers flew across the room, and the dancing started up again.[9]

Beatrice wiped a tear from the corner of her eye and looked around for the bar. It was time for another Negroni.

9. "99 Luftballons" is a 1984 hit from the singer Nena. It is very upbeat. According to the website Songfacts, "The song talks about Nena and the listener buying 99 red balloons in a shop and letting them go, for fun. ... The song, though difficult to understand, is about the dreams of the German people that were lost after World War II. The 99 balloons represent the many dreams that each person had" (see https://www.songfacts.com/facts/nena/99-luftballons).

CHAPTER SECHZEHN

BEATRICE DOWNED HER ESPRESSO AND FOLLOWED IT with a sparkling water chaser, leaving a bright red lipstick stain on both cups. The morning after the night before was warm, with bright sunshine bouncing off the crisp yellow leaves. A little too bright. Beatrice fished dark sunglasses out of her handbag. People chattered loudly in the lobby of the Hessischer Hof, and despite her hangover, Beatrice smiled. After all, she was a Scorpio: passionate, assertive and—Beatrice accepted this now—interested in the lives and culture of the people around her.

The solicitous young waiter with the chiseled jaw stopped by her table. "Breakfast for vun?"

"Zwei," Caspian cut in, arriving at the table after a short walk from the lift. Beatrice lowered her sunglasses and took in his neat uniform, clean shaven face and bright eyes. Overall, his appearance gave no hint of the celebrations that had continued long into the night. The party had moved from the Literaturhaus, to the Irish pub, to the Apfelwein bar, and finally, inevitably, back to the Hessischer Hof. Beatrice's suite. She pushed her sunglasses back up.

"Danke. We need more espresso. And pastries. And sausage. And perhaps some of that Frankfurter Schnitzel, the one with the green sauce."[1]

1. Frankfurter Schnitzel is a celebrated local dish which, according to legend (or this food blog, at least: https://gastrogays.com/frankfurt-schnitzel-green-soss/) contains

The waiter raised one eyebrow, then nodded, and left Beatrice and Caspian looking at one another across the white tablecloth.

"Caspian," Beatrice began, just as Caspian said her name. They laughed.

"I admire you so much," she continued, "Your humane political views, your taste in books, your wherewithal in the face of danger, and your unselfishness as a lover. But—"

Caspian's smile was quick and gentle. "Do not say anything more. I understand completely. You have my business card if you ever need to get in touch."

Beatrice grinned in relief. "I had a text from Lotte this morning. I need to meet her at the airport at noon." She nodded towards the wall, where her luggage was neatly stacked. "I just have time for breakfast before I head to the Flughafen." And with that, they tucked into a hearty meal, doing those choice morsels full justice with honest delight.[2]

* * *

The taxi wound along the Main River. Beatrice leaned forward in her seat, cherishing every glimpse of this bookish city, which she was soon to leave behind (at least for now) as she began her career as an International Publishing Consultant. Suddenly, her eyes narrowed. There, on the water... was that...could it be...a manboat?[3] She groaned.

---

seven different green herbs in precise amounts in its luminescent accompanying sauce: parsley, chervil, borage, chive, sorrel, cress, and lemon balm. For previous mention of schnitzel, see Chapter Zwei, page 37, note 14.

2. Reference to Charles Dickens, who often ends chapters with similar descriptions of hearty meals (see, for example, *The Pickwick Papers*).

3. As the multiple references to the article "Oh Look A Ferry" in this text illustrate, boats are something of a preoccupation for Squiscoll, Driscoll, and Squires. The textual insertion of a manboat in this chapter arguably harks back to an occasion when one of the three witnessed just such a manboat on the Yarra River around Christmastime (in Australian summer), probably a function, possibly for a workplace (of men). Another boat incident that is yet to be written into the Squiscoll oeuvre concerns a trip in a tinny (a small metal boat) across Sydney Harbour with multiple stops including one at Shark Island. On the way home from this outing, the tinny ran out of fuel and its passengers required rescuing by the New South Wales water police, who are affectionately known as the "Water Rats" (from the television show of the same name that screened between 1996 and 2001). It will be unsurprising if a lightly fictionalised version of this experience appears in a future Beatrice Deft adventure.

"What's the matter?" asked the driver.

"Boats with only male passengers. They're the worst. They remind me of manels."[4] Silently, Beatrice resolved that wherever she went in the future, one of her missions as International Publishing Consultant would be to work against manels of all forms. She hunted in her bag for a notebook and pen to jot this plan down as the car left the city centre and started to speed along the Autobahn to the Flughafen.

* * *

Beatrice settled in a high stool at the airport bar, a Negroni in hand, sunglasses still perched on her nose. She'd creased back the cover of one of the books she'd been tempted by at the bookshop, an irresistible display which included the latest Nora Roberts, the winner of the New Academy prize in literature Maryse Condé, and a travel guide for creative professionals.[5] Beatrice imagined how this time next year the shop would be populated by the titles that had been the buzz of this year's Buchmesse. The new titles Adriana would commission for Linksphilosophie Verlag, even. Her mind wandered from the page, as she thought about the past few days, all the people she had met, everything that went into the creation, circulation and consumption of books. The annual pilgrimages to the Buchmesse, the continuing international exchange of translation rights, cultures and ideas. Frankfurt lovers.

Beatrice took another sip of her Negroni, smiling at her recent memories of Caspian. She felt the heat of their bodies, as she span the ice around

---

4. The online *Macmillan Dictionary* defines a manel as "a panel of experts or participants, for example on a TV quiz show or at a conference, that consists of men only" (https://www.macmillandictionary.com/dictionary/british/manel). A 2019 article elaborating on the phenomenon also describes the manference: Holly Else, "How to Banish Manels and Manferences from Scientific Meetings," *Nature* 573, no. 7773 (September 10, 2019): 184–86. Manboat is as yet undefined in the *Macmillan Dictionary*.
5. Beatrice makes an eclectic choice of reading matter: a romance novel, the winner of the award which was temporarily set up to replace the non-awarded Nobel Prize in Literature of 2018 (see page 81, note 11, for more details) https://www.theguardian.com/books/2018/oct/12/alternative-nobel-literature-prize-maryse-conde-new-academy-prize), and a non-fiction guide which demonstrates her diligent approach to work (despite, or perhaps intensified by, her drinking of a strong cocktail before lunch).

in her glass, her fingers the only cool part of her. The immediate bitterness of the drink was tempered by its sweet finish, leaving her wanting more.[6]

She signalled to the waiter. She observed his broad-shouldered approach and knowing nod as he took her glass to make her another cocktail.

Her eyes drifted to the locations on the screens, which flicked over again. Guadalajara, Beijing, Sharjah, Bologna, New York…

The waiter returned. "You are waiting for Frau Frankel, I know," he said. "She has left this for you." Beatrice took the thick envelope—130 gsm, probably—and read her briefing.

* * *

The screens flicked once more. The gate for her flight came up. Beatrice texted Caspian one last goodbye, put the envelope and book back in her bag, and took her purse out to leave a tip for the solicitous waiter.

As she did so, her eye caught a woman facing her on the other side of the bar, unblinking. A strapping blonde. With a shock of recognition, Beatrice realised where she had seen her before. Guarding the first Kabuff.

For a moment the two women's eyes locked. The blonde lifted her glass to Beatrice, then turned back to her e-reader.

Beatrice gathered her hand luggage, and headed for the gate.

THE END—or is it

6. It is worth emphasising yet one more time the superlative nature of the Negroni.

Critical Essays

Genesis

KIM WILKINS

CAN CREATIVE WRITING BE TAUGHT?

I typed this burning question into Google in preparation for writing this essay, and discovered that *yes of course* it can and in *no way* can it be taught. I tend not to like paradoxes. They give me anxiety.

Being assigned an essay called "Genesis" also gave me anxiety. Given the creative genius of Blaire Squiscoll and the author's comfort with things outside the box, I spent a good deal of time crafting an essay that would cleverly and thematically lead from Genesis (the book in the Bible) to Genesis (the '70s progressive rock band) and then to Genesis (the luxury Hyundai spin-off). It was hopeless and not funny, and I balled up many pieces of paper and threw them in the bin, as all frustrated writers do. I mean, what do I know about the Bible or Hyundais (I admit to knowing a fair bit about prog)? Kim, I said to myself, you must *write what you know*. That is what people who believe that creative writing can be taught are always saying. It's not advice I've ever taken, but on this occasion I listened. It was preferable to trying to shoehorn Adam, Eve, Phil Collins, and the "athletic elegance" of the GV80 into a coherent narrative.

Full disclosure: I teach creative writing. I have for years and years, and I have mentored several bestselling writers and I have a carpet bag full of marvellous tricks to help people see narrative structure differently, so that they can write from beginning to end (which is the hard part). One fateful day in Frankfurt, Blaire Squiscoll, who had negligible fiction writing experience, asked me for a tutorial in how to write a novel.

* * *

I have argued elsewhere that creative writing pedagogy needs to be loosened from the academic environment and situated more within the real world of publishing, distribution, and reading.[1] When faced with teaching Blaire Squiscoll the structure of a novel, I had a ready-made test of my hypothesis right in front of me. Blaire may have been relatively new to writing fiction, but had a very, very strong knowledge of the world of readers and publishers. We were travelling together at the time. Blaire is exceedingly good company. Not unlike Beatrice Deft, truth be told, with a penchant for good shoes and good Negronis. Chapters unfolded in front of me in the hotel we shared in Frankfurt, where we had met for the 2018 book fair. I was something of a sounding board at first, having lines and ideas bounced off me, suggesting a phrase every now and again or sometimes even taking control of the keyboard while Blaire dictated, and I interjected. I thought we were playing a short-lived game; Blaire had loftier, longer-term goals.

By the time I realised that Blaire was, indeed, going to write an entire novel, we were about to go our separate ways. Wanting to leave some lasting advice, I hastily scribbled out a diagram for Blaire, as we stood at Frankfurt Hauptbahnhof. "Stories," I said, drawing a line, "have a beginning, a middle, and an end. The trick is knowing where the beginning ends, because that's where the middle begins, and so on." I took the nascent author through critical turning points, and how to maintain a balance between the pleasure principle (helping the reader to stay suspended in the moment of pleasure for as long as possible, through world building and fascinating characters) and the death drive (asking narrative questions so the reader was compelled to keep reading). I then helpfully marked on the page that a beginning should be roughly 25 percent of a story, a middle 50 percent, and the end the remaining 20 to 25 percent depending on how the other chapters have played out. I taught it like a rule.

The teacher was about to become the student.

* * *

I learned to write from Shakespeare. This sounds so desperately pretentious that I have to add the disclaimer that I hadn't read any Shakespeare until I was well into my twenties, when I attended a high school for adults so that I could qualify for university study. I should say I had written stories all my life, but it was in studying Shakespeare that I began to see their component parts and how they related to each other. The tighter and brighter those relationships, the better the story. Character, conflict, context, and style.

> Two households, both alike in dignity,
> In fair Verona, where we lay our scene,
> From ancient grudge break to new mutiny,
> Where civil blood makes civil hands unclean.
> From forth the fatal loins of these two foes
> A pair of star-cross'd lovers take their life...[2]

There it is. Character (dignified households, star-cross'd lovers), conflict (ancient grudges and new mutinies), context (fair Verona), and style (I mean... *all of it*).

But what really fascinated me about Shakespeare's plays was their structure, especially the tragedies. Reading them was like boarding a train. No matter how beautiful the places we might slow or stop, the drive of the story seemed inevitable and inescapable. It is from his plays that I derived my ideal plot structure, and wrote my first published novel.

(Years later somebody told me I should have just read Robert McKee's *Story*, which teaches a similar structure.[3] I like to think learning it the hard way also taught me forgiveness, that the structure must sometimes bend to submit to what the story needs. I still haven't read *Story*, but wouldn't discourage anyone from doing so.)

My "elements of story" and "three-part structure" principles were highly market-friendly, and it should come as no surprise that I am a great lover of genre fiction. As I have had so much success in the industry with my principles, I have taught them now for more than twenty years. It never occurred to me to consider the publishing environment again and consider how my work related to it; because, as we know, the publishing environment has changed a great deal since 1996 when my first book was acquired.

In the weeks following our Frankfurt trip, Blaire continued to upload chapters of *The Frankfurt Kabuff* to Wattpad. I could see the beginning finish and the middle begin. Excellent. I could see the middle end and the end begin. Well done. But then... Blaire added a little more than necessary to the end, and then a little bit that could have been middle-ish if looked at in the right light, then some character stuff that wasn't entirely necessary. It dawned on me that Blaire knew something I didn't: Wattpad isn't built for a tripartite structure. It's built for episode, for prolonging the fun, meandering here and adding non-essential detail there, drawing the reader into the world and inviting them to just be with the characters, rather than hurrying them to a thundering final cadence. The triumph of Blaire's work is that the novella-ist knew better than me what would work in a particular industry and readerly context. It turned my thinking about how to approach stories upside down.

* * *

As I write this, I am taking a writing break from a book that fictionalises the life of a fashion designer and bon vivant from twentieth-century Melbourne. Her story, like anyone's life, does not play out in a tidy three-act structure. How I tore my hair out looking for critical turning points to contain the damned thing. Until I asked myself: what would Blaire Squiscoll do?

Blaire would understand that twenty-first-century stories are evolving in structure, crossing platforms, indulging readers. Blaire would understand that now is the time to experiment, mix it up, tell the story a new way. I took my cue from Netflix and started writing the novel as a series of episodes, chapter by chapter, that would propel the reader not to an end 60,000 words away, but simply to the next chapter, in the hopes that the world and the character will engulf them and they will binge-read it. Is it the right thing to do? Who knows? I will find out when it's published, but given my role as a professor of creative writing who says she pretty much knows everything, I would be negligent if I didn't try something new in 2021.

I said at the start of this essay that paradoxes made me anxious, and they do. But sometimes they delight me. I am delighted to say that I taught Blaire Squiscoll to write, but it was me who learned the lessons.

Notes

1 Kim Wilkins, Helen Marshall, and Marina Tulic, "Emerging Writers/Established Publishers: A Ten-Year Study of the Hachette Manuscript Development Program," in *Creative Writing Scholars on the Publishing Trade: Practice, Praxis, Print*, ed. Sam Meekings and Marshall Moore (Abingdon, Oxon: Routledge, 2021), 19–32.

2 William Shakespeare, "Romeo and Juliet," in *The Norton Shakespeare*, ed. Stephen Greenblatt et al. (1597; repr., New York: W. W. Norton & Company, 2008).

3 Robert McKee, *Story: Substance, Structure, Style, and the Principles of Screenwriting* (London: Methuen, 1999).

Unplugging the Circuit

Historical Perspectives on Why Scholars Think Writing and Reading Books Is the Easy Part

LESLIE HOWSAM

IN CHAPTER ZWÖLF OF *THE FRANKFURT KABUFF*, WHERE the third excerpt of the Melbourne-set story-within-the-story unfolds, the protagonist Beatrice Deft engages in a quarrel with her unreliable boyfriend. Not only is Callum a pretentious and deluded small-press publisher whose physical appeal has waned, but he boasts a superficial knowledge of the theoretical scholarship in book history. This is obvious when he tells Beatrice—or rather "spits the words out"—that "'writing and reading books is the easy part... the difficult part of the book circuit is publishing it.'" Her response is impatient: "'Yes, Darnton's communication circuit,' I sigh. I can't believe we're going over this again. 'And you're also a hero struggling for symbolic capital.'"[1] Before Bourdieu or anyone else can make an appearance, however, their squabble is sidetracked by events: Callum has negotiated a distribution deal for his firm's latest book of poetry (after a disappointment on a funding subvention) and the resulting financial security will permit him to stop working with the sketchy character called Kev and even move to a more comfortable neighbourhood. But Kev's business blows up in the "chicken shop incident," and soon everyone is on the run.

This essay recognises *The Frankfurt Kabuff* as a light-hearted but ultimately serious critique of the interdiscipline of book history, and aims to show how a fresh model—rather like the fresh genre of an autoethnographic comic erotic thriller—might reorder a field of study where interdisciplinarity is, once again, running riot.[2] Blaire Squiscoll is particularly concerned with academic analysis of one integral part of that field, the contemporary global publishing industry. But book historians can also be literary scholars, librarians, and cultural historians—each of them drawing variously upon archival, bibliographical, ethnographic, and other methodologies and resources to do their work.[3] Does the tagline "Writing and Reading Books is the Easy Part" hold up when the book in question has been around for decades or centuries? Can Beatrice's Negroni be taken as a metaphor for the people, places, and objects that make up book history—a delicate and delicious mixture of elements where the bartender measures the ingredients with precision? Sweet and bitter; strong and cold; served with a twist, at just the right time and in exactly the right place?

No doubt many publishers have reflected on their role as crucial intermediaries, and believed their work to be more difficult, and less appreciated, than either the literary labour of authors or the interpretive task undertaken by readers. For the most part, though, it is historians of the book (not publishing entrepreneurs like Callum) who articulate this observation by evoking an essay first published in 1982, by a historian called Robert Darnton. Using a visual aid, Darnton sought to cut through all the complexity built up over centuries of bibliographical, literary, historiographical, and other kinds of discipline-bound scholarship about books in the past. He suggested that it might help scholars to think in terms of "the book" moving from the mind of an author to that of a reader, via a publisher and related agents, and—since readers may become authors—back to another author and eventually, another book. The publisher initially acts as gatekeeper and then oversees the transformation of the unpublished text into an object that is both material and commercial. They are implicitly doing the heavy lifting of putting "the book" into the world of "intellectual influences and publicity, economic and social conjunctures, and political and legal sanctions."[4]

For aficionados of book history, the Darnton communication circuit is simultaneously foundational and banal, as Beatrice's world-weary reaction suggests. A number of scholars have proposed revisions to the circuit that better capture their research perspective.[5] Virtually all introductory curricula include the essay or one of its several revisions or reinventions; and almost all compilers of textbooks and "readers" for the study of book history include an excerpt from Darnton's article in their section on theory.[6] As a result, thousands of students have learned that this simple but powerful model embodies the history of the book. The global organization whose conferences shape the world of Blaire Squiscoll, the Society for the History of Authorship, Reading, and Publishing, reinscribes the basic idea of the circuit in its title (although the crucial order of the book's progress from composer to consumer is disarranged for the sake of a pronounceable acronym, SHARP).[7] Scholars attending SHARP presentations groan when they see a slide depicting the circuit, because it's all so predictable and familiar.

The reliance on Darnton as a starting point was understandable during the 1980s, and perhaps even the 1990s, decades when book history in general (and SHARP in particular) began to take its place on university campuses, curricula, and conference circuits. But time has not stood still, nor have the geography and periodization of book history remained in the limited Anglo-American and post-medieval constraints that hampered its beginnings. People like Callum don't realise that Darnton's circuit doesn't work very well outside of eighteenth-century France, where it started. More importantly, as Beatrice intuits, it doesn't capture the fundamental mobility and mutability of an object—the book—whose history, while it does not end at the Frankfurt Book Fair, might have a significant encounter there. Publishers do undertake the initial transition of a book from text to physical object. But, as yet another theorist, D.F. McKenzie, observed: "the book is a friskier animal than the words 'physical object' will allow."[8] Blaire Squiscoll's novella offers the attractive possibility that book history, too, can be a friskier animal than the words "academic interdiscipline" will allow. In Sydney Shep's formulation, books travel, and they also transform.

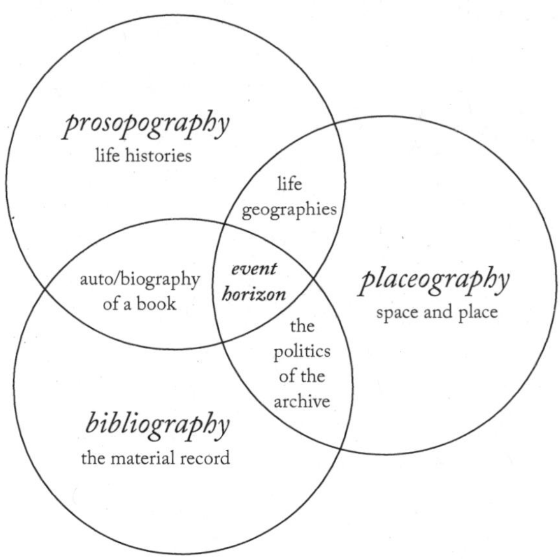

Modelling Situated Knowledges in Book History. Credit: Sydney Shep

Shep's challenge to the Darnton circuit was published in 2015, and workshopped three years earlier at a SHARP conference in Dublin (see figure on page 103). She suggests that the prevailing lack of attention to mobility and mutability "can be addressed by modelling the field of book history as one of *situated knowledges*. An examination of the complex, dynamic intercrossings between people (prosopography), places (placeography), and objects (bibliography) offers a quite different way of conceptualizing the ways and means by which books travel and transform through space and across time."[9] Unlike its predecessors, this is a model that puts scholarly methodologies (the several "ographies") in conversation with the narratives and arguments they interrogate—the life geographies of people and places, the politics of the archive, and the biography of a book.

While *The Frankfurt Kabuff* might be mapped onto the Darnton circuit and its variants, it works better with Shep's model of situated knowledges in book history. Certainly all the key nodes on the original circuit can be identified: the Turkish taxi-driving author whose manuscript can stop a bullet like a bible on a battlefield; the readers gathered together in Tante Fran's book club who can mobilise against the evildoers; the agents and rights managers who haunt the book fair; and most of all the publishers, from left to right the noble Kurt Weidenfeld (named for a renowned British bookman) and the evil White Storm with their new edition of *Mein Kampf* and their villainous leader, a rejected author. A close reading would identify many more characterisations of agents and representations of themes. But the novella also touches on the inherent mobility and mutability of books, the way their meaning changes across space and over time, and in the hands and minds of people with diverse values and objectives.

The (book) people, (book) places, and (book) things where Squiscoll's novella meets Shep's model can't be pinned down like the Darnton examples; revision happens, as do translation, suppression and transmediation. The co-authors' knowledge—both disciplinary and experiential—of the book trade is central to narrative and plot. The material record of the novella's own history, consisting of digital publication on such platforms as Wattpad and multiple printings in book form, is already complex and still evolving. The geographical settings, Melbourne and Frankfurt, are both inevitable and arbitrary as backgrounds for the action. The politics of the archive include, in this case, the tenacious insistence of the authors on a playful, even giddy, approach to a subject that is usually taken with preternatural seriousness. Especially in Australia, where the history of the antipodal book is fraught with colonial inferiority complexes; especially in Germany, where Gutenberg's claim to be the first printer in the western world is jealously guarded.[10] Certain spaces intrude upon themselves (ferries and conferences, for example), spaces where questions get asked and manels get challenged. In particular, we can think of the chicken shop and the Kabuff—where virtue confronts evil across the deep-fryer and inside a cobwebby and multi-layered cupboard—as contact zones, spaces where people and books come together and then disperse again to further adventures.

One subdiscipline of book history that is treated with particular respect by many scholars, but with flippant disrespect by the authors, is bibliography (the study of the book as a material object, which requires distinguishing minutely between different editions, multiple issues, and even individual copies of the same work). As Shep indicates, every copy tells a story, one that intersects with the stories of other copies that derived from different settings of type, or were reissued for another market, or acquired distinct marginalia by dint of going through the hands of multiple owners. Here the novella's authors—who presumably controlled the design and typesetting quite closely—have ended two of their sixteen chapters with a classic printer's error: the "widow," that word or phrase left awkwardly hanging at the top of a new page rather than skilfully fitted into the page that preceded it. This may be their subtle way of pointing out that the study of contemporary publishing has been treated with a certain amount of disdain by some book historians.

From the perspective of the open-minded book historian, however, *The Frankfurt Kabuff* captures something that is evanescent in the interdiscipline, something about strong emotions and unstable relationships. Beatrice can appreciate her policeman friend with the same passion that people express when they say they "just love books." Blaire Squiscoll can model, in their collaboration, an academic relationship where the fun is part of the intellectual package. Set at a book fair rather than a conference, the novella nevertheless invokes the centrality of exchange to academic life. When the characters have dealt with the challenges presented by the plot, they can gather at another event horizon—in this case the Literaturhaus and later at the bar of the conference hotel, where the Negronis are shaken, shared, refilled, perhaps ritualised as tradition, perhaps forgotten by next year. Both book fairs and conferences are marketplaces of ideas, but the latter are also spaces for trading in career prestige, where the currency is not so much a royalty agreement as the opportunity to present next year's keynote lecture, or a nomination for an annual award. Sydney Shep identifies "the book's historical research process as one of constant, energetic interplay between people, places and things."[11] Blaire Squiscoll gives a name to the place where the interplay happens, and it's the Kabuff (or perhaps the chicken shop). Publishing, writing, and reading books are *all* the easy part; what's hard is thinking about all three at the same time, while everything is in a state of transformation and constantly in motion.

Notes

1 Page 70 of this edition.

2 For "running riot" see Robert Darnton, "What is the History of Books?" *Daedalus* 111, no. 3 (1982), 67; for interdisciplinarity see Leslie Howsam, "Thinking through the history of the book," *Memoires du livre / Studies in Book Culture* 7, no. 2 (Spring 2016). https://doi.org/10.7202/1036851ar

3 Leslie Howsam, *Old Books & New Histories: An Orientation to Studies in Book and Print Culture* (Toronto: University of Toronto Press, 2006), 16–27.

4 Darnton, "What is the history of books?" 68. After the original 1982 *Daedalus* article noted above a slightly altered version of the circuit diagram was reprinted in *The Kiss of Lamourette: Reflections in Cultural History* (New York: Norton, 1990), 112. See also Darnton's self-criticism after 25 years: "'What is the History of Books?' Revisited," *Modern Intellectual History* 4, no. 3, 2007: 495–508.

5 Thomas R. Adams and Nicolas Barker, "A New Model for the Study of the Book," in *A Potencie of Life: Books in Society*, ed. Nicolas Barker (London: British Library, 1993), 5–43. Padmini Ray Murray and Claire Squires, "The Digital Publishing Communications Circuit." *Book 2.0* 3, no. 1 (2013): 3–24. https://doi.org/10.1386/btwo.3.1.3_1

6 Examples include *The Book History Reader*, ed. David Finkelstein and Alistair McCleery (London: Routledge, 2002; 2nd edition 2006), 12; and *The Broadview Reader in Book History*, ed. Michelle Levy and Tom Mole (Peterborough: Broadview Press, 2015), 234.

7 SHARP was founded in 1992; the organization initiated a listserv and a newsletter, and held its first conference in 1993. https://www.sharpweb.org/main/purpose-history/.

8 D.F. McKenzie, "The Sociology of a Text: Orality, Literacy and Print in Early New Zealand," *The Library* 6th series, 6 (1984), 334.

9 Sydney Shep, "Books in Global Perspectives," in *The Cambridge Companion to the History of the Book*, ed. Leslie Howsam (Cambridge: Cambridge University Press, 2015), 65–66.

10 Martyn Lyons, "National Histories of the Book in a Transnational Age," *Memoires du Livre / Studies in Book Culture* 7, no. 2 (Spring 2016). https://doi.org/10.7202/1036855ar. Adrian Johns, "The Coming of Print to Europe," in *The Cambridge Companion to the History of the Book*, ed. Leslie Howsam (Cambridge: Cambridge University Press, 2015): 107–24.

11 Shep, "Books," 66.

An Excellent Rectangle

The Shape of The Frankfurt Kabuff

IAN GADD

This is an excellent rectangle.
—Ron Swanson[1]

. . . to turn little slices of life into rectangles rife with metaphor.
—Deborah Copaken Kogan[2]

WHEN BEATRICE DEFT FIRST SPOTS THE FRANKFURT Kabuff as a part of a scale model of Hall 3 of the Frankfurter Buchmesse, it has no name: it is simply "a tiny cardboard cupboard."[3] It is the sinister Vice President of the Buchmesse who calls it a Kabuff: "a cupboard, a cobwebby cupboard where things are hidden."[4] Later, when, like a latter-day Alice, Beatrice steps into the Kabuff, its precise shape remains indistinct as the darkness forces her to use "her hands to see, feeling coats, bags, bottles, and cardboard boxes" (page 56), relying on a kind of *fingerspitzengefühl* ("fingertips feeling," to adapt the German word for intuition). For all the Kabuff's apparent "shapelessness," however, we can infer a definitive rectangularity to the door through which Beatrice enters and to the trapdoor through which she leaves as well as to the boxes she fumbles past. In fact, rectangularity pervades *The Frankfurt Kabuff*: cigarette packets, suitcases, tote bags, bills, business cards, envelopes, newspapers, windows, boxes, flags, stands, posters, greeting cards, doors, walls, mobile phones, computer screens, iPads, notebooks, trapdoors, red carpets, papers, laptops, clipboards, pages, e-readers, and above all else, books.

This should not surprise us. We inhabit a "highly carpentered" world of rectangles.[5] Most of us live in rectangular spaces, only accessible by walking through a rectangle; many of these same spaces are themselves constructed from smaller rectangles. From inside these spaces, we look out at the world through rectangles. We sleep on rectangles, we work at them, we pay with them, we gaze upon them, and we are buried in them. Much of what we buy comes in rectangles that were packaged inside larger rectangles and were shipped inside even larger rectangles. Films, TV programmes, photographs, even social media posts all appear as rectangles; much of Western visual art is similarly framed within rectangles. Even the striking rectangularity of the Frankfurter Buchmesse in which thousands of rectangular books are promoted within hundreds of rectangular stands inside almost a dozen rectangular halls, only differs from other rectangular workplaces or homes by degree.[6]

Yet, for all this, we do not *see* the rectangles. We have become so habituated to them that their rectangularity is largely invisible to us. (The statement by the artist Nathan Swaya's that "I see the world in rectangles" is exceptional.[7]) We do not think about their rectangularity, unless they fail in some way or intrude unexpectedly. That rectangles *frame* so much of our visual art and multimedia suggests they are fundamentally non-aesthetic:

> That one directional, clear rectangular form [is] not used because it's the most beautiful form; it's just the practical thing. That's why our TVs are rectangles.[8]

The paradox of the unseen yet ubiquitous rectangle is reflected in a quirk of the English language. While we have everyday words for most three-dimensional shapes—spheres, cubes, cones, pyramids, diamonds—there is no commonly used term for a three-dimensional rectangle. Even mathematicians use a range of different terms: cuboid, hyperrectangle, rectangular parallelepiped, right rectangular prism, orthotope, orthopiped.[9] Put another way, the English language does not have an agreed word for the shape that, beyond any other, defines so much of our human-made world.

Perhaps this is why we do not need to be told that the Frankfurt Kabuff is rectangular: its three-dimensional rectangularity is there to be inferred rather than described. Counterintuitively, the same is true for *The Frankfurt*

Kabuff, that is the book itself: its undeniable rectangularity as it sits in our hands is unremarkable because books, at least in the West, have been rectangular for millennia. In fact, the Western reading "space"—whether papyrus scroll, wax tablet, manuscript or printed page, or digital screen—is invariably rectangular.[10] Moreover, like the Frankfurter Buchmesse, these reading spaces contain rectangles within rectangles: within the rectangular space is an invisible rectangle within which the written or printed text is bounded while, for many centuries, the printed book was rectangles all the way down to the individual letter. There are striking continuities in terms of the size and proportionality of these readerly rectangles which reflect, in part, how developments in technology or media often deliberately echo earlier forms but also underline how books, at least since the emergence of the codex, have long been valued for their portability. In fact, there is an enduring association between a book's size and particular kinds of texts, whereby more "intimate" genres (such as devotional works or novels) use more mobile ("handy") book sizes than grand works of scholarship. Thus, the size of *The Frankfurt Kabuff* (178mm x 108mm) is typical of the so-called A-format used for mass-market paperbacks but it is almost exactly the same size as duodecimo-format novels of the mid-eighteenth century, and only a little taller and wider than a large smartphone (another kind of intimate readerly object). Books are not just expected to be rectangles: their very contents determine their likely size and proportionality.

As is the case for so many other rectangular objects, the rectangularity of the book is fundamentally practical. For centuries, this has allowed book-makers to gather together folded sheets in a way that compresses an enormous amount of textual space without sacrificing portability or accessibility. (The combined surface area of a single copy of *The Frankfurt Kabuff* is just under $2m^2$, meaning that a mere twelve copies would pretty much fill the floor space of the Buchmesse's largest "Classic" stand of $24m^2$.) Yet, again like so many other rectangular objects, the book's rectangularity is not truly *seen*. Andrew Piper has marvelled at the typical book's "shapeliness" that "fits it to our hands" which may seem a curious statement when there are other shapes that are much better suited to our hands and our bodies.[11] What Piper means by "shapeliness," though, is not intrinsic to the object but has had to be actively learned by each reader: as any parent or kindergarten teacher can confirm, we have to handle many books before we are so confident in their use that their rectangularity seems to disappear in our hands.

Repeated encounters with books throughout a lifetime mean that we develop an intimate haptic knowledge of books as objects. As Sydney Shep has noted, "every physical feature of a book shapes the reading experience and constitutes a kind of material thinking that impacts the processing of information" but few readers are conscious that they are finding meaning in a book's size, shape, heft, and surfaces.[12] Just like Beatrice in the Kabuff, readers "use [their] hands to see," capable of identifying the genre, contents, and even publication dates by touch alone, but a book's tactility is often considered to be a distraction, an anomaly, or even a fetish that ought to lie beyond the scope of reading.[13] The reader of a modern novel should not be conscious of themselves as readers, meaning that the materiality of the book itself cannot become a distraction: to paraphrase the subtitle of a highly influential twentieth-century essay by the typographer Beatrice Warde, the book should be invisible.[14] The "readability" of a novel is itself the consequence of a series of conscious practices by typographers, book-designers, and printers, refined over centuries affecting the size of the book, the proportions of the page and page-opening, the margins, the typeface and type size, the line spacing, the line lengths, the spacing between words and even individual characters on the page—all of which operate in a tightly rectangular world.[15] In other words, Western readers have repeatedly encountered written objects whose physical form and design have been, in certain fundamental ways, unchanged for centuries, enabling readers to trust the immutability of the book as an object: no matter what happens to Beatrice Deft, the material form of *The Frankfurt Kabuff* is reassuringly predictable. The effect for modern readers, who learned the necessary skills and conventions so young that they cannot remember *how* they learned them, is an illusion of disembodiment, a sense that they are reading not with the eyes or the hands but "with the heart," to use the fifteenth-century French term (*lire au coeur*) for silent reading.[16] *The Frankfurt Kabuff* plays with this paradox of the ubiquitous but invisible book, simultaneously absent and present: only by discovering the unseen (in all senses) Kabuff can Beatrice truly see the hidden world of publishing that lies behind all the bookish rectangles.

Rectangles delimit the human-made world. Linear, bounded, and Cartesian, they contain us as much as they define us. In the final scene of *The Frankfurt Kabuff*, Beatrice sits in an airport bar surrounded by rectangular screens, reading a printed book, only to lock eyes with the woman who had guarded the (rectangular?) Kabuff: "The blonde lifted her glass to Beatrice, then turned back to her e-reader."[17] The menace of this new technology is palpable but for all that the digital might one day displace print, the textual world remains resolutely rectangular. Books, it seems, will always be Kabuffs: small cobwebby rectangles, full of secrets and hidden in plain sight.

Notes

1 "Farmer's Market," *Parks and Recreation*, NBC, Series 6, Episode 12, January 23, 2014, 15:09.

2 Deborah Copaken Kogan, *Shutterbabe: Adventures in Love and War* (Edinburgh: Mainstream Publishing Company, 2002), 15.

3 Page 52 of this edition.

4 The real Frankfurter Buchmesse offers only cubicles rather than Kabuffs: see "Prices & Products 2021" (Frankfurter Buchmesse, March 2021), 16–17, https://www.buchmesse.de/files/media/pdf/exhibit-prices-frankfurter-buchmesse-2021.pdf. These are all rectangular.

5 The phrase comes from Marshall H. Segall, Donald T. Campbell, and Melville J. Herskovits, "Cultural Differences in the Perception of Geometric Illusions," *Science* 139, no. 3556 (February 1963): 769–71, which suggested that people exposed to "highly carpentered, urban, European environments" perceive depth differently—the so-called "carpentered world hypothesis." The term "carpentered" is a nineteenth-century coinage (*OED*, *s.v.* 'carpenter', *v.*) but Segall et al. seem to be the first to apply it to rectangular environments.

6 With the exception of the historic Festhalle and the stadium-shaped Hall 3, every hall of the Messe Frankfurt is emphatically rectangular: "Site Map Messe Frankfurt," Messe Frankfurt, accessed September 19, 2021, https://www.sitemap.messefrankfurtlocations.com/. Stands at the Frankfurter Buchmesse are only available in rectangular form: see "Prices & Products 2021," especially 11–14. Intriguingly, the central action of *The Frankfurt Kabuff* takes place in the non-rectangular Hall 3.

7 Quoted in Giulia Rhodes, "Nathan Sawaya: The Artist Making Sculptures from Lego," *The Guardian*, September 22, 2014, https://www.theguardian.com/lifeandstyle/2014/sep/22/nathan-sawaya-artist-sculptures-lego.

8 Pipilotti Rist quoted in Haley Weiss, "Performing with Pipilotti," *Interview Magazine*, May 18, 2015, https://www.interviewmagazine.com/art/pipilotti-rist-soluna.

9 See for example, Abraham Miller, "'Cuboid' Not the Correct Name for 3d Rectangle?," Mathematics Stack Exchange, December 15, 2019, https://math.stackexchange.com/questions/3476760/cuboid-not-the-correct-name-for-3d-rectangle, and Abe, "What Is the Name for a 3-d Rectangle?," *What Is Today?* (blog), April 21, 2020, https://www.whatistoday.net/2020/04/cuboid-dilemma.html.

10 See, for example, the statue of an Egyptian scribe dating from c.1400BCE in the Brooklyn Museum, and illustrated in Keith Houston, *The Book* (New York: W.W. Norton & Company, 2016), 246. Such readerly rectangles are usually oriented as "portrait," that is with a distinctive text-area that is taller than it is wide even if, as

with scrolls and codices, the reader is presented with an opening rather than a single "page" unit.

11 Andrew Piper, *Book Was There: Reading in Electronic Times* (Chicago: University of Chicago Press, 2012), 2.

12 Sydney J. Shep, "Book," in *Literature Now: Key Terms and Methods for Literary History*, ed. Sascha Bru, Ben De Bruyn, and Michel Delville (Edinburgh: Edinburgh University Press, 2016), 41–42.

13 D. F. McKenzie, *"What's Past Is Prologue": The Bibliographical Society and History of the Book* (London: Hearthstone Publications, 1993), 3–7; Ian Gadd, "From Printing Type to Blackboard™: Teaching the History of the Early Modern Book to Literary Undergraduates in a 'New' UK University," in *Teaching Bibliography, Textual Criticism, and Book History*, ed. Ann R. Hawkins (London: Pickering & Chatto, 2006), 65.

14 Beatrice Warde, "The Crystal Goblet, or Printing Should Be Invisible," in *The Crystal Goblet: Sixteen Essays on Typography*, ed. Henry Jacob (Cleveland and New York: The World Publishing Company, 1956), 11–17. Italo Calvino's *If on a Winter's Night a Traveller*, trans. William Weaver (London: Vintage, 1998) directly subverts this expectation, by opening "You are about to begin reading Italo Calvino's new novel, *If on a winter's night a traveler...*" (3).

15 See for example, Warde, *passim*; Jan Tschichold, *The Form of the Book: Essays on the Morality of Good Design* (Point Roberts, WA: Hartley & Marks, 1991), 36–64; Robert Bringhurst, *The Elements of Typographic Style*, 2nd edition (Point Roberts, WA: Hartley & Marks, 1999), 143–78; Geoffrey Dowding, *Finer Points in the Spacing & Arrangement of Type* (London: Wace & Company Ltd, 1995).

16 Paul Saenger, "The Impact of the Early Printed Page on the History of Reading," *Bulletin Du Bibliophile*, 1996, 268. I have written more extensively on how modern reading practices are pervaded by the "ambience of absence": Ian Gadd, "Ready Reader One: Recovering Reading as an Ambient Practice," in *Ambient Literature: Towards a New Poetics of Situated Writing and Reading Practices*, ed. Tom Abba, Jonathan Dovey, and Kate Pullinger (Cham: Palgrave Macmillan, 2021), 27–51.

17 Page 93 of this edition.

Signature Cocktail

Negronis as Method in The Frankfurt Kabuff

JULIE RAK

> Do you have a drink to hand? Are you ready for the job that will be done?
>
> —Driscoll and Squires, "The Epistemology of Ullapoolism"[1]

IN *THE FRANKFURT KABUFF*, BEATRICE DEFT REALLY orders only one cocktail: a Negroni. The novella opens with her drinking one as "her first meal of the day"[2] as she gloomily sits in a hotel bar, the pall of the Australian chicken shop incident still upon her. She has the cocktail five times in the course of the story, which ends with her expecting a sixth to arrive. She does turn down the offer of a Negroni once in favour of tea, but she regrets the decision almost immediately in the wake of a bomb threat that slightly rattles her nerves. When the sexy and well-read police officer Caspian hands her a glass of German Sekt at a posh book fair reception, Beatrice enjoys the drink in the wake of her success at capturing neo-Nazis and obligingly sways with her companion to strains of Kelis's "Milkshake." But still, she has "another Negroni" after that, a decision that means she has had one already, and that probably leads to her drinking espresso and water with Caspian the next day, without a single regret.[3]

Like her fondness for red lipstick and quality shoes, the ruby tinge and sharp taste of the Negroni is Beatrice's "signature," as Jacques Derrida would term it, a sign of Beatrice's presence that is both original and repeatable as it should be for any good genre fictional heroine. Like James Bond saying his name and then ordering a Martini the same way no matter what year or film it is, Beatrice drinks Negronis and signs herself into the action each time as a literary and a secret agent. The Negroni is a mark of who she is, even as it leads to another, a floating signifier served ice-cold. What does that mean for Beatrice, and for the method of *The Frankfurt Kabuff*? The mark of presence in the signature is also an absence, since a signature marks the condition of possibility for presence at the same time that it marks the condition of impossibility of presence within language itself. It is worth noting that even Derrida needs a drink after saying this, calling his argument "this *very* dry discussion" before playfully appending his signature to the whole thing, a wink at his audience which proves his point.[4] This gesture is often used to explicate deconstruction in ways that seek to recoup play into something that is thematic, ponderous and not much fun.[5] But Derrida was a teller of jokes—he told the one about the panda that "eats shoots and leaves" at a dinner one time, and his jokey signature at the end of his critique of Austin points out the silliness of Austin's own exclusion of jokes from his explication of the performative.[6] "Whatevs," you can almost hear Derrida thinking, as he signs his own essay with a flourish after telling everyone how meaningless the signature is. The signature *is* method. Derrida eats, shoots, and leaves with it.

Beth Driscoll and Claire Squires are doing something similar with Beatrice Deft in *The Frankfurt Kabuff*, which I have called "the MOST serious, scholarly and thorough methodological experiment at SHARP, hands-down."[7] I stand by that tweet. As they have written about elsewhere, the adventures of Beatrice at the Frankfurt Book Fair represent a way to do research in publishing studies differently, because the emphasis on big data collection in publishing studies cannot impart what the experience of being at a book festival is actually like.[8] And having fun, including making fun of other people, is an important part of what happens in the book business, especially at Frankfurt, the centre of international rights sales and the location of book launches, prize ceremonies, no doubt a lot of posturing, and, of course, the presence of amazing canapés and accompanying drinks. Although phenomenological and autoethnographic methods can help to track what the "individual and interior" experience of book festivals feel like,[9] the Frankfurt Book Fair is a *book business event* marked by competitiveness between publishers, confidential book deals, gossip, the circulation of ephemeral forms of cultural capital, and the economic basis for the fair itself. Driscoll and Squires had tried different forms of research intervention in book festivals, including the use of the Sleaze-O-Meter to track sexism at events and the invention of the Author Yurt account on Twitter to lampoon the pretentiousness of the Edinburgh International Book Festival's take on the green room,[10] but the study of a book business event where business is done requires different kinds of interventions. As the Frankfurt Book Fair says of itself, "after all, in-person encounters are what generate unexpected business opportunities, surprising moments and innovative ideas."[11] If that is the case, how can researchers interested in the largest book trade fair in the world study the unexpected and the clandestine? Methods must also reflect research ethics concerns "as book cultures researchers actively drift between work and leisure settings,"[12] particularly when they involve alcohol or socialising that could compromise the integrity of researchers and their subjects. How to do research within publishing studies that breathes life into the work, without compromise?

It is hard enough in publishing studies to find out whether bestseller lists are a marketing fiction or actual evidence of sales,[13] or whether publishers are telling the truth about their work[14] without having to take into account the complexities of contemporary publishing and marketing processes themselves. Somewhere along the way, two things can be lost: the need to critique methods that pile up data without telling us anything new[15] and the importance of research as a "minor gesture" that incorporates creative methods as a critique of mainstream methodologies and their accompanying policing in the academy.[16] Driscoll and Squires call this the "off-to-the-sideness" of studying book cultures, and observe that this "is what enables book culture studies to be playful and even satirical, to be a space where life can be breathed into academia and society."[17]

Through this study of minor forms Driscoll and Squires can advocate for research methods which move beyond the description of literary capitalism in order to become activist and interventionist in their aims and refuse academic capitalist systems that validate the creation of big data and downplay the analysis of experience and affect.[18] *The Frankfurt Kabuff* is an innovative way to track the complicated journey of a book from a self-publishing platform to its readership, to critique the androcentric nature of much publishing in its creation of a feminist detective heroine who is a researcher in her own right, and to describe and satirise the preoccupations of book fair business in its creation of "a pacy, pocket-sized political thriller," as its 2019 book announcement promises. But (and this is important) Ullapoolism as research is also about having a lot of fun along the way, without ethical compromise. Therefore Beatrice can have cocktails, engage in lighthearted intimate encounters, and investigate suspected neo-Nazis when it would not be ethical or perhaps even that much fun for real-life publishing scholars embedded in a research site to do any of those things.

And so, Beatrice's fondness for Negronis in excellent hotel bars constitute that "minor gesture" Erin Manning talks about as so necessary for good research. It is a detail that signifies who Beatrice is, whose interests she serves and which methods she uses to ferret out the truth, which include collaboration, interviewing, deductive reasoning, participant observation, and action research—especially when neo-Nazis need to be stopped. The Negroni is perfect for Beatrice's purposes because, like Beatrice herself in freshly applied lipstick, it's eye-catching and is anything but frivolous. Toby Cecchini, who modernised the Cosmopolitan and is the author of an excellent memoir of the same name that Beatrice and Caspian would probably want to read, calls the Negroni "one of the most perfect drinks in existence" because of its balance between spicy, sweet and sour, and because it "catches the light like a polished ruby" in a way that makes everyone want to order it.[19] The Negroni is a classic cocktail with legions of dedicated devotees. Unlike other cocktails invented in the United States such as the Martini, the Moscow Mule, or the Sidecar,[20] the Negroni is a European drink. It was invented in Italy as a collaboration between thirsty expatriate Americans and European royalty or pseudo-royalty, depending on who tells the story.[21] It is a challenging cocktail for some because of the bitterness of Campari, but that is also the source of its cult status.[22] The politics and style of the Negroni are Beatrice's, too. The Negroni is democratic because it only has three ingredients and anyone can make it, yet it imparts sophistication in its looks and flavours which bely its simplicity. It is classic, it is contemporary, and it has none of the self-conscious pretentiousness of red wine, the drink of the academic intelligentsia. Not coincidentally, red wine is Beatrice's ex-partner Callum's drink of choice as he sells poetry chapbooks and makes dubious business deals.[23] It is no wonder that Beatrice prefers the Negroni, and that Kurt Weidenfeld, the left-wing publisher of philosophy Beatrice vows to protect, has a Campari and soda himself during their first meeting.[24]

And so, there is method in Beatrice Deft's cocktail choices, and in Blaire Squiscoll's use of them too. But there are signs that during the pandemic, Beatrice has had to improvise: after the London Book Fair is cancelled due to COVID-19, in *The Corona Kabuff* she has a round of Bellinis with Caspian in Venice. Forced into lockdown with her favourite police officer, Beatrice exchanges books for "black market beers" to sustain them both.[25] But I anticipate that, before long, as the borders loosen and book fairs forego the pleasures of Zoom to offer canapés and sparkling wine once again, Beatrice will be back in action fighting for freedom of expression and an end to patriarchy in the world of books and hopefully everywhere else. To that end, I consulted with a friend of Blaire Squiscoll's, the mixologist and cultural theorist Janielle Frak, to see what in the world Beatrice might be drinking next. After some consultation with their local book and canoe club, they came up with the two cocktail recipes found below, one with alcohol and one without, both as delicious and as much fun to drink as *The Frankfurt Kabuff* is to read. I hope to see Beatrice enjoying these in Paris, Helsinki, and perhaps Ullapool, floating lemon twists like signifiers and leaving a trail of well-developed admirers behind her.

THE SUMMER COLOPHON
Shake over ice equal measures of dry gin, Lillet, sweet vermouth, and St. Germain with a dash of orange bitters.[26] *Serve with a lemon twist.*

THE BITCH GODDESS
Stir together 2 parts cranberry juice and 1 part ginger beer with a dash of Angostura Bitters. Pour into a glass with ice and garnish with a slice of orange.

Notes

1 Beth Driscoll and Claire Squires, "The Epistemology of Ullapoolism: Making Mischief from within Contemporary Book Cultures," *Angelaki* 25, no. 5 (September 2020): 137-55, https://doi.org/10.1080/0969725X.2020.1807147, 137

2 Page 28. All references to the text of *The Frankfurt Kabuff* are from this edition.

3 Page 89.

4 Jacques Derrida, "Signature, Event, Context," trans. Alan Bass, in *Margins of Philosophy* (Chicago: University of Chicago Press, 1982), 20.

5 Nicole Anderson, "Free-Play? Fair-Play! Defending Derrida," *Social Semiotics* 16, no. 3 (September 2006): 407–20, https://doi.org/10.1080/10350330600823989.; Jeffrey T. Nealon, "Jokes and the Performative in Austin and Derrida; or, The Truth Is a Joke?" *Cultural Critique* 95 (Winter 2017): 1–24, https://doi.org/10.5749/culturalcritique.95.2017.0001; Michaela Fišerová, "Pragmatical Paradox of Signature," *Signata. Annales Des Sémiotiques / Annals of Semiotics*, no. 9 (December 2018): 485–504, https://doi.org/10.4000/signata.1599.

6 Elizabeth Rottenberg, "The Laughter of Jacques Derrida," *Oxford Literary Review* 36, no. 2 (2014): 296–97, https://doi.org/10.3366/olr.2014.0137.

7 @rak_dr, "#sharp19 The Frankfurt Kabuff Is the MOST Serious, Scholarly and Thorough Methodological Experiment at SHARP. Hands-down.

@ClaireSquires @Beth_driscoll," *Twitter*, July 18, 2019, https://twitter.com/rak_dr/status/1151920518079098887.

8 Beth Driscoll and Claire Squires, "Serious Fun: Gaming the Book Festival," *Mémoires Du Livre / Studies in Book Culture* 9, no. 2 (May 2018): 1–37, https://doi.org/10.7202/1046988ar.

9 Beth Driscoll and Claire Squires, "Experiments with Book Festival People (Real and Imaginary)," *Mémoires Du Livre / Studies in Book Culture* 11, no. 2 (June 2020): 1–40, https://doi.org/10.7202/1070271ar.

10 Claire Squires and Beth Driscoll, "The Sleaze-O-Meter: Sexual Harassment in the Publishing Industry," *Interscript*, March 8, 2018, https://www.interscriptjournal.com/online-magazine/sleaze-o-meter; Driscoll and Squires, "Experiments with Book Festival People."

11 "Frankfurter Buchmesse," accessed August 8, 2021, https://www.buchmesse.de/en.

12 Driscoll and Squires, "The Epistemology of Ullapoolism."

13 Laura J. Miller, "The Best-Seller List as Marketing Tool and Historical Fiction," *Book History* 3 (2000): 286–304, https://doi.org/10.1353/bh.2000.0012.

14 Janice Radway, *A Feeling for Books: The Book-of-the-Month Club, Literary Taste, and Middle-Class Desire*, Revised edition (Chapel Hill, NC: University of North Carolina Press, 1999).

15 Paul Feyerabend, *Against Method*, 4th edition (London: Verso, 2010).; Beth Driscoll and Claire Squires, "Book Commerce Book Carnival: An Introduction to the Special Issue," *Mémoires Du Livre / Studies in Book Culture* 11, no. 2 (June 2020): 1–17, https://doi.org/10.7202/1070262ar.

16 Erin Manning, "Against Method," in *The Minor Gesture* (Durham: Duke University Press, 2016), 26–45.

17 Driscoll and Squires, "The Epistemology of Ullapoolism."

18 Driscoll and Squires, "The Epistemology of Ullapoolism."

19 Toby Cecchini, *Cosmopolitan: A Bartender's Life*, Reprint (New York: Crown, 2004), 232.

20 William Grimes, *Straight up or on the Rocks: The Story of the American Cocktail* (New York: North Point Press, 2001).

21 Gary Regan, *The Negroni: Drinking to La Dolce Vita, with Recipes & Lore*, Illustrated edition (Berkeley: Ten Speed Press, 2015); Matt Hranek, *The Negroni: A Love Affair with a Classic Cocktail* (New York: Artisan, 2021).

22 Bill Rowland, "The Negroni: Sophistication in a Glass," *The Cocktail Novice* (blog), July 17, 2014, https://thecocktailnovice.com/negroni-sophistication-in-a-glass/; Mark Ellwood, "How The Negroni Became Today's It Cocktail," Condé Nast Traveler, August 24, 2015, https://www.cntraveler.com/stories/2015-08-24/how-the-negroni-became-todays-it-cocktail.

23 Page 58.

24 Page 36.

25 Blaire Squiscoll, *The Corona Kabuff: A Beatrice Deft Short*, 2021, https://www.wattpad.com/story/216487145-the-corona-kabuff-a-beatrice-deft-short; also included in assemblages section of this edition, on page 231.

26 Thanks to Claire Squires for suggesting the addition of orange bitters. Janielle Frak approves this change.

The Frankfurt Kabuff and the Historical Sociology of the Detective Genre

BRIDGET FOWLER

> "Years ago you [R.W.] remarked to me that it would be perfectly possible to take a popular format like a thriller and put it to good use."
>
> —Raymond Williams, quoting his publisher, *Politics and Letters*[1]

The Frankfurt Kabuff: *Fissures and Contradictions*

BLAIRE SQUISCOLL'S *THE FRANKFURT KABUFF* IS A SCINtillating example of the detective novel genre. As tautly fast-moving and urbane as a Dashiell Hammett novel and as innovatively realist as a China Miéville or Christopher Brookmyre, it plays havoc with certain classical features of the genre. Not least, it subverts the standard opposition between the professional masculine hero and the bureaucratic police. Squiscoll's heroine freely enters into an erotic adventure with a decidedly nonbureaucratic police inspector, signalling, in turn, a rupture with the hegemonic masculinity of the professional detective and the compliant femininity of the Amateur.[2] For it is to the fearless and decisive Beatrice Deft in *Kabuff* that the targeted male victim turns. Threatened as he is by a lethal neo-Nazi faction, she is assisted in her mission to foil the conspirators by a sensitive, well-read police officer, Caspian Schorle, and by a group of literary women whose knitting needles serve—somewhat comically—as unanticipated weapons. In brief, the novella offers the excitement of acting on humanist values together with the sublimated erotic pleasures of the detective form or the romance.

Yet *Kabuff* invokes further problematic issues that belie its surface simplicity and lightness, not least, the predicament of Europe's refugees. In this context, I am thinking, particularly, of the conversation in Melbourne where Beatrice talks to her Australian partner, Callum, citing Robert Darnton's "communication circuit." More than an engaging intertextual allusion, this is surely an indicator of the author's own reflexivity about the hurdles to be surmounted in transgressing the conventions governing popular fiction in the publishing world.[3]

Darnton's vivid study of eighteenth-century popular books and pamphlets culminates with one of the best models yet devised of the literary artworld: that is to say, writers, readers, and those whom Becker calls "support-personnel": publishers, printers, and booksellers.[4] This communication circuit was originally conceptualised to display the interrelations of readers and subversive bestsellers like Mercier's utopian *L'An 2440* (1771), which served a vital role in *delegitimising* the monarchy of Louis XVI.[5] Pierre Bourdieu later paid tribute to Darnton: indeed this particular communication circuit model is an important predecessor to Bourdieu's conceptual models. But Bourdieu's own research has focused on the later, more fragmented or "chiasmatic" French literary field, after Louis-Napoleon III's authoritarian rule helped to establish the new era of capitalist industrialization.[6]

The contemporary German social order depicted in Squiscoll's novella appears at first sight to be functioning effectively. Yet, as in all memorable detective novels, fissures or cracks appear in the structures governing everyday life, emblematic of wider contradictions.[7] In this particular case, what is at stake is the Frankfurt Book Fair's ceremonial symbolic recognition of Kurt Weidenfeld, a Jew, for his lifelong commitment to the publication of radical philosophy. White Storm, a neo-Nazi organisation, aims to massively disrupt this consummate expression of the fair's liberal autonomy, provoking memories of the "men in dark times" of 1930s and '40s Germany.[8]

This particular threat to the Frankfurt Book Fair has further connotations. It recalls earlier troubled periods in the long history of the fair, which was already operating in 1478, soon after the Gutenberg printing press and "the coming of the book."[9] In the late feudal and early modern period, the Frankfurt and other book fairs represented what might be labelled an ascendant progressive bourgeoisie, circulating books in Latin across European borders in alliance with artisanal workers.[10] As Febvre and Martin's illuminating history reveals: "until 1625 this town remained the headquarters of the European book-trade."[11] Indeed: "Frankfurt was the 'new Athens' where you could see celebrated scholars talking and debating amongst themselves in Latin before an astonished public."[12] In turn, such fairs—which were initially organised around gift exchanges in kind as well as money—facilitated book production.[13]

Yet, around 1630, the annual book fairs had to contend with the growing fragmentation of the European linguistic market resulting from the rise of literature in the vernacular: the consequence of Benedict Anderson's national "imaginary communities."[14] Later, in the sixteenth and seventeenth centuries, merchants and printers at the Frankfurt Book Fair met with even graver vicissitudes as France and other Counter-Reformation countries introduced the death penalty for publishing the Bible or the Reformers' texts in the vernacular. The ensuing Wars of Religion put an end to the Frankfurt Book Fair's cosmopolitan, cross-border progressive mission for many years;[15] indeed, it was only after the Second World War, in 1949, that the fair was fully reinstated.

Thus, beneath the narrative pleasures of the *Kabuff* text, the novella possesses further hermeneutic depth as the bearer of collective memory. For the White Storm conspiracy of *Kabuff* kindles an awareness of deeper threats to "free exchange" of books, a trade historically more fragile than might at first sight appear. The neo-Nazis distribute a new edition of Hitler's *My Struggle*: not Knausgaard's recent "amoral" memoirs of the same title, as Beatrice had hoped.[16] They plan to abort the bestowal of official recognition on the publisher, Weidenfeld. Give or take a twist of given names, this protagonist is based on a world-historical figure, the ennobled British publisher George Weidenfeld (1919–2016), himself no stranger to antisemitic persecution.[17] The allusion is surely no accident, despite the author's claim to be fictional. It jolts us into reflecting on the antisemitism sweeping over contemporary Europe, or what the lawyer Philippe Sands has called the return of these "poisonous wells" of nationalism.[18]

In a different key, the novel alerts us to other fissures in the smooth structures of publishing and book-retailing, notably the alienating effects of the long-term subordination of women staff. In this context, the novella's utopian ending not only foils the conspirators and further legitimates Weidenfeld's consecration. It also figures the long-overdue promotion of such minor characters to influential positions within the publishing world.

Other contradictions hinted at in the novella relate not just to the Frankfurt Book Fair and the globalised publishing world, but to the deficits in the cultural recognition of authors within the broader literary field. In part, the motivating device for Beatrice's departure from Melbourne for Frankfurt is her ambivalence about her former partner, Callum. Callum, a small-press poetry publisher, is said to be starved of any "symbolic capital."[19] His depression registers the harsh reality of contemporary disregard for the poet: "[that] belated small-scale producer of private mythologies [who makes it] easier to cut through dead metaphors and go straight to the principle of mythopoeic practices."[20] Indeed, we could extrapolate from the middle-aged publisher's distress a wider uncertainty in modernity as to the author's social worth, familiar to cultural producers such as Kafka, who were only posthumously legitimated. In Bourdieu's simple but poignant phrase, they spend their lives agonised by whether they really *are* a writer.[21]

Theorising the Detective Genre: Bourdieu and the Literary Field

How can we theorise the very diverse sources of unease depicted in this novel? We should certainly turn to Bourdieu as one of the foremost sociologists of culture, especially for his illumination of the different literary fields. In particular, his empirical studies of cultural production and reception re-established the well-known bifurcation between fast-selling profitable books (from which flowed the fame of Chandler, Fleming, Forsyth, and other thriller writers) and the slow-selling, more experimental literary fiction (of Kafka, Beckett, Saramago, etc).[22] When gradually consecrated via the curriculum, once formally challenging works offer secure back-list sales profits. Thus, for commercial reasons as well as for publishers' literary self-image, such books remain in print. But, as I shall show, Bourdieu came to see that such literary publishing of *new* or insufficiently recognised writers face fresh threats.[23]

Bourdieu's brilliant socioanalysis of cultivated and popular tastes in *Distinction* is fed by theoretical reflections relating as much to Voloshinov/Bakhtin's work on the carnivalesque and their depiction of popular culture's celebration of bodily excesses as to Kant's legitimate aesthetic judgement.[24] Yet the sociologist has relatively little to say about what he calls "popiliterature": the field of popular literature. When interrogated about the literary consecration of popular texts, Bourdieu invariably responded that this was exceptional.[25]

This rarity derives in practice from the demanding intellectual and material preconditions for producing those few distinguished literary works that are subsequently consecrated. Amongst these, not least telling are the long years of experimentation necessarily spent in the metropolis. Such a formation is open to very few writers from the subordinate classes, especially those from the provinces or producers in "small languages."[26] While Bourdieu is right about such practical barriers, French sociologists, such as Bernard Lahire,[27] as well as American and Australian cultural theorists, such as Beth Driscoll,[28] have challenged this theoretical approach, viewing it as out of touch with writers' support from "day jobs" as well as potential literary legitimation from less academic judges of literary texts, such as the Oprah Book Club or the Man Booker Prize.[29]

In particular, it is striking that otherwise appreciative readers of Bourdieu, such as Jacques Dubois and Joseph Jurt, have challenged Bourdieu's blanket pessimism in this respect. They have noted in particular that popular texts inspired by nationalist or other popular movements can later undergo forms of canonisation.[30] More sociological work needs to be done here, especially showing the vital role of those relatively rare literary critics who have themselves experienced unorthodox, minority trajectories. It is mainly this group who have pioneered the literary consecration of certain popular writers after the mid-nineteenth-century split between "serious literature" and mere genre works.[31] But it is also true that, since the 1970s, the fierce struggle in the field of power between the two *fractions* of the dominant class—the dominant fraction (financial and entrepreneurial elites, generals, right-wing politicians) and the dominated fraction (academics, artists, professionals)—has led to the much-increased prominence of the former with its wider range of tastes and suspicion of "intellectuals'" cultural capital.[32]

The Historical Sociology of the Thriller

Beyond these Bourdieusian parameters, the historical sociology of popular cultural genres *has* flourished, from as early as the 1920s onwards. Thus, ironically, to understand *The Frankfurt Kabuff* we need to return to the Frankfurt School itself on the genesis and modalities of the detective novel, notably to the interwar theories of that "eccentric Marxist," the Frankfurt-based Siegfried Kracauer. Indeed, the form of this novella complies broadly with the general portrait of the detective novel (dating from the 1850s) given by Kracauer:

> The detective novel [...] has gradually been promoted to a position, the status and significance of which can surely not be denied. [...] In its exemplary creations it has long since ceased to be an impure mixture [...] but rather constitutes a particular stylistic genre which decisively presents a complete world with its own aesthetic means.[33]

The world of this stylistic genre can be sketched out in broad brushstrokes. First, the narrative is organised around the existence of a secret. As Simmel showed, secrecy—especially secret societies or conspiracies—produces a type of social interaction hinged on concealment and ignorance. Such secrecy is more easily maintained in the opaque and complex division of labour of capitalist modernity.[34]

Secondly, the detective novel genre can only be conceived in the multiple realities or compartmentalised fields of modern societies. It takes for granted their multiple perspectives.[35] Thirdly, the detective operates in a world lacking the *gemeinschaft* (community) of tradition, stripped of the meanings once endowed by religion. As Kracauer emphasised, the detective novel is dominated by a social order of fragmented relationships, linked together only by a God-like detective. The detective succeeds by uncovering a purely formal reason ("ratio") operating within social action. Ultimately, as Frisby emphasises, for Kracauer, narrative closure is achieved only by revealing coincidences at play: their sublimated form refracts the fortuitous combinations of those separate, disparate ends underlying urban capitalism.[36]

Kracauer's study of detective novels was based on Holmes, Gaboriau, and Leblanc.[37] He does not address the "hardboiled detective form" published a few years later in the interwar period, most notably by Chandler and Hammett. These famously, in Chandler's terms, "gave murder back to the kind of people that commit it for reasons, not just to provide a corpse." Frisby's writings examine the contemporary coexistence of the two genres of the detective novel—the ratiocination type, or, in Frisby's phrase, the "Golden Age of the puzzle type," and the hardboiled form, where the locus of the detective's work is famously Chandler's "mean streets."[38] Like Kracauer, Frisby focuses on the genesis of the detective novel: for him, it is the refracted literary form of the *transformations* of the metropolis in modernity. He pinpoints particularly the emergence of segregated areas of urban deprivation characterised by labyrinthine networks of sunless streets; the growth of a money economy, where the mere passing of a cheque can render a person rich;[39] and the appearance of the flâneur, even in the unhygienic metropolitan "abyss." Indeed, the flâneur, first described by Benjamin, is the precursor of the urban detective, not to speak of the sociologist.[40]

It is well known that Dashiell Hammett himself once worked in Pinkerton's, the leading American detective agency. Yet, as Frisby shows in his meticulous study of the Pinkerton archives, a striking disparity exists between the mundane world of the detectives' reports collected together in the files, and fictional portrayal of such agencies in the hard-boiled genre. The novelists' conventions of romanticism veil the surveillance and strict regulation which all such detectives historically had to endure. Thus, Pinkerton's *General Principles* and *Rules* (dated 1873, 1878, and 1916) ensured that the operatives were in fact controlled by rigorous rational–legal bureaucratic rules, whether they were "shadows," following the "Yeggmen," or "ropers," agents who discovered secrets by strategic conversation. The Pinkerton Rules ensured that the detective's financial interests were restricted entirely to their salary, forbidding any private payments, specified a precise and hierarchical division of labour, and enforced a demanding work ethic.[41]

Even more telling, the actual reality of detection at Pinkerton's reveals a clear link with those aspects of production relations usually omitted from the Chandler and Hammett novels, notably, the anti-union activities of detective agents, who were forcibly drafted in to discover the names of labour organisers and to break strikes.[42] Conversely, in the novels—even the hard-boiled genre—the detective is portrayed as a highly-autonomous figure with the capacity for discretion and individual judgement.

A further fertile development within the historical sociology of the thriller is Palmer's influential analysis.[43] Like Kracauer and Frisby, Palmer goes beyond conventional "internalist" analyses that situate the thriller's history in terms solely of its literary provenance. First, the structuralist dimension of his analysis uncovers the two essential features of the detective/thriller genre—the conspiracy, which threatens societal disintegration, and the charismatic detective hero who acts as an insider-outsider to re-found the State.

Secondly, Palmer is at his most telling in elucidating the economic and legal preconditions for the thriller form. He argues persuasively that the isolated detective hero emerges in the Hobbesian world of a competitive "possessive individualism" underlying the emergence of rational bourgeois capitalism. Further, he links the perpetual fear of conspiracy which the hero must quell to the crucial change in the legal constructions accompanying capitalism. In particular, he examines traditional jurisprudence which had operated with a clear distinction denoting *mala in se* (e.g., murder) as heinous, and *mala prohibita* (other prohibited acts, such as wilful destruction of the lord's property, theft) as less significant. In the new nineteenth-century "reformed" philosophy of punishment, property crimes acquired the same severity as murder. The thriller's conspiracy has its origin in this undifferentiated abhorrence of crime and the moral panic about the "dangerous classes" who perpetrated it:

> Since the thriller was born at this time [mid nineteenth century] it is plausible that it was, in some sense, "caused" by the shift in public attitudes towards economic crime, specifically by the conflation of all offences under the new general category of offences against the social/natural order. By concentrating on crimes that everyone agreed were "offences against nature" criminality and policing could be presented, as it were, by sleight of hand, as a unitary and immensely threatening phenomenon. [...] The thriller conspiracy is a pathological irruption into an otherwise ordered world [...] because it is a breach of the natural order, and any breach of the natural order is by definition without reason, i.e. incomprehensible.[44]

Recently, the French sociologist Luc Boltanski has made a memorable intervention within this sociological field.[45] He elaborates further on significant determinants of both the detective and spy novel forms, distinguishing the imperialist/right-wing espionage genre (epitomised in John Buchan) from that of the political left (Eric Ambler, Orwell, and others).[46]

Perhaps his most fruitful analytical achievement is to connect the flourishing detective and spy genres from the end of the nineteenth century and early twentieth century, in France and Britain, to the political and scientific consciousness of this period. More specifically, he links both these genres to the cultivation of biopower and nationalism as part of each imperial country's hegemonic project, which in turn fostered a subversive *populist* nationalism. Whilst the nation-state became increasingly credited with monopolising the only legitimate perspective on social reality, in these fictions the gap between the official rhetoric and social reality is laid bare—hence, the figure of the traitor, mole, and hostile spy.

The threats at the heart of the detective or spy novel also stem from the new field of psychiatry in the late nineteenth century, particularly, the influential diagnoses of paranoia and schizophrenia. More broadly, the rise of social science, especially in works such as Durkheim's *Suicide*, had illuminated the underlying social determinants motivating individual and collective action. These disciplines provoked awareness in the general public of a more complex model of multiple social realities—an everyday "reality" of appearances concealing a deeper "*REALITY*" [*sic*].[47] Hence, in contrast with the picaresque novel, the detective in the new genre operates in a perspectivist and disenchanted world, free of miracles, and must comply with the logic of science.[48] The ordered social world thus appears more fragile, hiding another reality, more real:

> It [the idea of objective description, governed by laws] accompanied the development of statistics, political economics and then—shortly before the appearance of the detective story—sociology. It was also in this intellectual context and by relying on these new ways of envisaging the human environment, that the social novel [naturalism], took shape, a genre that flourished to an extraordinary degree in the nineteenth century, and of which the detective story is, in part, a belated transformation.[49]

Boltanski is acutely aware of the tension in the late nineteenth century between the pervasive idea of the closed and ordered nation-state, and the "profoundly fluid," cosmopolitan, international character of finance and industrial capitalism,[50] figured simultaneously by the Jewish banker and the uprooted or stateless revolutionary.[51] Indeed, he regards the detective novel as also undertaking the exposure of contradictions to the maximum intensity—an attribute which Williams earlier had viewed as the concern of the mid-nineteenth-century "Question of England" novels.[52]

Within these novels, revolving generically around enigmas, conspiracies, and investigations, it is Kafka's *The Trial* that ultimately makes a major symbolic revolution. For this freshly unveils the disquieting nature of social reality which, in Chesterton, Christie, et al., is concealed by anodyne forms of a healthy social order recuperated.[53]

Most strikingly for Boltanski are national types of detective novel. Thus, Conan Doyle's Sherlock Holmes novels—with their split between the brilliant Holmes and the unimaginative Watson—are an ideal-typical exemplar of the British genre. Crucially, Boltanski links the Sherlock Holmes series to the precocious development of capitalism in Britain, notably, the acquisition of capitalist interests by the agrarian bourgeoisie (the former aristocratic class), the continued *political* importance of the nobility, and a highly developed distinction between private and public interests. Holmes's acute perceptions relate to the incipient breakdown of this order, thus producing enigmatic troubles which must be confronted: in other words, Holmes works on the contradictions typical of this form of social order.[54]

In contrast, Georges Simenon's Maigret is a policeman hero, the representative of the State who stands above all competing corporate interests. Unlike the patrician Holmes, Maigret embodies the meritocratic ideals of the French Republic, the hidden object underneath the web of the intrigue.[55] Faced with erupting social pathologies, as Boltanski comments, he bravely eradicates them, much like a Weberian bureaucratic functionary, without ire or passion. But although thus disciplined as a bureaucratic official, in his private life Maigret is a humanist. Indeed, Boltanski credits Simenon's hero with healing the splits between the republican democratic left and the monarchist/imperialist right, more vulnerable to disintegration in France than in the British longer-lasting historical coalition of nobility and bourgeoisie.[56]

Thus, in a telling departure from Bourdieu, Boltanski argues that "the detective gradually came to constitute a specific literary genre, with its own agencies of consecration: that is, as it became a *field*."[57] In these terms, Sherlock Holmes has an "art for art's sake"[58] of detection yet this is anchored in the "moral sense" of "common sense."[59] Unlike Maigret, he is "the detective of the great" but he always champions "morally superior goals."[60]

Gilloch has rightly complimented Boltanski for his revelation of the nature of abstract reason in the detective novel—"the central conception of the Ratio" and for his perceptive yoking of this genre to the general condition of modernity.[61] But I would suggest that Gilloch has underplayed the latter's rigorous sensitivity to different *national* histories in his sociology of the detective form, as briefly sketched above. Boltanski is particularly demystifying in discussing the British right-wing spy story, revealing, for example, the rabid antisemitism on which the celebrated Buchan novels are hinged.

Recent Transformations and Literary Struggles

We might make one criticism of Boltanski. For despite Boltanski's earlier wide-ranging research on abortion,[62] he fails to confront the extraordinary continuity of *patriarchal* representations in the detective novel, within both classical "Golden Age" and hardboiled forms. Yet in the novels of late capitalist modernity the female detective hero—following Christie's Miss Marple—has now indisputably come to the fore, either acting alone or within the police. Indeed, she is emblematic of the new entry of women into the ranks of waged labour, freed from private patriarchy, able to roam the world and thus liberated to be exploited everywhere.[63] In this respect, Gilloch is more telling in recognising the distinctiveness of the "Scandi-noir" (the disenchanted Scandinavian genre) of the last few years, noting the transformations in the genre contingent on the rise of the female detective.[64]

In fact, this phenomenon is not unique to Scandi-noir—it has been a prominent element of Scottish so-called "tartan-noir," the French TV series *Engrenages* (*Spiral*), and well beyond. In this new subgenre, women are elevated as central protagonists in the quest for a just order. In the distinctive case of *Kabuff*, the narrative also breaks decisively with the traditional romantic resolution. The heroine collaborates autonomously with Caspian, a police officer, to foil the ultra-right plot, and also initiates an erotic relationship with him, not unlike Kollontai's ideal of free love.[65] Following the elimination of the neo-Nazi conspiracy, the novella magically resolves other contradictions too: the status of women is re-examined, for example, allowing them to rise to unusual occupational heights, both within the administration of the Frankfurt Book Fair and more widely within the bookselling industry. This narrative imaginary thus represents a new kind of utopian function in literature.[66]

Writing this in the wake of the Afghan tragedy of 2021, not least the downfall of Afghan women's hopes for equal participation in the economy, this utopian function attains a fresh urgency. Yet… the novella also reminds me of Fraser's perceptive critique of contemporary *uses* of feminism within neoliberal hegemonic projects, where it is in danger of provoking ideological elements in the "new spirit of capitalism" mentioned already:

> Disturbing as it may sound, I am suggesting that second-wave feminism has unwittingly provided a key ingredient

> of the new spirit of neoliberalism. Our critique of the family wage now supplies a good part of the romance that invests flexible capitalism with a higher meaning and moral point. Endowing their daily struggles with an ethical meaning, the feminist romance attracts women at both ends of the social spectrum [...] At both ends, the dream of women's emancipation is harnessed to the engine of capitalist accumulation.[67]

Perhaps we should extend Fraser's malaise even further, to the organisation of the publishing world itself? Despite savouring the tranquil resolution of *Kabuff*, we could point to further hidden structural conflicts which the novella cannot resolve, linked to Callum's longing for symbolic recognition mentioned above. These relate to the nature of the contemporary book market and the structural hurdles recently set up that limit writers' opportunities, especially those writers operating in the restricted literary field.[68]

In one of his last works, Bourdieu notes the qualitative changes possessing all the "scale" and "brutality of structural disruptions brought about over the last twenty years by the irruption of an uncompromising financial logic into the relatively protected [...] world of French publishing."[69] Due, especially, to increased concentration of capital and the rationalizations resulting from control over such capital, this has led many companies to "abandon literary policies in favour of strictly commercial ones."[70] This logic applies even if subsidiary companies are afforded a nominal degree of literary independence. The most lucid of the authors thus rebuffed can see the game clearly for what it is. The ensuing appointments of corporate CEOs with no literary competence follow from this commercial logic. Eschewing the experimental methods that were the mark of Zola or Joyce, they impose a business plan drawn from the world of entertainment, especially the "American model."[71] Thus, for Bourdieu, the rare contemporary descendants of the nineteenth-century "heroic modernists"[72] are those small publishers who dispense with literary agents and read the manuscripts submitted by authors or translators themselves.[73]

Bourdieu has been far from alone in expressing disquiet about the globalised publishing industry. André Schiffrin, a Franco-American publisher of great distinction, has written a similarly damning portrayal of the enhanced concern for profitability in large-scale publishing. Unlike in earlier periods, he argues, this imperative of profit is now applied to every title.[74] A more nuanced but equally disturbing account is John Thompson's study based on interviews with publishers and literary agents.[75] Attacking contemporary "myths" concerning the transgression of all literary norms in the contemporary publishing "oligopoly," his research nevertheless makes starkly apparent the degree to which the humanist ethos once characterising the field has indeed succumbed to a new economic logic.[76]

Conclusion

Popular culture, from Dickens on, has not infrequently combined its authors' erudition and wide-ranging lived experience with fast-moving plots, engaging characters, and utopian endings, all of which *Kabuff* possesses. I have argued that *Kabuff* is part of a detective novel genre which emerged with nineteenth-century capitalist modernity. Indeed, the genre was only possible from this period, given the individualism and the legal changes in crime and punishment which were then instituted. The form has undergone various transformations, including—most recently—the imaginary of non-patriarchal gender relations. But I have also suggested that alongside the dangers represented with considerable plausibility by *Kabuff*'s antisemitic conspiracy, we might add another looming crisis in the literary world that is in danger of being neglected: not an illiberal and repressive conspiracy but an even harsher competition for material interests in a globalised world. This threatens to erode the continuation of a space for literary values, undermining what Bourdieu calls the "conquest," from the mid-nineteenth century, of the "restricted field" of artistic innovation.[77]

Notes

1 Raymond Williams, *Politics and Letters* (London: NLB, 1979), 297.

2 The figures of Detective and Amateur are elucidated in Jerry Palmer, *Thrillers: Genesis and Structure of a Popular Genre* (London: Edward Arnold, 1978).

3 Robert Darnton, *The Forbidden Best-Sellers of Pre-Revolutionary France* (London: HarperCollins, 1996), 183, see also 187.

4 Cf. Howard Becker, *Art Worlds* (Berkeley: University of California Press, 1982), 40–67.

5 Darnton, 231.

6 Pierre Bourdieu, *The Field of Cultural Production: Essays on Art and Literature*, trans. Richard Nice (Cambridge: Polity, 1993); Pierre Bourdieu, *The Rules of Art*, trans. Susan Emanuel (Cambridge: Polity, 1996).

7 John Holloway, *Crack Capitalism* (London: Pluto Press, 2010).

8 Hannah Arendt, *Men in Dark Times*, (London: Cape, 1970).

9 Lucien Febvre and Henri-Jean Martin, *The Coming of the Book: The Impact of Printing, 1450-1800*, trans. David Gerrard (London: NLB, 1976), 229.

10 Febvre and Martin, 139–40.

11 Febvre and Martin, 193.

12 Febvre and Martin, 230.

13 Febvre and Martin, 226. cf Pierre Bourdieu, *Anthropologie Économique* (Paris: Seuil, 2017), 45–46.

14 Febvre and Martin, *The Coming of the Book*, 330–32.

15 Febvre and Martin, 196.

16 Page 60. All references to the text of *The Frankfurt Kabuff* are to this edition.

17 Lord Weidenfeld was in fact the recipient of a Lifetime Achievement Award for International Publishing at the London Book Fair in 2007. (https://en.wikipedia.org/wiki/George_Weidenfeld,_Baron_Weidenfeld).

18 *2017 Holocaust Memorial Lecture with Professor Philippe Sands*, YouTube video (University of Glasgow, 2017), https://www.youtube.com/watch?v=I_f6Y31nDdM. Cf. also Robert Fine and Phillip Spencer, *Antisemitism and the Left* (Manchester: Manchester University Press, 2017).

19 Page 70.

20 Pierre Bourdieu, *The Logic of Practice*, trans. Richard Nice (Cambridge: Polity, 1990), 94.

21 Pierre Bourdieu, *Sociologie Générale, Vol 2* (Paris: Raisons d'Agir/Seuil, 2016), 181–96. Beatrice's books for her journey home combine authors from both the restricted and the expanded fields (see page 92), a cypher for the utopian desire to transcend this characteristic division of modernity.

22 Pierre Bourdieu, *Distinction*, trans. Richard Nice (London: RKP, 1984).

23 Pierre Bourdieu, "A Conservative Revolution in Publishing," trans. Jerôme Bourdieu, *Translation Studies* 1, no. 2 (May 2008): https://doi.org/10.1080/14781700802113465.

24 Jeremy Lane, "Sociology as Dialogics: Pierre Bourdieu, Mikhail Bakhtin and the Critique of Formalist Aesthetics," in *Face to Face: Bakhtin in Russia and the West*, eds. Carol Adlam, Rachel Falconer, Vitalii Makhlin, and Leslie Pinfield (Sheffield: Sheffield Academic Press, 1997).

25 Pierre Bourdieu, *Sociology in Question*, trans. Richard Nice (London: Sage, 1991).

26 Bourdieu, *The Rules of Art*. Cf. Pascale Casanova, *The World Republic of Letters*, trans. M.B. Debevoise (Cambridge, Mass: Harvard University Press, 2004).

27 Bernard Lahire, *La Condition Littéraire: La Double Vie Des Écrivains* (Paris: La Découverte, 2006), 41; 498–99.

28 Beth Driscoll, *The New Literary Middlebrow* (London: Palgrave Macmillan, 2014).

29 Driscoll, 15–16, 45–72.

30 Jacques Dubois, *L'Institution de la Littérature* (Brussels: Ferdinand Nathan, 1978); Joseph Jurt, "Le Champ Littéraire Entre Le National et Le Transnational," in *L'Espace Intellectuel En Europe*, ed. Gisèle Sapiro (Paris: La Découverte, 2009), 213–32.

31 See, for example, the case of Raymond Williams—himself from working-class origins—and especially his championing of Mrs. Gaskell and Thomas Hardy. Raymond Williams, *The English Novel from Dickens to Lawrence* (London: Chatto and Windus, 1971).

32 For this argument, see John Guillory, *Cultural Capital* (Chicago: University of Chicago Press, 1993), 45–46.

33 Siegfried Kracauer, 1971: 105, cited Graeme Gilloch, "'Hamlet Wird Detektiv': Reflections on Kracauer, Benjamin and (Neo-)Noir," in *The Detective of Modernity: Essays on the Work of David Frisby*, ed. Georgia Giannakopoulou and Graeme Gilloch (London: Routledge, 2021), 190.

34 Georg Simmel, *The Sociology of Georg Simmel*, ed. Kurt Wolff (New York: Free Press, 1955), 330–75.

35 Derek Robbins, *The Bourdieusian Paradigm* (Manchester: Manchester University Press, 2020), 7; 20–37.

36 David Frisby, *Fragments of Modernity* (Cambridge: Polity, 1985), 132–33.

37 Frisby, 127.

38 Chandler famously wrote: "Down these mean streets a man must go who is not himself mean, who is neither tarnished nor afraid. The detective in this kind of story must be such a man." For this and the quotation in the body of the chapter, see David Frisby, *Cityscapes of Modernity: Critical Explorations* (Cambridge: Polity, 2001), 61, 92.

39 Georg Simmel, *The Philosophy of Money*, ed. David Frisby (London: Routledge, 1978).

40 Janet Wolff, "The Invisible Flâneuse. Women and the Literature of Modernity," *Theory, Culture & Society* 2, no. 3 (November 1985): 37–46, https://doi.org/10.1177/02632 76485002003005; Georgia Giannakopoulou, "Unmasking the Flâneur," in *The Detective of Modernity: Essays on the Work of David Frisby*, ed. Georgia Giannakopoulou and Graeme Gilloch (London: Routledge, 2021), 212–15.

41 Frisby, *Cityscapes of Modernity*, 64, 78, 81.

42 Michael Denning, *Mechanic Accents* (London: Verso, 1987); Frisby, *Cityscapes of Modernity*, 65.

43 Palmer, *Thrillers*.

44 Palmer, 201.

45 Luc Boltanski, *Mysteries and Conspiracies: Detective Stories, Spy Novels and the Making of Modern Societies* (Cambridge: Polity, 2014).

46 See Bridget Fowler, "Figures of Descent from Classical Sociological Theory: Luc Boltanski," in *The Spirit of Luc Boltanski: Essays on 'the Pragmatic Sociology of Critique,'* ed. Simon Susen and Bryan Turner (London: Anthem, 2013), 71–74; Gilloch, "'Hamlet Wird Detektiv,'" 187.

47 Boltanski, *Mysteries and Conspiracies*, 1–39, especially 21.

48 Boltanski, 5–7.

49 Boltanski, 22–23.

50 In this respect, it is no coincidence that Boltanski is the co-author (with Eve Chiapello) of *The New Spirit of Capitalism* which also draws on the contradictions between the fluid, cross-national travel of globalised capitalism for elites and the more restrained expectations of the domestic world for others.

51 Boltanski, *Mysteries and Conspiracies*, 129; 145–50.

52 Williams, *Politics and Letters*, 253–56; 267.

53 Boltanski, *Mysteries and Conspiracies*, 268–73.

54 Boltanski, 98–103.

55 Boltanski, 117–18.
56 Boltanski, 110; 116–18.
57 Boltanski, 36.
58 Boltanski, 51.
59 Boltanski, 49; 50.
60 Boltanski, 64.
61 Gilloch, "'Hamlet Wird Detektiv,'" 187.
62 Luc Boltanski, *La Condition Fœtale: Une Sociologie de l'engendrement et l'avortement* (Paris: Gallimard, 2004).
63 This sentence paraphrases Sylvia Walby's *Theorizing Patriarchy* (Oxford: Blackwell, 1990), 201.
64 Gilloch, 182.
65 Cf. Pierre Bourdieu, *Masculine Domination*, trans. Richard Nice (Cambridge: Polity, 2001), 110–12.
66 Cf. Ernst Bloch, *The Utopian Function of Art and Literature*, trans. Jack Zipes and Frank Mecklenberg (Cambridge, Mass: MIT Press, 1988).
67 Nancy Fraser, *The Fortunes of Feminism* (London: Verso, 2013), 220–21.
68 Bourdieu, *The Rules of Art*, 344–47.; Pierre Bourdieu, "A Conservative Revolution in Publishing," *Translation Studies* 1, no. 2 (May 2008): 123–53, https://doi.org/10.1080/14781700802113465.
69 Bourdieu, 145.
70 Bourdieu, 145.
71 Bourdieu, 146. Bourdieu sees these changes reflected in the way the Frankfurt Book Fair now structures advertising space to prioritize German and Anglophone literatures: "All other literatures, especially those of smaller countries, are relegated to the margins" (2008: 146 n46). The fair's mirroring of wider geopolitical and economic power within its own geographical structuring of central and peripheral halls is emphasized in Beth Driscoll and Claire Squires, *The Frankfurt Bookfair and Bestseller Business* (Cambridge: Cambridge University Press, 2020), 46; 65; 101.
72 Bourdieu, *The Rules of Art*, 47–112.
73 Bourdieu, "A Conservative Revolution," 148.
74 André Schiffrin, *The Business of Books* (London: Verso, 2000).
75 John Thompson, *Merchants of Culture* (Cambridge: Polity, 2010).
76 Thompson, 139–42.
77 Bourdieu, *The Rules of Art*.

Tinker, Tailor, Driscoll, Squires

Book Fairs and Liberal Bookism in The Russia House *and* The Frankfurt Kabuff

MARK BANKS

WHAT HAPPENS AT A BOOK FAIR? PROBABLY NOT MUCH, you'd be forgiven for thinking. Certainly, the idea of the book fair as providing the dramatic setting for a novel—and a *thriller* at that—might not seem so promising. Yet, in two remarkably similar (though, as we will see, also quite different) thrillers, John le Carré's 1989 *The Russia House*[1] (*TRH*) and Blaire Squiscoll's 2019 *The Frankfurt Kabuff* (*TFK*), the book fair provides the principal theatre for both tension and action. Indeed, the book fair is cast as its own vital and animating agent. By this, I mean that in both *TRH* and *TFK* the book fair *does things*. It pulls people together and shapes and contours their social and personal exchanges. It also creates unforeseen possibilities and foments different motives and desires. Things also happen at book fairs, more or less visibly, but rarely without import or consequence. In addition, we can say in both novels that the book fair is also imagined to possess a grander and more epochal agency, in that it provides a setting for both *diagnosing the present* and *predicting the future.*

In the following I will offer some general observations on the similarities and differences between *TRH* and *TFK*[2] with respect to their depiction and understanding of international book fairs. What such fairs are imagined to be for, and what they can usefully do in their particular and different settings, is the primary focus of discussion. I will also include some parallel observations on how *TRH* and *TFK* reflect differently on the nature of books themselves—as reliable or useful objects. I'll then consider how both the depiction of book fairs and books, and a wider sense of bookism,[3] might suggest how le Carré and Squiscoll are located somewhat differently, politically, with respect to book culture. Such differences might be said to mirror a transition that seems somewhat characteristic of the current period—crudely summarised as a shift from liberal trust in the civilising power of books, to a more ironic and qualified scepticism about the innate virtues of books and bookishness.

The Russia House, *or the Book Fair as Liberal Fantasy*

The Russia House is a spy thriller set in mid-1980s Moscow, amidst the waning years of communist rule. Our hero is an Englishman—a semi-derelict, middle-aged publisher named Bartholomew ("Barley") Scott Blair. Barley is the frontman for "Abercrombie & Blair," a small, genteel, and commercially struggling publishing house. He is a regular visitor to Russia where he tries to drum up trade and hangs out with the arts *nomenklatura*, while lamenting his broken love life, unfulfilled dreams, and the usual range of disappointments. He is a classic le Carré type—the jaded, compromised, and morally-ambiguous Company Man.

TRH opens at the British Council's "first ever" Moscow audiobook fair, taking place in the upper room of "an ornate and hideous" Stalin-era hotel.[4] The fair is meandering to its inauspicious end, with the prevailing mood more like "the last hours of sinking liner than launch of a great initiative."[5] The crowd is a mix of curious onlookers and people in the book trade. The Russians have come for the opportunity to meet available Westerners or merely for something to do. At the closing cocktail party, the Russians enjoy their rare chance to dress up, while the sombrely clad British maintain a "monotone of socialist austerity."[6] A senior British diplomat who is "not quite the Ambassador" has conscientiously "shook the better hands," and women in pinafores have assiduously dispensed the "curling salami sandwiches and warm white wine."[7] The visible guards look on, impassively. The invisible watchers are assumed. It's a glum prospect. Despite the novelty of the fair, this is an ossified scene: we are very much in a Cold War cultural exchange. Nothing untoward can happen here. Yet, we are on the cusp of something. This is the era of an emergent *glasnost* ("openness") and *perestroika* ("restructuring"), where the winds of change are blowing in, and the Soviet state is in peril—not least from itself.

A mysterious and beautiful woman enters the fair—Katya. Katya is nervous but also determined. She is looking for Barley in order to give him a package. Finding Barley absent, Katya entrusts the package to another bookseller, Niki Landau. In hushed tones, the impassioned Katya informs Landau the package contains a literary work of the utmost importance and significance. A "great novel,"[8] she claims, no less. The novel has a "message that is important for all mankind" but it "cannot yet be published in the Soviet Union" since it "demands action and rejects all cosmetic change."[9] Katya claims that Barley has promised to publish the novel, once it is conveyed to England. Landau—intrigued—agrees to take the package and hand it over to Barley in London. In entrusting Landau, Katya chooses her Mercury wisely. Landau is a natural romantic who cannot resist a desperate woman's plea. He's also a proud Pole with no love for Mother Russia. There is a deft exchange of packages between Landau and Katya. As we later discover, the palimpsest secrets of an Empire (theme: the necessary collapse of all prevailing ideas) have been swapped for *A Midsummer Night's Dream* (theme: the necessary difficulties of love).

Landau, arrived in London and unable to locate Barley, takes the package to the Foreign Office. The "novel," we now discover, is a set of scribbled notebooks that appear to contain some coded and highly sensitive Russian nuclear secrets. From here on, the decidedly non-genteel apparatus of the British and American security services kicks into gear. Barley, eventually found sunning himself in his Lisbon *pied-à-terre*, is hauled in to explain his connections. It's revealed that the author of the "novel" is a man known as "Goethe," a casual acquaintance Barley met on a previous visit to Russia. It transpires that the hapless Barley is not himself a spy but merely befriended one at a boozy party, impressing "Goethe" with his drunken loose talk about the implacable follies of the superpowers and the futility of the nuclear struggle.

"Goethe," it emerges, is actually one of Russia's top nuclear physicists, a man named Yakov. Yakov is determined to hand over his trade secrets to the opposition, entrusting that the shambling but dauntless Barley (identified by his Russian acquaintance as a "decent human being"[10]) will publish this illicit material, so helping precipitate the end of the Cold War, and, by dint, the collapse of the Soviet Union.

So what is the role of the book fair here? We might venture to say that the book fair is first serving as a threshold or inception point. Katya is a messenger from a future still in the making. Not only is the fair offering her a gateway to encounter the necessary other, but it also provides the conditions of liminality that both stimulates and facilitates her desired transgression. The book fair—ironically—provides the means to transmit the unsayable and the unpublishable, and the book itself (in this case an initially indecipherable bundle of notebooks) is the vehicle that conveys the possibilities of tomorrow. It is notable that Yakov's scientific secrets are hidden amongst an apparent chaos of jottings, slogans, aphorisms, and line drawings ("meaningless scribblings, done by a lunatic...at breakneck speed and furious angles"[11]). Katya tellingly describes Yakov as "more like an artist than a scientist,"[12] and his livid and declamatory prose, laid down in coarsely assembled notebooks, stinking and stained, resembles a kind of Walter Benjamin "dream diary" or story of a world *in potentia*.[13] Like Benjamin, Yakov is showing the future through allegory, allusion, and play, yet deep within lie dark secrets that must be teased out for progress to be made.

Le Carré is implying here that the literary (rather than the merely scientific) book—and spaces of literary exchange—provide the most effective means for both imagining and obtaining another kind of (better) world. Here, Katya, the emissary, is perfectly cast as an agent of change. It is her formal and proper exterior as an editor in a Soviet state publishing house that provides the alibi for her presence but also the cover that conceals what Landau identifies as the "conviction"[14] within. "I am a humanist,"[15] she later declares; we learn how she was radicalised at the age of 16 in the insurgent heat of 1968, where "she had read Erich Fromm and Ortega y Gasset and Kafka and seen *Dr Strangelove.*"[16] Katya lives in political hope. The "great gesture"[17] made by Yakov—the revelation of state nuclear secrets—is made in both his and Katya's impassioned belief in the necessity of peaceful disarmament, and in the potential of (an as yet unformed) universal democracy to rescue Russia—and America too—from tragic illusions. Le Carré is therefore telling us that the old order is disintegrating (as Yakov has it, "the Soviet knight is dying in his armour"[18]) and the transmission and exchange of forbidden literature is an effective way to accelerate its demise. The book fair, therefore, also serves as an interstice, or zone of transient passage; a place where the Rubicon might be crossed and a new world called into being—one both formed and inspired by books, aesthetic education, and literary exchange.

Later, Barley, the reluctant spy, is played back into Russia under the guise of a new Anglo-American publishing venture ("Potomac & Blair"). He contacts Yakov, through Katya, under orders from his British and American spymasters to establish Yakov's bona fides. Inevitably, Barley and

Katya fall in love, and when Yakov is taken and Katya detected by the KGB, Barley finds a way to play the Russian and American intelligence agencies against each other, making a bold and skilful trade that extracts him (and Katya) from both obligation and repercussion. *TRH* then concludes one year on, with Barley living free and settled in his Lisbon hideaway, waiting optimistically for a reunion with Katya, who—we are led to assume—is in transit. In essence, we can regard *TRH* as a darkly satirical critique of the immorality underpinning the military-industrial complex of the superpowers, and, more ostensibly, a somewhat telegraphed romance about the choices one might make between human beings and abstract ideas. Barley's refusal to see the necessity of taking sides in the "corrupt and anachronistic equation"[19] of the Cold War sees him trade secrets for love, or "real people in exchange for unreal arguments."[20] Systems and ideologies melt in the heat of a true heart's desire.

A further publishing party, this time at the prestigious Moscow Book Fair, provides the animating context for the novel's climax. We enter the festivities where the CIA shell that is "Potomac & Blair" is hosting a "great glasnost launch party"[21] to signal its arrival on the Russian literary scene. Staffed by intelligence agents, and marketing books that will never exist, Potomac & Blair is presented as a new entrepreneurial venture to cement East-West relations amidst the rapidly liberalising (and nascently capitalistic) new Russia. Here—unlike the audiobook fair—the atmosphere is vibrant and heady. Russians, Americans, and British are drinking together, making merry and eyeing future opportunities. The Russians swap jokes about the new *perestroika* and its putative freedoms, while le Carré injects some of his trademark cynicism about the motives of Americans:

> Henzinger [a CIA agent under cover] is making his speech. It is a masterpiece of unconscious hypocrisy [...] "Let's make each other rich!" he cries [...] "Let's make each other free! Let's trade together, and let's talk together and let's drink together, and let's make the world a better place. Ladies and Gentlemen—to you and to Potomac & Blair and to our mutual profit—and to the *perestroika*—good health! Amen!"[22]

Far from signalling the advent of a new and mutual peace, the emergent *perestroika* is viewed by the Americans as an opportunity to undermine the rival super-power while also opening up new opportunities for US capital interests. The *glasnost* book fair and the new publisher party are symbols of this duplicity, and so it is left to Barley and Katya to remind us of the high ideals that are supposed to underpin these kinds of cultural and literary exchanges:

> **BARLEY:** "We had this vision, all of us, for years, of great Russian artists waiting to be discovered [...] The secret continuation of the nineteenth century. 'And when the thaw comes, they'll all come out of the ice and dazzle us," we told each other. So, where the hell are they, all these geniuses? What if they froze to death in the ice? Maybe the repression worked. That's all I'm saying."
> **KATYA:** "The Russian talent exists and has always existed, Barley, even in the worst times. It cannot be destroyed [...] Perhaps it will first have to adjust itself to the new circumstances, but soon it will express itself brilliantly. I am sure that is what you wish to say."[23]

While the book fair and books—and the liberal exchanges they require and demand—are seen as susceptible to appropriation and corruption, le Carré wants us to hold faith in the essential goodness of books and the people who write (and appropriately sell) them. Not only have Katya and Barley helped Yakov advance the cause of a more liberal peace through transmission of the written word, the actions of those who use books and publishing to mask their own venal interests (governments, security services, and vulgar businessmen alike) is contrasted with the always higher aims of our more humane protagonists. Barley and Katya, through their (heavily stereotyped) combination of innate English "decency" and native Russian "conviction," have sought to uphold the liberal ideal that invests books and bookselling with autonomous grace. The thaw is coming, and in the "new circumstances" it is anticipated that Russian creativity, artistry, and democratic expression will once more flourish. Barley and Katya use the threshold setting of the *glasnost* party to not only air their liberal views, but as a catalyst to consummate their relationship, and plan their future escape. For le Carré, the book fair acts again as crossing-point and passage to a more pacific world of free intellectual exchange and mutual and borderless love.

It's worth noting that the innate good of books and bookishness is a familiar theme in le Carré's work. Yet it's also fair to say that books have sometimes been viewed less idealistically. In his first major success, *The Spy Who Came in From the Cold* (1961), we find Liz, the librarian girlfriend of Leamas, portrayed as a tragic naïf whose rose-tinted and book-learnt communist sympathies are ruthlessly exploited by the British secret service. Here, the enlightened and abstract ideal is shown to offer no protection against the cruelties of international *realpolitik*. Yet, for le Carré, books and bookism have more often featured as powerful symbols of liberal enlightenment. In his masterpiece, *Tinker, Tailor, Soldier, Spy* (1974), we once again find books doing good work. Firstly, the wannabe Russian defector, Irina, uses her secret diary to communicate both the existence of a "mole" at the heart of British intelligence, and her love for the English, especially her confidante, the "English gentleman"[24] and British agent Ricki Tarr, with whom she desires to live freely, beyond "fear" and "lies."[25] Secondly, rare books, German literary antiquities in particular, are the primary intellectual interest of le Carré's most famous creation, British agent George Smiley. Early in *Tinker, Tailor, Soldier, Spy*, we encounter a cash-strapped Smiley "wrapping up an early edition of Grimmelshausen" in order to sell at "Heywood's Hill bookshop in Curzon Street,"[26] before arriving home later in anticipation of a delivery of the latest edition of *Philology*, or *German Life and Letters*. Through reading and genteel book trading, Smiley fashions himself a reliable sanctuary from the compromising demands of his employers at the "Circus" and the troubling ambiguities of his intelligence work. Yet this literary inclination is also a symbol of Smiley's political faith. Smiley's enduring bookism has tended to serve as a recurrent signal of that which le Carré himself always held dear—strong faith in European liberal democracy and in the post-WWII project of cultural reparations, free expression, and mutual exchange. In *A Legacy of Spies* (2017), we find the now-ancient Smiley in his Freiburg hermitage immersed, as ever, in obscure German books, still hoping for some political *rapprochement* and peaceful adjustments to a more liberal enlightenment. Fully aware of the renascent energies of European right-populism (including Brexit), Smiley's final appearance provides le Carré the opportunity to have his best-loved character ventriloquise what we might now regard as the author's own political epitaph:

> I am European [...] If I had a mission—if I was ever aware of one beyond our business with the enemy, it was to Europe. If I was heartless, I was heartless for Europe. If I

> had an unattainable ideal, it was of leading Europe out of her darkness towards a new age of reason. I have it still.[27]

In le Carré's liberal cosmos, the book and bookism, while open to abuse, are to be trusted, and invested in, and the goods they convey regarded as intrinsic. In *TRH* as elsewhere in le Carré's work, books, bookishness, and bookism stand as reliable symbols of good faith, as well as of enlightenment and passage. The open society and free unfettered expression are self-evident goods worth striving for. Books and bookish exchange provide the light to lead us out of the darkness and away from the shadow of an intolerable unreason. This is a markedly European reason, much less an American one. It is staffed and administered with both "decency" and "conviction"—by Barleys, Katyas, Irinas, Smileys, and other "apostles of negation"[28] who have committed themselves to destroying illiberal views and the corruptions of warring nations. "I ask you to show this book to English people who think as we do,"[29] Barley is urged, and who the "we" might be is always heavily signalled within le Carré's oeuvre. Yet, today, the gradual evolution to a more liberal and enlightened Europe looks a somewhat less than secure proposition—and perhaps also a more controversial one than it might have seemed, say, in 1974 or 1989. A short reading of *The Frankfurt Kabuff* might help us to understand why this might be the case.

The Frankfurt Kabuff, *or the Book Fair as Cultural Battleground*

If *TRH* is a novel about book fairs in 1989—and the state of the world—then *TFK* is also very much of its moment. Like *TRH*, the narrative of *TFK* pivots around book fairs and publishers' parties. But the book fair in *TFK*—the Frankfurter Buchmesse—is less a stable signifier of an expanding enlightenment than a locus for its now resurgent others: free speech anxieties, "culture wars," and fascist revival.

The *TFK* is of course a self-identified "comic erotic thriller"—a parody of the kind of novel that was le Carré's stock in trade and indeed took very seriously (though his work was not without humour). However, the satirical edge in *TFK* comes less in spoofing the conventions of the thriller and more in acerbic commentary on books, the book trade, and the ambivalences of contemporary book culture.

First, though, there are some striking similarities between *TRH* and *TFK*. In both novels, the drama begins and ends with a publisher's party. In *TFK*, our hero, Beatrice Deft, overhears plans to destroy the Buchmesse at a subterranean Frankfurt soirée, while waiting to be served her customary Negroni. Her suspicions are further confirmed when she subsequently meets a publisher of left-wing philosophy, Kurt Weidenfeld, who informs her that a fascist organisation—"White Storm"—is plotting to destroy the Buchmesse unless it can be turned into their "exclusive platform."[30] What follows—as readers will doubtless recall—is a breathless series of capers, culminating in Beatrice and her aides thwarting the ignoble efforts of White Storm to assassinate Weidenfeld and blow up the Buchmesse. The final extravagant party has all the hallmarks of a cosmopolitan European order restored to rightful place: a return to a permissive exchange and pleasurable, cosmopolitan (and bookish) life:

> With Caspian by her side, Beatrice approached the Literaturhaus, a smile playing on her lips and her heart leaping in time with the deep bass beat [...] They pressed through the chatting crowd on the steps, a merry babel of languages from all around the world surrounding them over the robot sounds of Kraftwerk's "Trans-Europe Express."[31]

Amidst this enduring sonic signifier of a mobile and literate European modernity, the party escalates. There is frenzied dancing, the quaffing of Sekt, the consumption of "ingeniously designed canapés," and some impromptu cloakroom sex. Kurt Weidenfeld is awarded a prize for his "open submissions policy and an even-handed embrace of both paper and digital formats."[32] Beatrice basks in the glow of having saved the Buchmesse and "rediscovered her interest in both books and physical pleasure."[33] But while parties provide the bookends for both *TRH* and *TFK*, and the suggestion of similar kinds of closure—a victory for liberal bookism, a fulfilment of desire, a promise of further free expression and emancipation to come—*TFK* casts more doubt on the both the stability of the present and the prospects for the future. Within this, and compared to *TRH*, the inherent goods of the book fair—and books themselves—are made ambivalent, or thrown more markedly into question.

To demonstrate this difference, and ambivalence, I'll conclude with three illustrative points. Firstly, today, the liberal freedoms of Europe and the West—so strongly championed in 1989 and exemplified in Francis Fukuyama's (1989) notorious "end of history" polemic—no longer seem so self-evidently good. Liberalism has failed not only to deliver enlightenment, but also justice, equality, and sufficiency for all. Financial crisis—and now pandemic—has further exposed the illusions under which the West has too long laboured. No longer can European (or any) societies take for granted the primacy of liberal institutions, market "freedom," and the inevitability of elevation to the sunlit uplands of a more inclusive social settlement. The complacency of the liberal worldview is variously skewered in *TFK*'s barbs about the Buchmesse. The glitz of the book fair is contrasted with the poverty and inequality that surrounds it; the book trade is seen as shallow and commercially corruptible; the Buchmesse is militarised and masculinised—the protection of freedom requires a certain kind of repression. The Anglo and Eurocentric worldview—exemplified in le Carré's Cold War thrillers, as well as the modern global publishing industry—is rendered unstable. At the end of the book, and in her newly awarded capacity as "International Publishing Consultant,"[34] Beatrice is made aware of the need to consider Global South writers and locations, and is already herself familiar with the inequities of the international book trade through her previous experience of teaching refugee students with authorial ambitions. Squiscoll's questioning of the sanctity of the book fair as a symbolic passage to (European) enlightenment, or a route to some stable future order, is all part of a now necessary undoing.

Secondly, *TFK* is written in an era where the meaning of free expression and free speech has become more troublesome and thorny, especially in the so-called liberal societies. In the public imagination—as in many novels and commentaries of *TRH* era—Western ideas of free speech and free creative expression were celebrated as incontrovertible rights, or as unqualified goods in which all would eventually share. Yet the resurgence of virulent European nationalisms, enduring racism and hate speech and the unwelcome rise of the kind of nativism satirised in *TFK*, indicate some of the tensions inherent in even the most banal endorsements of liberal free speech. "The robust exchange of ideas is our raison d'etre" exclaims the (secretly fascist) Vice President of the Buchmesse; but, as Weidenfeld astutely observes, "White Storm poses more than an ideological threat!"[35] As *TFK* shows us, an assumed freedom to speak can mean an assumed freedom to speak without consideration of context or consequence, and demands to be heard even if what is said is hateful and despicable, or oppressive to social minorities. While, in *TFK*, White Storm might temporarily be defeated, we are left feeling they are likely to return—and that, regardless, many people would continue to defend their fundamental right to speak (or be published). The liberal book fair is now a more complex and disputed territory[36]—perhaps why at the conclusion of *TFK* we see Beatrice equipped with her new roving role to help the book trade "chart a moral path between the freedom to publish and the need to support marginalised voices"[37]; to defend free expression without providing a platform for the social violence being increasingly inflicted on stigmatised and racialised others.

Finally, where le Carré reveres books, even fetishises their power, Squiscoll is much more ambivalent about their value and reliability. Beatrice herself has fallen out of love with books. Her publisher boyfriend, Callum—immediately signified as suspicious through possession of a man-bun—props up his business through shady trades with gangsters in the local Melbourne chicken shop: books are, by necessity, a dirty business. When Angela Carter's "feminist reworking of *Bluebeard*" is used as distraction in a criminal scam, Beatrice wonders "when even the best books could be turned to evil purposes, what use were they?"[38] She flees Callum for Frankfurt. "Do you like books?" a waiter asks. "I did. Once," she replies.[39] Books and authors (Dickens, Bourdieu) are the subject of deflating jokes; absurd titles and ideas are floated as potential bestsellers—we get the sense that books are a dangerous liability and bookselling a rackety kind of trade. The polite and vestigial petty capitalism signified by the likes of Abercrombie & Blair (and Smiley) is absent from the world of the *TFK* Buchmesse, where international publishing mega-corps and the Google Play stand compete for attention from the "suited men and chicly dressed women"[40] who make up the acquisitive throng. "I've seen the damage books can do,"[41] Beatrice opines, and unlike in much of le Carré's work, the book is not taken to be inherently good but often suspect and untrustworthy; part of a commercial culture marked by a deep-rooted and encroaching cynicism, rather than an unimpeachable symbol of an enlightened modernity. Yet, crucially, and returning us to something of le Carré's perspective, in *TFK* books *are* still regarded as salvageable and the book trade redeemable, so long as vigilant and diverse communities are prepared to stand up for the right values and to "troubleshoot political extremists"[42] who might seek to usurp the infrastructure that supports normatively respectful and inclusive literary exchange. A key difference between *TFK* and *TRH*, therefore, is that the former recognises the now radical instability of liberal freedoms, their ethnocentricity, and relative contingency, while the latter—in the manner of its time—somewhat takes these as a given. Both have merits as diagnoses of their present, but only *TFK* leaves open the possibility of an unresolvable future.

Notes

1 This chapter contains spoilers.
2 *TRH* is a long book, *TFK* a very short one. Their relative lengths are reflected in the treatment of each offered here.
3 A proposed Ullapoolist term, with open meaning. I propose it to signify non-individualised bookishness.
4 John le Carré, *The Russia House* (1989; repr., London: Penguin, 2020), 1.
5 Le Carré, 1.
6 Le Carré, 2.
7 Le Carré, 2.
8 Le Carré, 7.
9 Le Carré, 7–8.
10 Le Carré, 78.
11 Le Carré, 17.
12 Le Carré, 203.
13 Walter Benjamin, *The Storyteller: Tales out of Loneliness*, trans. Sam Dolbear, Esther Leslie and Sebastian Truskolaski (London: Verso, 2016).
14 Le Carré, 7.
15 Le Carré, 197.
16 Le Carré, 200.
17 Le Carré, 11.
18 Le Carré, 20.
19 Le Carré, 356.
20 Le Carré, 429.
21 Le Carré, 367.
22 Le Carré, 401.
23 Le Carré, 401.
24 John le Carré, *Tinker, Tailor, Soldier, Spy* (London: Hodder and Stoughton, 1974), 71.
25 Le Carré, 71.
26 Le Carré, 21.
27 John le Carré, *A Legacy of Spies* (London: Penguin, 2017), 351.
28 Le Carré, *The Russia House*, 197.
29 Le Carré, 78.
30 Page 38. All references to the text of *the Frankfurt Kabuff* are to this edition.
31 See page 83 and its footnote on "Trans-Europe Express." A tune that George Smiley would undoubtedly have approved of politically if perhaps not aesthetically.
32 Page 88.

33 Page 87.
34 Page 80.
35 Page 51.
36 It's worth noting that the "White Storm" narrative was inspired by events that occurred at the actual Frankfurter Buchmesse, as Beth Driscoll and Claire Squires (2020) have documented.
37 Page 80.
38 Page 71.
39 Page 29.
40 Page 33.
41 Page 80.
42 Page 81.

Romancing Book Culture

SARAH BROUILLETTE

THE FRANKFURT KABUFF FIRST CIRCULATED IN SERIAL form on Wattpad, a self-publishing platform that has become a disruptive force within the contemporary book industries. Wattpad upends the traditional model for book publishing, replacing the top-down system in which editors unearth saleable talent with a bottom-up method in which work that is selected for formal publication has already achieved measurable popularity via the Wattpad platform.[1]

Technically anyone with a digital device and internet subscription can publish via Wattpad, and most of the people who read narratives on Wattpad do so for free. Like other social media platforms, the company gathers information about users' online behaviours and its revenue streams depend upon strategic use of this data. Primarily, Wattpad hosts advertising. In addition, though, for a cut of the deal, Wattpad works with other media companies in books, film, and television to supply content that has already proven popular. Wattpad also now has its own publishing division, Wattpad Books, which reshapes and repackages content for sale as complete monographs in print and ebook formats.

Aside from being mainly free, part of what distinguishes Wattpad from other self-publishing options, such as Amazon's Kindle Direct Publishing, is the way it has managed to foster a supportive community of readers and writers who identify as embracing diversity and promoting inclusion within the activities of reading and writing. A distinct feature of reading via Wattpad is interacting with comments from other readers. People create community around their reactions to stories. In turn, by identifying as a writer's fans, users shape their own online identities while helping to market the work that they enjoy. Many Wattpad readers have experienced it as a form of reliable respite and community in troubled times. As a result, it is now the biggest repository of narrative fiction online, and it has more than 90 million users, notably predominantly women between the ages of 18 and 30.

There is an important book industry context for what Wattpad does. A massive focus of interest within the publishing industry and among its observers over the past decade has been its relative homogeneity, especially its Whiteness.[2] It is a hard industry to get a foothold in, especially if you do not happen to come from a wealthy background to support expensive university training, or if you cannot shoulder burdens of debt and perhaps work for free as an intern while you try to get your foot in the door—living in London or New York City, no less, among the most expensive cities in the world.

This is the milieu that Wattpad enters, making opportunities available where they otherwise would basically not exist. Many of the most successful Wattpad authors actively identify as defying the usual publishing industry standard narrative of wealthy, university-educated, White, able-bodied, cis heteronormativity. Wattpad's top content is in genres that are popular with audiences more diverse than those in the literary niche: young adult (YA), romance, and fan fiction, with many authors focusing specifically on development of non-normative protagonists. You do not need a creative writing degree to write for the site, nor specially networked contacts to grease the wheels. Anna Todd wrote the first installments of *After*—a massively popular YA fan fiction romance about a young woman who falls in love with a bad boy based on One Direction's Harry Styles—on her phone, between domestic tasks and when standing in line at the shops. The Wattpad company, which thrives more the more contributions it receives from unpaid writers, naturally welcomes such writers with open arms, in part by offering a lot of free training to aspiring writers, in everything from building a platform, to designing a cover, to personal branding, to hooking readers between each exciting, serialised segment. Wattpad's reliance on freely contributed material, and the work involved in cultivating a fan base, in turn shape how writers who identify with the platform conceive their work—as, for example, labour-of-love care work before original self-expression.[3]

It is no surprise that the fiction itself is often enough pedagogically inflected, sentimental models of acceptance despite difference. My own recent research has studied what I call Wattpad's "bibliotherapeutic forms": the platform itself, and the narratives it hosts, often emphasise the mental health benefits of seeing yourself reflected in fiction, and having your non-normative experiences valorised as worthy of representation.[4] The nerdy nobody unites with the former school jock who became a reject after turning depressive and suicidal; the girl who is not as thin and pretty as everyone at her new school finds release in making artworks that also happen to earn her respect, including from one of the hottest guys at school; girls whose private photos have circulated around the school join forces to fight "slut shaming" double standards.[5] The chief evils of these works are comparing yourself to others, striving for popularity, and being rigidly normative about who should date whom and how coupledom should work.

Put simply, these are stories about being accepted and embraced for who you are, which have an understandable appeal for young women living so much of life online today. It is the romance of community rather than of coupledom, with many stories ending not in pairing off but, more ambiguously, in compatible friendship or contented singledom. In accessing these narratives via Wattpad, readers are not just encountering stories of acceptance and inclusion. They are themselves having an approximation of an inclusion experience, in the form of connections made online to like-minded readers and to authors who work carefully to cultivate caring relationships with them.

The Frankfurt Kabuff is thus very much an exemplary Wattpad text. Though it uses fiction as a means of semi-academic autoethnographic observation about contemporary book cultures, it is written in a form familiar to Wattpad readers, one that was available to them to intervene within via feedback on installments of the work as it emerged. It in turn playfully references transformations in the publishing industry, while yearning for expanding access and inclusion beyond the usual White wealthy ranks. To be clear: this is a romantic thriller in which a gang of left-leaning heroes, brought together by fate and shared allegiances, come to fight an insurgent Nazi movement threatening to take over the Frankfurt Book Fair. Like most generic romance novels, it presents idealised scenarios that provide symbolic resolution to real problems that might plague readers in their personal and professional lives: here, problems such as loving books but hating the Whiteness, patriarchy, and normativity of traditional book culture; loving sex but resisting coupledom. It even imagines a police officer who does not serve to uphold White supremacy but rather works to defeat it (what?!), all the while fixated on pleasing his new lover, our protagonist Beatrice, with expert cunnilingus!

Atop all these romantic imaginings sits the desire to reconcile the old traditional culture of the printed book, for which the centuries-old Frankfurt Book Fair is a starred brand, with the new transformative force of the Wattpad smartphone novel. The novel is in this way a romance with book culture itself, about the possibility that old and new could be reconciled in a harmonious way in a fantasy industry that is devoted to promoting progressive social goods rather than maximising profits. Our left-liberal heroes hate not just outright Nazis but everything stemming from "economic inequality." They oppose how the book fair, and publishing more broadly, has tended to give priority to White wealthy voices.

Consider that Beatrice's intellectual ex-boyfriend justifies getting tangled up with a local Melbourne crime ring because his small-press poetry work has been failing to pay. "I've been telling you for years how hard making a living as a poetry publisher is," he complains. He has lost his Australia Council funding because, by his own lights, "our list wasn't hitting 'equalities targets.'" He says, "you know how good our books are, Bea... I only see excellence."[6] To continue to publish his "excellent" White poets, he has to commit crimes that end up threatening the actual lives of some refugees from Sudan now living in Melbourne. Again, the pedagogy is key: Beatrice's ex-boyfriend is basically the opposite of everything that Wattpad is about. He is elitist, pretentious, and violently committed to the idea that he is uniquely able to identify innately good writing and bring it to the world. It just so happens to be inordinately White! He can't help that! (Insert eyeroll here.)

When the novel closes with Beatrice taking on a new job that entails charting "a moral path between the freedom to publish and the need to support marginalised voices," we know she is over her terrible ex.[7] Her new official job title is "International Publishing Consultant," but her real work will be travelling the globe to rout out fascist movements parading under the language of "free speech" all over the world. That the publishing industry would offer lucrative employment in such work is both a delightful fantasy and a convenient opening to a series of sequels, one hopes! Indeed, is *The Frankfurt Kabuff* not precisely about becoming a franchise romance heroine? When we first meet Beatrice, she is disenchanted with romance and with books, and her journey is thus about fighting to rearrange the terms of engagement with publishing, and with men, in a way that makes it possible for her to reignite her passions. The resolution she arrives at is an invitation to seriality: there is no dearth of fascists to takedown, nor of men available for temporary, fortuitous alliances. It is in the nature of the romantic form to slyly index all the real unmet needs that the fantasy narrative world is there to redress. As Arielle Zibrak has recently written of the idea of the "guilty pleasure"—"a descriptor of what it feels like to be female"[8]—why fault anyone for enjoying imagining all the delightful ways in which they might be useful, wanted, accepted, and embraced?

Notes

1 Aarthi Vadde, "Platform or Publisher," *PMLA* 136, no. 3 (2021): 455–62; Melanie Ramdarshan Bold, "The Return of the Social Author: Negotiating Authority and Influence on Wattpad," *Convergence: The International Journal of Research into New Media Technologies* 24, no. 2 (April 2018): 117–36, https://doi.org/10.1177/1354856516654459; Rosamund Davies, "Collaborative Production and the Transformation of Publishing: The Case of Wattpad," in *Collaborative Production in the Creative Industries*, ed. Alessandro Gandini and James Graham (London: University of Westminster Press, 2017), 51–68.

2 Shelly Romero and Adriana M. Martínez Figueroa, "'The Unbearable Whiteness of Publishing' Revisited," *Publishers Weekly*, January 29, 2021, https://www.publishersweekly.com/pw/by-topic/industry-news/publisher-news/article/85450-the-unbearable-whiteness-of-publishing-revisited.html; Richard Jean So, *Redlining Culture: A Data History of Racial Inequality and Postwar Fiction* (New York: Columbia University Press, 2020); Anamik Saha and Sandra van Lente, "Rethinking 'Diversity' in Publishing" (London: Goldsmiths Press, 2020), https://research.gold.ac.uk/id/eprint/28692/1/Rethinking_diversity_in_publishing_full_booklet_v2.pdf.

3 I discuss Wattpad authors' extensive labour and accompanying self-conceptions in detail in Sarah Brouillette, "Wattpad, Platform Capitalism, and the Feminization of Publishing Work," *Book History*, Forthcoming.

4 Sarah Brouillette, "Wattpad's Fictions of Care," *Post45*, July 13, 2022, https://post45.org/2022/07/wattpads-fictions-of-care/.

5 These are the plots of three Wattpad Books in the YA category: Sky Chase's *Saving Everest* (2019), Jo Watson's *Big Boned* (2021), and Natalie Watson's *Revenge of the Sluts* (2021), respectively.

6 Page 70. All references to the text of *The Frankfurt Kabuff* are to this edition.

7 Page 80.

8 Arielle Zibrak, *Guilty Pleasures* (New York: New York University Press, 2021), 26.

Politics at Play in the Kabuff

The Buchmesse as a Political Space

CORINNA NORRICK-RÜHL

IN *THE FRANKFURT KABUFF*, A KEY SCENE TAKES PLACE between Kurt Weidenfeld, the publisher of left-wing philosophical texts, and the protagonist Beatrice Deft. Weidenfeld is explaining that he and other left-wing publishers have received threats from the (fictitious) radical right-wing publisher White Storm, intimating that they should stay away from the Frankfurt Book Fair (FBF). What happens when political ideas and ideologies clash at the fair? Beatrice Deft is initially surprised that White Storm has tried to control the discourse at the fair in this way. As she says, "Frankfurt Book Fair is about the exchange of ideas."[1] This is certainly part of the fair's appeal, and its emphasis on openness and exchange is closely connected to its history and revival after the Second World War.[2] To this day, FBF is a complex space infused by expectations from all sorts of different attendees—from international exhibitors to local book aficionadas, from publishing students seeking an internship to big-name celebrities basking in the media attention, signing books piled high.

Among these varied attendees with their different agendas and accessories are, as *The Frankfurt Kabuff* highlights, political publishers but also politicians, eager to network and be seen, and to be associated with the cultural values and economic largesse on display. Local, regional, national, and even international politicians receive guided tours of selected booths, orchestrated perfectly for maximum media attention and accompanied by an entourage of journalists. Onsite, there are plenty of interview opportunities, and big-name politicians are invited to speak at the opening or closing ceremonies. This intermingling of politicians and the fair has an advertising and amplifying effect for both. The German market research centre INFAS has even shown that popularity rates of politicians increase directly after public fair visits.[3]

Given the book's dual status as a cultural object and a commodity, it seems obvious that economics and culture meet at the fair, and that these systems have different logics and currencies within themselves. I have argued elsewhere that it can be fruitful to apply systems theory to the analysis of FBF. Besides the two separate systems of economics and culture, the system of politics can be considered relevant to the analysis of FBF. Here, the currency is power.[4]

The FBF website tends to vagueness when acknowledging its role as a political space. Until mid-2021, under the heading "Politics and Society," the English-language version of the FBF website read, "Knowing what moves the world—big questions, strong opinions and uncomfortable truths."[5] At time of writing—September 2021, during the run-up to a hybrid attempt at FBF after 2020's online-only iteration—the English-language website states rather blandly:

> Frankfurter Buchmesse is one [of] the world's most important stages for current debates on international and socio-political events. In Frankfurt, we bring together the people whose business is ideas, open a constructive dialogue on pressing issues, and meet on equal footing with those who have different views.[6]

Given these opaque statements on the FBF website, this essay considers (some of the) politics at play at FBF more closely.

Around the occasion of the 50th anniversary of its modern incarnation in 1999, FBF received increased attention from German book studies scholars, with the edited collection *50 Jahre Frankfurter Buchmesse: 1949–1999*[7] and Sabine Niemeier's *Funktionen der Frankfurter Buchmesse im Wandel.*[8] In 2003, former FBF director Peter Weidhaas published his memoir/history of the book fair, which covered not only his tenure, but also contextualised the history of the FBF going back to the fifteenth century.[9] Importantly for our context, a 2007 edited collection on the politicization of the book industry in the 1960s contained a long chapter by Ulrike Seyer on the politicization of FBF during this very turbulent period, with massive student protests almost leading to FBF being closed to the public.[10] The student protests broke open the political dimension of FBF, which had been simmering under the glossy veneer of the event. As Seyer discusses, contemporary critics noted the fair's thorny relationship with and incorporation of the German Democratic Republic's publishing scene, its increased commercialization during a phase of rapid industry conglomeration, and the controversial choice of the 1968 FBF Peace Prize winner, the Senegalese president Léopold Sédar Senghor. After the 1970s, the political dimension once again retreated to a more subliminal level, with some exceptions, as we will see later. Recently, new scholarly attention has been awarded to literary events such as festivals and fairs, and scholars, including Beth Driscoll and Claire Squires,[11] Roanna Gonsalves,[12] and Luise Hertwig[13] have used FBF as a site for contemporary book studies research.

To focus on a different phase, let us briefly go back in time, either in imagination or using the Ullapoolism time machine,[14] to 13 October 2009, the day of FBF's opening ceremony in the fairground conference centre. The FBF opening ceremony is usually held in this building located at the gates of the fairgrounds, which connect the fair to downtown Frankfurt, just a stone's throw away from the central train station. Here, the fair is opened in a select and exclusive ceremony with big-name, and frequently political, speakers. In 2009, the headline speaker was Dr. Angela Merkel, then the German Chancellor. This year was particularly interesting for a variety of reasons, many of them political. Most visibly and importantly, China had been invited to present its literature as Guest of Honour that year, which had already occasioned heated debates about censorship, platform, and freedom of speech in the run-up to the book fair. Similar debates had accompanied the 2004 presentation of the "Arabian World," with journalists speculating about which authors would receive official invitations to attend and which wouldn't.[15] In 2009, in a debate in German parliament, FBF's politics were denounced as "opportunistic"[16] by Hans-Joachim Otto, a member of the Bundestag. In response, Jürgen Boos, FBF director, made blanket statements about FBF not being "controllable"—and admitted to compromising with the Guest of Honour China and its plans.[17] The Guest of Honour system is, perhaps, "uncontrollable" in that FBF offers the guest the venue space free of charge but does not contribute any funding. The FBF, then, only has limited influence on what is presented, which themes are emphasised, and who is (or isn't) invited.[18]

The 2009 opening ceremony, punctuated with a jazz big band which the reporting journalist Bartels claimed gave the event the character of a late-night show,[19] ended with Merkel's speech. Given Merkel's ongoing flirtation with the economically powerful China as a possible investor in Germany,[20] journalists and critics were not surprised that she avoided the topics of censorship and freedom of speech. However, her speech was ridiculed for its focus on "curiosity." Merkel appealed to her audience in the conference centre, but also to the wider German public: "I ask everyone to be curious and avoid prejudices. Don't be shy to ask questions which might lead our Chinese partners to think: 'Do they know anything about our country?' Only curious questions lead us into discussions so we can learn to understand each other better."[21] The politics at play here are diffuse. China as an economic partner was too important to criticise in a forthright manner, but the heated preliminary debate in the news media made some sort of nod towards the discussions around censorship necessary. So, instead of going into more detail about the German-Chinese relationship, Merkel talked about her personal experiences living in the German Democratic Republic and seeing censorship enacted: "I always hoped to find acquaintances and relatives from the West who would be willing not only to send a box with soap and citrus fruit, but also to smuggle a book, for which you needed to be quite courageous."[22] Bartels criticised the speech—and indeed, the whole ceremony—as "beautiful backdrop magic", meant to distract journalists and the audience from the negative press that had circulated before FBF.[23]

The "backdrop" metaphor brings us full circle, then, to Beatrice Deft and the Kabuff. Cobwebby, empty spaces between booths and behind walls, created by fair management to give the effect of a fuller hall, are simultaneously the opposite of the glossy, happy-go-lucky opening ceremony and its prerequisite. FBF refuses to be pinned down with a political identity, welcoming controversial Guests of Honour, avoiding confrontational language—all in the name of freedom of speech.

The Frankfurt Kabuff is fiction, to be sure, but the conflict at the heart of the comic erotic thriller is a real one, seething beneath the bright red-and-white logos of FBF. Frankfurt may be home to the "Buchwelt" ("the world of books"), but it is located in Germany, which has its own history and political upheaval to contend with. In recent years, with right-wing radicalist parties such as Alternative für Deutschland on the rise, more attention has been given to the types of publishers exhibiting at the fair. In 2017, the political tensions at the fair escalated, with protests and tumult reminiscent of the late 1960s.[24] Nonetheless, FBF decided not to exclude any publishers from the fair in preparation for 2018; these decisions were debated throughout the year and reflected in Leipzig Book Fair's inclusion of right-wing publishers. As with her 2009 speech, Merkel's remarks on occasion of the opening of Leipzig Book Fair in March 2018 ignored the ongoing tumultuous relationship between German right-wing radical publishers and book fairs, focusing instead on "reading being the elixir of life," and recommending German classics (such as Erich Kästner, Wilhelm Busch, and Johann Wolfgang von Goethe) alongside Shakespeare and Tolstoi.[25] These somewhat uninspired comments about well-known authors increased suspicions among the feuilleton journalists that Merkel is not, in fact, a reader of literature. But apparently, as one commentator summarised, for the chancellor with a PhD in physics, this lack of reading verve has not proven to be a disadvantage in the political realm.[26]

The backlash and discussions surrounding these decisions are not unique to German book fairs. As Christian Lenemark has shown in his work on the Gothenburg Book Fair, the inclusion of extreme-right publishers and publications is a minefield in Sweden as well. In Gothenburg, the fairs in the years 2016 and 2017 were dominated by discussions surrounding the presentation of the extreme-right newspaper *Nya Tider.* Lenemark emphasises, "above all, the question raised by *Nya Tider*'s participation was about whether the Book Fair should be considered part of the public sphere or not."[27] After much deliberation, the Gothenburg Book Fair excluded *Nya Tider* from the fair in 2018.

FBF has chosen a different way forward. For 2018, FBF strategised to minimize protests but stopped short of disinviting any publisher. Instead, they relocated most of the right-wing radical publishers to a cul-de-sac in hall 4.1, near antiquarian booksellers and away from the big crowds and potential walk-ins. Was this relegation to the background political? Was it an implicit political statement? Was it merely a pragmatic decision to facilitate easier access for police and security personnel? The stance of FBF (or rather, its lack of one) was hotly debated in the feuilleton and beyond. German philosopher Svenja Flaßpöhler, known for her willingness to engage with contemporary debates, suggested in a philosophical magazine that tolerance of the publishers was the right way forward. Given the political developments in Germany, Flaßpöhler argued, it is certainly risky to allow right-wing radical publishers to use FBF as a stage. Simultaneously, Flaßpöhler believed that it was a necessity according to agonistic democratic theories.[28] The fact that FBF has uploaded a PDF of Flaßpöhler's article to their website hints that FBF is perhaps more worried about its reputation than it lets on. As Lotte indicates in *The Frankfurt Kabuff*, "chart[ing] a moral path between the freedom to publish and the need to support marginalised voices"[29] is a twenty-first century challenge for the book industry—including for the FBF.

As researchers of contemporary book culture and publishing, we attend, observe, and sometimes shape FBF and other book and cultural events. As we evaluate and re-evaluate FBF and similar events, it seems important to include the political dimension to a greater degree than we have so far. If the political dimension is relegated to the metaphorical Kabuff, or real-life cul-de-sacs in far-flung fair halls, we may overlook necessary debates. In 2020, during the first-ever fully digital iteration of FBF, Jürgen Boos was quoted as saying that "the Buchmesse has always been a political platform and will remain one."[30] As book studies researchers, we should hold FBF to that standard, interrogating closely in which instances FBF chooses to emphasise the political—and it which it recedes from the discussions in favour of an allegedly more neutral standpoint. Like archives, libraries, and museums,[31] the fair can and should no longer pretend to be neutral.

Notes

1 Page 38.

2 For contexts, see Urs Büttner and Corinna Norrick-Rühl, "Commerce, Culture—and a Camel: The Re-Establishment of Frankfurt Book Fair as an Institution of Literary Circulation after World War II," in *The Value of Literary Circulation/Der Wert der Literarischen Zirkulation*, ed. Michael Gamper et al. (Berlin: de Gruyter, 2022), 205–22.

3 See Carsten Dierig, "Der Werbeeffekt ist groß," *Die Welt*, April 2, 2013, https://www.welt.de/print/die_welt/article114925237/Der-Werbeeffekt-ist-gross.html.

4 See Corinna Norrick-Rühl, "'Die Buchwelt zu Gast in Frankfurt': Understanding the Impact of the Guest of Honour Presentation at Frankfurt Book Fair on the German Literary Marketplace," *Mémoires Du Livre / Studies in Book Culture* 11, no. 2 (Spring 2020): 1–34, https://doi.org/10.7202/1070263ar.

5 Frankfurter Buchmesse, "Politics and Society," accessed July 15, 2021, https://www.buchmesse.de/en/highlights/reader-delights/politics-society.

6 Frankfurter Buchmesse, "About Us," accessed September 10, 2021, https://www.buchmesse.de/en/about-us.

7 Stephan Füssel, ed., *50 Jahre Frankfurter Buchmesse: 1949–1999* (Frankfurt: Suhrkamp, 2000).

8 Sabine Niemeier, *Funktionen der Frankfurter Buchmesse im Wandel* (Wiesbaden: Harrassowitz, 2001).

9 Peter Weidhaas, *Zur Geschichte der Frankfurter Buchmesse* (Frankfurt: Suhrkamp, 2003).

10 Ulrike Seyer, "Die Frankfurter Buchmesse in den Jahren 1967–1969," in *Die Politisierung des Buchmarkts: 1968 als Branchenereignis*, ed. Stephan Füssel (Wiesbaden: Harrassowitz, 2007), 159–241.

11 Beth Driscoll and Claire Squires, *The Frankfurt Bookfair and Bestseller Business* (Cambridge: Cambridge University Press, 2020).

12 Roanna Gonsalves, "The Survival of the Friendliest: Contemporary Indian Publishing in English at the Frankfurt Book Fair," *Cultural Sociology* 9, no. 3 (September 2015): 425–46, https://doi.org/10.1177/1749975515590244.

13 Luise Hertwig, "State-Funded Support of International Trade in Rights and Licenses. Translation Funding Programs of Guests of Honour Argentina and France at the 2010 and 2017 Frankfurt Book Fair," *Mémoires Du Livre / Studies in Book Culture* 11, no. 2 (Spring 2020): 1–38, https://doi.org/doi:10.7202/1070264ar.

14 Beth Driscoll and Claire Squires, "The Ullapoolism Time Machine: Travels Through Periodicity in Book History," https://wwuindico.uni-muenster.de/event/366/attachments/76/680/Moving%20Texts_Conference%20Programme.pdf, 13.

15 Frankfurter Allgemeine,"Gastland Arabien: Wer zur Buchmesse kommt," July 7, 2004, https://www.faz.net/aktuell/feuilleton/buecher/frankfurter-buchmesse-gastland-arabien-wer-zur-buchmesse-kommt-1178995.html.

16 Quoted in "Buchmesse als opportunistisch kritisiert," *Zeit*, September 10, 2009, https://www.zeit.de/kultur/literatur/2009-09/frankfurt-china-buchmesse." All translations of German quotes by the author.

17 Quoted in "Buchmesse als opportunistisch kritisiert."

18 For more detail see Norrick-Rühl, "'Die Buchwelt zu Gast in Frankfurt.'"

19 Gerrit Bartels, "Schöner Kulissenzauber," *Zeit*, October 14, 2009, https://www.zeit.de/kultur/literatur/2009-10/buchmessen-eroeffnung.

20 Noah Barkin, "Rethinking German Policy Toward China," *Chatham House*, May 26, 2021, https://www.chathamhouse.org/2021/05/rethinking-german-policy-towards-china/merkels-approach-china.

21 Angela Merkel, "Bulletin 103-2: Rede von Bundeskanzlerin Dr. Angela Merkel zur Eröffnung der Frankfurter Buchmesse am 13. Oktober 2009 in Frankfurt am Main," *Bundesregierung*, October 14, 2009, https://www.bundesregierung.de/breg-de/service/bulletin/rede-von-bundeskanzlerin-dr-angela-merkel-799194.

22 Merkel, "Bulletin 103-2."

23 Bartels, "Schöner Kulissenzauber."

24 For more details, see Nikola Roßbach, *Achtung Zensur! Über Meinungsfreiheit und ihre Grenzen* (Berlin: Ullstein, 2018), 151–155.

25 Gerrit Bartels, "Leipziger Buchmesse: Diese Bücher sind Angela Merkels 'Lebenselixier,'" *Tagesspiegel*, March 15, 2018, https://www.tagesspiegel.de/kultur/leipziger-buchmesse-diese-buecher-sind-angela-merkels-lebenselixier/21056562.html.

26 Bartels, "Leipziger Buchmesse."

27 Christian Lenemark, "Negotiating Value: A Case Study of the Gothenburg Book Fair," *Mémoires Du Livre / Studies in Book Culture* 11, no. 2 (Spring 2020): 1–42, https://doi.org/10.7202/1070266ar.

28 Svenja Flaßpöhler, "Wie viel Meinungsfreiheit verträgt die Demokratie?," *Philosophie Magazin*, October 15, 2018, https://www.buchmesse.de/files/media/pdf/PMD_2018_06_72dpi_einzelseiten.pdf.

29 Page 80.

30 Quoted in Claus-Jürgen Göpfert, "Direktor der Buchmesse im Interview: 'Der Mythos Buchmesse lebt weiter,'" *Frankfurter Rundschau*, October 10, 2020, https://www.fr.de/frankfurt/frankfurter-buchmesse-direktor-juergen-boos-corona-zeiten-digitalisierung-politik-90066043.html.

31 On the discussion of the pseudo-neutrality of memory institutions, see for example Nathan Mudyi Sentance, "Your Neutral Is Not Our Neutral," *Archival Decolonist* (blog), January 18, 2018, https://archivaldecolonist.com/2018/01/18/your-neutral-is-not-our-neutral/.

Charting a path for social change, one Negroni at a time

The Frankfurt Kabuff

DORIS RUTH EIKHOF

AS ALL GOOD (COMIC EROTIC) THRILLERS SHOULD, *THE Frankfurt Kabuff* opens with a Negroni, sunglasses, and bright red lipstick. Beatrice, a 32-year-old Scorpio who once loved books, is in self-care mode, medicating jadedness and jetlag in autumnal Frankfurt.[1] Eighty-some pages later, with her passion, assertiveness, and interest in the "lives and culture of the people around her"[2] restored, Beatrice embarks, another Negroni in hand, on an alluring future as International Publishing Consultant.

Between *Kabuff*'s first and last Negroni lies the Frankfurt Book Fair. A glitzy world in which the "milling intelligentsia and cultural entrepreneurs"[3] float between grand hotels and executive clubs with tinkling Bösendorfers, parties in pole-dancing clubs, and the Literaturhaus's trendy cocktail of canapés, Sekt, and Kraftwerk. Erotic art, Primal Scream, and Nena frame expensively cut suits, "heel[s] that meant business,"[4] 100% Egyptian cotton sheets, and 300 gsm business cards. So many business cards.

But this glossy incarnation of the upper-left quadrant in Bourdieu's social space diagram is under grave threat. From the cobwebby, pitch-dark underbelly of the Buchmesse stands blows the White Storm, "a network of newspapers and zines dedicated to reviving the worst ideas and policies of the twentieth century."[5] A white-capped bunch of brutes that, after the 2021 insurgence on Washington's Capitol and COVID conspiracy theorists, looks a much less exaggerated depiction of the threats to the woke world as we'd like to know it than when *Kabuff* was published. Beatrice, the jaded Australian Scorpio, is drafted in to "confront the evil despoiling the heart of the publishing industry and culture more broadly."[6] *Kabuff* takes us along for the ride, deftly (sorry) taking in every available cliché about the international publishing industry.

Beyond the canapés and comic-erotic action, the tongue-in-cheek characterisations of *Kabuff*'s cast lend themselves to timely explorations of who gets to drive social change—and with what legitimacy. At the centre of it all is Beatrice Deft, the big-hearted schoolteacher from Melbourne. Beatrice used to be "interested in every human being"[7] but a sinister accident in the neighbourhood chicken shop involving her migrant protégé pupil Amina, unscrupulous money launderers, and Beatrice's partner has "wrung her dry."[8] She escapes to Frankfurt and, clinging to Negronis and cigarettes, hides her once-flirtatious eyes behind dark sunglasses: "some spark inside her had gone out, and remained unlit for months now."[9] Beatrice is clearly a woman in need of more than a change of clothes and new lipstick, not ready yet to surrender to the "genuine enthusiasm"[10] of the publishing party's chic crowd or the bashful advances of Polizeiobermeister No. 6969.

Beatrice's self-care trip is summarily interrupted by Kurt Weidenfeld, a "famous publisher of left-wing philosophy"[11] known to even the Turkish taxi driver. Weidenfeld has been warned off attending the Buchmesse by the neo-Nazi publisher White Storm. But, as he explains to Beatrice, his small Linksphilosophie Verlag "requires international rights sales to survive,"[12] and so Weidenfeld calls on Beatrice to be his "eyes and ears"[13] while he attends business meetings to secure the future of freely published left idea(l)s.

An eminent lefty maybe, but Weidenfeld's warfare is distinctly more James Bond than Audre Lorde, with cryptic messages and hotel lounge meetings straight out of the master of all secret agents' toolbox. He guilt-trips Beatrice with fond memories of her mother's care for others and calls her "Liebchen,"[14] a German version of "darling" so antiquated and patronising that any native speaker and literary type of Beatrice's age would be hard-wired to invoke Goethe's indignant Gretchen: "bin weder Fräulein, weder schön, kann ungeleit nach Hause gehn"[15] ("am neither miss nor beautiful and can go home unescorted").

Weidenfeld has long-standing, and, as we learn as the *Kabuff* gathers pace, highly effective connections to Tante Fran and her book club. Themselves no strangers to behind-the-scenes scheming, this sisterhood comes armed with knitting needles, a Goodreads page, and handy access to

Frankfurt's police force, courtesy of Tante Fran's nephew, Polizeiobermeister Caspian. The "feminist solidarity"[16] from these "formidable women"[17] who read Marcuse and Luxemburg and paint slogans (on Fridays) further affirms the "debonair"[18]-looking Weidenfeld's grounding in the intellectual grassroots of good causes.

With Weidenfeld also comes Adriana, the rights director of Linksphilosophie Verlag. We meet her as the publisher's sidekick, possibly more his special agent, who at Weidenfeld's whisper "smooth[s] her skirt"[19] and goes to distract the White Storm stall minder. But Adriana is not only schooled in the smooth operations of secret agenthood; she also knows the realpolitik of social change. When Weidenfeld announces the former asylum seeker as the new Publisher at Linksphilosophie Verlag, she does not take up the invitation to talk about her story of injustice and harm. Instead, she quickly assures the audience that she won't let her story "stand between you and more canapés"[20] and allows *Kabuff* to surefootedly swing back from substance to style and Negronis, complete with Nena's soundtrack of hope after destruction—"Hab' 'n Luftballon gefunden, Denk' an dich und lass' ihn fliegen" ("and here is a red balloon, think of you and let it go").

To cut a not-very-long story even shorter, *Kabuff* draws Beatrice into the fight against the White Storm and into the developed biceps of Polizeiobermeister Caspian Schorle ("flawless tanned skin, straight nose, full lips,"[21] "shapely uniformed shoulders"[22]). In thigh-high, red-laced black leather boots and a succession of "shapeless yet stylish"[23] dresses, Beatrice strides through "moment[s] of smouldering intensity,"[24] smoke grenade attacks, and the non-metaphorical networks that connect everything at the Buchmesse. With Caspian at her side, secret agent assistance from Adriana and Weidenfeld, and decisive combat action from Tante Fran and the book club, Beatrice dismantles the bomb threat, fends off White Storm (for now), and secures the Buchmesse's exchange of ideas (also for now).

The rewards, all paid in the literary field's customary currency of symbolic capital,[25] are plenty: Caspian is promoted to Polizeihauptmeister, Lotte Frankel to the Buchmesse's Vice President, and Adriana to Publisher at Linksphilosophie Verlag. The eminent Weidenfeld is awarded the Buchmesse's Peace Prize. Beatrice is handed a whole new career as an International Publishing Consultant, with business cards and the brief to keep political extremists from destroying all that book fair champions "hold dear."[26] After some more Polizei-escorted partying and a hearty breakfast for two, Beatrice heads off to the airport. With her lipstick slightly worn but her sense of self intact (and her dress probably shapeless but stylish, though for once *Kabuff* does not mention her outfit), she boards the flight to her first assignment. Which, as we know by now, is probably not THE END.

The *Kabuff* is an entertaining tale of how Beatrice's propensity to care for others is reactivated through the comic, erotic, and thrilling events at the Buchmesse, and reinvented as the foundations of a new career in social change. *Kabuff* is also clever commentary on the publishing industry and the academic analysis of it. But what makes *Kabuff* interesting from a drivers-for-social-change perspective is its playful packaging of Beatrice's conversion to a professional force for good with style, consumption, and distinction. Hardly a paragraph goes by without reference to sartorial choices, tastes (literal and Bourdieusian), textures, audio-visual and tactile sensations, and aesthetics. What, then, can *Kabuff* tell us about style, substance, and the fight for social change?

Kabuff juxtaposes Beatrice's Negroni-fuelled care for others with two long-standing forces for change. Firstly, and most prominently (we are at the Buchmesse, after all), there is the scholarly intellectualism of Kurt Weidenfeld, Tante Fran, and the book club. Theirs is a learned approach, one that combines the study of history and theory with ritualised and institutionalised publication practice—left-wing philosophy for Weidenfeld, weekly painted slogans for the well-read sisterhood. Action has its place here as well, from Weidenfeld's secret messages to the book clubs' bomb-dismantling knitting needles, but the underlying motivation is a scholarly understanding of the problem and its theoretically reasoned solution.

The second force for change is the first-hand experience of injustice and harm, alluded to in the figure of Adriana, the former asylum seeker at the Linksphilosophie Verlag. We learn little about her, mainly through Weidenfeld, who tells us that Adriana has taught him of "horror I could only imagine"[27] and reaffirmed his belief in "cultural interchange."[28] That is as much voice of the underprivileged as *Kabuff* will allow itself. Adriana's future as the newly appointed head of the Linksphilosophie Verlag remains as unknown as that of Beatrice as an International Publishing Consultant. Will she exploit her knowledge of the establishment to drive radical change or will the rage management project that is respectability politics[29] keep her in check? Will she buckle under what Sara Ahmed describes as energy-sapping "diversity work"?[30] Will she be allowed to be more than a poster child for inclusion, a children's TV presenter-figure showcasing palatable social change, the kind that looks good on social media and otherwise keeps the established world-order intact? *Kabuff* doesn't say (yet).

A few lone comments on shoes (the sisterhood), "dramatically made-up" eyes[31] (Adriana), and "debonair"[32] looks (Weidenfeld) aside, *Kabuff* does not afford these seasoned fighters for social change much style or sumptuous adjectives. Instead, almost behind everyone's back, it joins their forces in the story's only conventionally recognisable advance towards social change when Weidenfeld, the linksintellektuelle 007 with the penchant for hotel lobby drinks and Liebchens, hands the reigns of Linksphilosophie Verlag to Adriana. Intellectualism and scholarship remain valued in Weidenfeld's new assignment as Editor-at-Large, of course. But the eminent White publisher vacating a position of visibility and power in favour of a young migrant is activism as per the textbooks of decolonisation and inclusive practice; it is a quiet counterpoint to Lotte Frankel's power-tooled corporate intervention to make the furniture arrangements of the Buchmesse's executive club "more inclusive, less fringing"[33] (deck chairs and ocean liners—ferries?—spring to mind).

Where does that robustly grounded pursuit of social change leave Beatrice, in her shapeless yet stylish dress, with her red lipstick and nice but vague interest "in every human being"?[34] She shares Tante Fran's love for good shoes but not the depth of the book club's insight into radical theory. And while bad things have happened in her life, we don't get any indication that they were horrors of the magnitude that Adriana had to endure. Are we allowed to roll our eyes at her self-care and navel (or slightly below) gazing, her fascination with business cards, her international assignments, and her hotel/airport lounge Negronis?

To stay in the realm of the superficial for a moment: social change has become fashionable. From jumpers that proclaim "On Wednesdays We Smash the Patriarchy" to disabled children in chips commercials, appeals for social justice and inclusion sell. The capitalist economy has once more turned its critique into a marketable commodity,[35] blending BLM insignias with Moleskine notebooks and reusable coffee mugs. Alexandria Ocasio-Cortez's online make-up tutorial for *Vogue* was a shiningly awkward example: it blurred the lines between product recommendation and left-wing politics until substance blended into style more seamlessly than the US congresswoman's concealer into her foundation. In Beatrice's defence, the world around her offers plenty of opportunity to overlook that while caring for others and a Stila lipstick (shade Beso) are not mutually exclusive, they are also not all there is to "chart[ing] a moral path."[36]

Of course, viability and opportunity alone do not justify choice. Wariness of performative diversity is undoubtedly justified. "Woke washing"[37] is real and social change can likely take only so many canapés and rainbow-framed social media profile pictures without compromising its integrity. And although, corporate capitalism is to blame for a lot,[38] there will always remain an individual responsibility to distinguish a stance that, in Helen Lewis's words, "makes demands on power" from what "is really self-help under a thin, sugary glaze of activism."[39]

At the same time, social change has a practical problem if it insists on only recognising those as legitimate agents of social change who can draw on either first-hand experience of injustice or a rigorous theoretical-historical understanding of problems and potential solutions. Social change of the kind alluded to in *Kabuff* requires myriad little changes. The majority of people who need to make those changes can draw on neither first-hand experience nor theories of injustice. They will come to social change through other paths, from the diffuse caring for others and primary school "kindness" imperatives to slogan T-shirts and Instagram posts. They will not have head-space, resource, or inclination to first write a PhD on social justice movements. And even if they did, we'd need them on board a little more quickly. And the obvious moral problems of asking anyone to catch up on the first-hand experience of harm aside, how much harm would one need to endure to accrue legitimacy? How many school years of being bullied for dyslexia equal one experience of sexual assault? Plus, if first-hand experience and scholarly understanding of injustice were all it took to affect social change, "the revolution would have long since come,"[40] as Black feminist Britney Cooper puts it. Humanity's past two millennia have had plenty of both.

"One doesn't knowingly determine the circumstances of one's birth," writes Emma Dabiri, "It's not about guilt-tripping anyone for having unearned wealth and privilege."[41] A similar argument applies to taste and consumption. Libraries full of social research demonstrate that even in our choices of lipsticks and dresses we are only partly able to change the course of the travels through spaces of perception and practice that chance has flung us on. What matters is what we make of, and with, both the style and the substance of our privilege. Will the International Publishing Consultant Deft secure the "continuing international exchange of translation rights, cultures and ideas," capsizing a few manboats along the way? Or will she become like the "wealthy, upper-middle class white people"[42] Emma Dabiri recounts, who asked her for anti-racist resources to read or watch, only to then overlook substantive opportunities to deliver on promises made in the "anti-racist frenzy of the summer of 2020"?[43]

What we imagine Beatrice's and Adriana's futures to be will say more about our own attitude to who does social change than about *Kabuff*'s cast of characters. "Writing and reading books is the easy part,"[44] comments Blaire Squiscoll. Or, in Britney Cooper's words: "It's fine to quote Audre Lorde to people and tell them, 'The master's tool will never dismantle the master's house.' The harder work is helping people find better tools to work with."[45]

THE BEGINNING—or is it

Notes

1 Page 27. All references to the text of *The Frankfurt Kabuff* are to this edition.
2 Page 90.
3 Page 66.
4 Page 43.
5 Page 37.
6 Page 75.
7 Page 45.
8 Page 27.
9 Page 28.
10 Page 33.
11 Page 44.
12 Page 38.
13 Page 38.
14 Page 37.
15 Johann Wolfgang von Goethe, *Faust. Der Tragödie Erster Teil* (Stuttgart: Reclam, 1986), 75.
16 Page 77.
17 Page 76.
18 Page 50.
19 Page 56.
20 Page 88.
21 Page 34.
22 Page 35.
23 Page 80.
24 Page 44.
25 Pierre Bourdieu, "The Field of Cultural Production, or: The Economic World Reversed," *Poetics* 12, no. 4 (November 1983): 311–56, https://doi.org/10.1016/0304-422X(83)90012-8.

26 Page 81.
27 Page 88.
28 Page 88.
29 Britney Cooper, *Eloquent Rage. A Black Feminist Discovers Her Superpower* (New York: Picador, 2018).
30 Sara Ahmed, *Living a Feminist Life* (Durham and London: Duke University Press, 2017), 91.
31 Page 87.
32 Page 50.
33 Page 81.
34 Page 45.
35 Luc Boltanski and Eve Chiapello, *The New Spirit of Capitalism* (London: Verso, 2006).
36 Page 80.
37 Arwa Mahdawi, "Woke-Washing Brands Cash in on Social Justice. It's Lazy and Hypocritical," *The Guardian*, August 10, 2018, https://www.theguardian.com/commentisfree/2018/aug/10 fellow-kids-woke-washing-cynical-alignment-worthy-causes.
38 Owen Jones, "Woke-Washing: How Brands Are Cashing in on the Culture Wars," *The Guardian*, May 23, 2019, https://www.theguardian.com/media/2019/may/23/woke-washing-brands-cashing-in-on-culture-wars-owen-jones.
39 Helen Lewis, *Difficult Women: A History Of Feminism in 11 Fights* (London: Jonathan Cape, 2020), 203.
40 Cooper, *Eloquent Rage*, 266.
41 Emma Dabiri, *What White People Can Do Next: From Allyship to Coalition* (Dublin: Penguin Random House, 2021), 120.
42 Dabiri, *What White People Can Do Next*, 119.
43 Dabiri, *What White People Can Do Next*, 120.
44 Page 205.
45 Cooper, *Eloquent Rage*, 274.

A Frankfurt Memoir

(inspired by The Frankfurt Kabuff*)*

ARPITA DAS

ON MY FLIGHT BACK FROM FRANKFURT IN 2018, MY IN-FLIGHT reading happened to be a little book called *The Frankfurt Kabuff* by an author with the highly improbable name Blaire Squiscoll. I read it from cover to cover during the eight-hour flight with a short break to watch the first two episodes of the first season of *Killing Eve*. The vividly narrated details of stand parties, pints of Guinness at 5 p.m., the travails of wearing heels at the fair, and moments of transnational dynamics which often went awry in translation took me back forcefully to my first time at the Frankfurt Book Fair, in 2006. This, dear reader, is my recollection of that time, and whether it is a tad or more coloured by my reading of Squiscoll's *Kabuff* will forever be consigned to the confines of conjecture.

* * *

South Asians can be tall. But I am not one of them. Being short is something I came to terms with long ago, in late adolescence/early adulthood, when it finally sank in that I would not be growing those few necessary inches that would make me stand out in a packed room. So, I had to hustle to make sure that my height did not get in the way of how much attention I needed to garner at any given time. I honed my public speaking skills, made sure my voice would carry over sundry conversations, and learned not to be shy about cracking a well-timed joke.

Once I started working, however, I found that sometimes it helped to be able to blend in more easily than others while trying to read the room before being spotted by someone, or to grab snatches of conversation while being "invisible," which would help me start a speech on the right note. You might be wondering what I do. I am an independent publisher and commissioning editor, and to be able to read the room is often important in my line of work—whether it is what to say as I introduce an author that will make every audience member queue up to buy her book; or what ingredient to promote at a sales pitch; or even what to order while meeting an author I want to sign up, so that I strike a chord strong enough for her to want to work with my deeply reputable but tiny house.

Having honed my short-person social skills for almost a decade, I felt confident about tackling the most discerning book business crowd from around the world when in 2006 I was invited to be part of the coveted Invitation Programme for publishers at the World Cup of the publishing industry, the Frankfurt Book Fair. The Invitation Programme has been run with great commitment by the fair for a few decades now, and it brings together publishers from the Global South under one roof (albeit of a hotel) for a few days, making it possible to interact with each other and get valuable exposure to the German publishing industry in the week before the fair. Once the fair starts, the programme generously offers stalls for each of the invited publishers, a luxury and an experience that many of us would not be able to afford otherwise.

As a result of the bonhomie during the preceding week, therefore, I was even more confident about tackling with aplomb what the fair would bring to the table. I was reassured by the number of POCs in the Invitation Programme as well as the ease with which Latin American and East European publishers could understand my challenges and aspirations, not to speak of the Middle Eastern and African ones. On the first day of the fair, climbing out of the subway and being carried up the stairs into the Messe by the colossal body of book industry people from across the world was a heady experience—I felt like I belonged to a worldwide community for the first time, something I had imagined ever since joining the industry in India and starting up my own little house. On that day, it felt tangible for the first time. Do remember, dear reader, that this was not yet the era of social media making the world a village the way it has subsequently. I did not even have a Facebook account at that point; Twitter had just opened its doors two months before and none of us knew anything about it at that point. Despite having been a postgraduate student in London in the previous decade, this experience felt like first contact with a worldwide community and industry in a way that remains memorable to this day.

The sheer size of the Messe complex left me speechless and somewhat paralysed at first. We are talking of 400,000 square metres of space with travelators to take you from one corner to another of the multiple mammoth halls hosting thousands of book stalls and meeting spaces for book people from across the world. Having found my stall after surprisingly few hurdles (German signage is legendary in effectiveness) and arranged my few first titles on its shelves, I sat back to take in my immediate environs. Even an avid smoker like myself was taken aback at the ashtrays kept thoughtfully on every table in every stall. Book people have always been smokers, but to be so liberally welcoming of smoking in a venue full of such combustible material as volumes and volumes of books was perplexing to say the least. At the rear of the event stage right next to my stall was a Lavazza stall where a lovely Italian man with twinkling eyes served the nicest coffee I would find that week—as many demi-tasses as you liked, free of cost! For a South Asian like myself, who values complimentary giveaways greatly, this was a boon. Fortified with tobacco and caffeine and feeling very much at home, I turned my attention to my specially purchased appointment book.

As soon as I had received the offer for the Invitation Programme, which was months before the actual fair, veterans in the Indian book industry had advised me to write to publishing professionals attending the fair with whom I wanted meetings. They had warned me that appointment books get jam-packed really quickly. After I had pored over the bulky fair catalogues (the print version, the reader will do well to remember) and had 20 names—I thought of them as my A-list and felt sure they would find my fledgling publishing catalogue interesting—I wrote them all what I thought was a charming email: not too effusive yet enthusiastic enough to evince interest. Two wrote back to say they had no slots left in their appointment books. By September, the month before the Buchmesse, I had progressed to List K and I had two paltry appointments per day for my five days at the Fair to show for it.

These ten precious appointments of mine were mostly with foreign rights agents of various Western publishing houses. But first, for the entirely uninitiated reader, here's some background on the most important attendee of the fair from across the world—the publishing rights agent. Non-publishing but book-reading people might be familiar with the literary agent, whose job is to represent the author and negotiate the best possible deal for them with a publisher. The foreign rights agent in a publishing house also represents the author, but indirectly via the publisher. Unlike literary agents, who usually read an author's work fairly rigorously in manuscript form, i.e., before publication, foreign rights agents mostly read an author's work after publication, as they rush to catch a flight to a book fair where they hope to sell subsidiary or translation rights for that author to other publishers from across the world. In that short transit time, they speedread all the books they are pitching at the fair and finalise the pitches for them. In many ways, therefore, you could say that they are a book agent-meets-PR person enabling the publisher/author to put their best foot forward in a foreign market. Pretty impressive job description. What it also means is that they are notoriously short on attention, almost always in a flurry of activity, hardly ever making eye contact. Once, having listened to a detailed twenty-five-minute pitch about a rights agent's titles (mostly entirely inappropriate for my list), I tried valiantly to use the last five minutes of the appointment to share details of a title on my list that I thought might work perfectly for her house. Her eyes glazed over, she slid to the edge of her seat and reminded me that this was something the editors in her house handled. There was only time to respond that I was aware of that, but since I was a cash-strapped independent South Asian publisher unlikely to visit her country any time soon and was meeting only her, would she be kind enough to carry the information sheet for said book to her editorial colleague as a favour to me. The ambiguous nod from her made me glance over at the brimming trash can in the corner of her stall, which I was sure would receive the information sheet soon after my departure. This happened to me again and again at the meetings I had set up at the fair that year. Over the years, I have learnt that I was not wrong about most unsolicited book information sheets landing in trash cans at Frankfurt.

A more singular problem that developed for me during these meetings, especially when saying hello and goodbye, was that all the agents were head and shoulders taller than me. Old demons crept into my head as I wondered if they weren't making eye contact with me because it was more convenient for them to look over my head. Or would they have taken my titles more seriously towards the end of the meeting if I had been taller? Often as a parting shot I would be told that the title I had suggested from my list might be a tad too South Asian for their house. This was usually said with an apologetic smile standing up at the end shaking hands, even as I stared up getting a crick in my neck, thinking, well, aren't the multiple titles you have pitched to me too American/French/Norwegian/German/

Swedish/Australian/New Zealander for my South Asian house! To mitigate the problem somewhat, I wore high-heeled boots on the second day to gain a few inches and be taken more seriously. That was a terrible mistake, as I found out by the end of the day. The sheer volume of walking that I had to do during the day meant that by the evening I was crumpled on a sofa baulking at the thought of the subway ride to my hotel in the suburbs of the city. By the third day I was back to wearing sensible flats, ready to be overlooked and spoken to over the top of my head.

One of the first editorial people I managed to meet at my first Buchmesse was a feminist icon of a publisher. Unfortunately, I arrived a full five minutes late to meet her (it was the day I was trying to wear heels). She was stern through most of the meeting and non-committal when I showed her our beautifully produced catalogue, except to say, "this is expensive paper; you must be rich!" I wondered whether I should tell her, no, my father does not own my company but was far too intimidated to do so: the shock and awe of her reputation, her sternness resulting from my late arrival, and the sheer sense of gratitude that she had actually agreed to meet me meant I mumbled something entirely incoherent in response to her comment.

That evening, though, when I bumped into her at the Ireland stalls for their Music and Guinness evening (yes, this happens every year), she hugged me warmly, air-kissing both my cheeks, and introduced me to another publishing woman, saying, "her books are marvellous!" Now this was a publishing agent with an American university press who bought rights to two of our books next year. I learnt then that Frankfurt is as much about the booze-ups in the evenings as the appointments. There was one of these booze-ups, sometimes more than one, every evening at some stall or the other, and I befriended people at these chaotic soirées whom I keep in touch with even today, and not just for business.

On the penultimate day of my first Frankfurt Book Fair, a distinguished-looking Englishman and his colleague who was dressed like a university student arrived at my stall, and apologised for not having fixed a prior appointment with me. They proceeded very seriously to tell me that since I am the only South Asian publisher with a sexualities (i.e., LGBTQ+) list, they felt their catalogue was perfect for me. The catalogue emerged a little later, somewhat surreptitiously, and as I started looking through it, I realised what they might brand as edgy erotica was what the burly customs officer at the Indian airport would certainly categorise as hardcore porn. I explained this conundrum to them, aside from the fact that we published LGBTQ+

writing and not erotica (to which he said that he "did not see a problem there") but they suggested I hold on to the catalogue. It was a quick learning curve for me in terms of how much Frankfurt can just be about hopes, crossed wires, lost-in-translation moments, and yet, infinite possibilities; on the last day I gave the catalogue to my Italian Lavazza kiosk friend.

A rather grim incident on the last day of the fair peppered my memories of my first time at Frankfurt. Another fellow publisher on the Invitation Programme was a charming, astoundingly professional, and heavily pregnant children's book publisher from Lebanon. On the morning of the last day, we found men in plain clothes, but clearly wearing their security credentials across their bland faces, surrounding her in her stall. It turned out that someone had reported (to whom, we never found out) that she had a book in her stall which was set in Palestine whose main protagonist was a child who had lost both his parents in the conflict. As per German law at the time it meant that her stall had to be "examined" for more "antisemitic" material, which meant that all her books were confiscated within the hour. It was horrifying to watch her stand there, tears streaming down her face, her tone determined yet helpless. Some of us on the Invitation Programme decided to quickly pen a petition criticising the Fair authorities for letting this unfortunate incident occur. A couple of friendly South Asian publishers warned me that I would never again be invited to Germany as a publisher if I did this.

I went ahead and signed the petition anyway, and received a second generous offer from the Frankfurt Book Fair to be on their Invitation Programme the subsequent year. German fairness and intellectual maturity is something I have fallen in love with over my decade and a half of travelling to that country, and to the fair.

* * *

Years later, as the captain announced that we were minutes away from landing in New Delhi, I closed my copy of *The Frankfurt Kabuff* misty-eyed, confounded, and more than a little buzzed from the dodgy wine. How could Blaire with the impossible last name have known of all my experiences from that first time in Frankfurt! Then I sprang to attention, whipped out my fair notebook and made a quick note so I would not forget to book an appointment with Adriana, now the director of Linksphilosophie Verlag, the next time I was in Frankfurt. What a chinwag we would have!

OuFiPo

Hypothetical Film Criticism (or Kabuff! *The Film Musical)*

ELIZABETH EZRA

THE FRANKFURT KABUFF IS NOT A FILM (OR AT LEAST, not yet), but what if it were? What kind of film would it be? Would it be a German Expressionist film, all dark shadows and sharp angles? Would it be a French Poetic Realist film, with shiny streets and a desperate hero hiding out from the law? Would it be an Italian neo-realist film, complete with rubble from bombings and post-war deprivation, or a Nouvelle Vague film, with a youthful sense of exhilaration, irreverence, and disregard for the cinematic conventions of its predecessors?[1] And what genre would the film be? Would it be a Western, with black- and white-hatted cowboys locked in a stand-off over world English-language rights? Or a sci-fi film, whose high-concept parallel universe can be accessed by consuming a red lipstick-coloured pill? Or a paranormal horror film about a ghostwriter roaming the corridors of the book fair in search of his kill fee? Clearly the book could be any of these kinds of film, but for the purposes of the present analysis, it will be a twenty-first-century Hollywood movie musical. This essay comprises the first known example of a new field I am calling Hypothetical Film Criticism, or the analysis of the films that books could be but are not.

Hypothetical Film Criticism builds on André Malraux's *musée imaginaire*, a museum without walls or an ideal art collection unconstrained by the usual material limitations of physical presence,[2] and made possible by the proliferation of photographic representations of art works in what Walter

Benjamin has called the age of mechanical reproduction (or the "era of mechanical reproducibility," depending which translation of the German one reads)[3] when the advent of technologies such as photography made art much more accessible to the masses. The *musée imaginaire* is a mental repository as capacious as the storage facility that houses Indiana Jones's lost ark or Charles Foster Kane's childhood sled, limited only by human beings' capacity for synthesis and imagination. Similarly, film viewers have arguably been assembling what we might call *cinématheques imaginaires* since long before the advent of online streaming services, but there is no doubt that the increasingly virtual nature of film spectatorship in the post-mechanical era has helped create the conditions of possibility for the birth of Hypothetical Film Criticism. I hope to chart not the decline but the re-imagining of materiality in the digital age by positing the (non-)existence of the *film imaginaire*, an object that paradoxically combines the inherent fungibility of post-mechanical reproduction with the utterly unique vision of a work such as Blaire Squiscoll's *The Frankfurt Kabuff* and other books (un)like it, resulting in a vast imaginary cinematic *oeuvre* that can only be described as NAFF (Not Actually Fungible Film).

The film's setting of a book fair—like the novel's—provides grist to the mill of the Kultur-Industry: a book fair industrialises culture, and a novel about a book fair adds a meta-cultural layer to the phenomenon, which is augmented by a collection of scholarly essays forming part of what will no doubt come to be known as the Frankfurt Kabuff School. The sale of film rights is one of the principal activities that takes place at a book fair—indeed, such a sale arguably represents at least one measure of a novel's success, the fulfilment of a book's cinematic potential. Each novel or novella, then, as well as being a work in its own right, would be a potential film. There is a need for a virtual or hypothetical workshop—like a sewing room, say—in which to conceive of, contemplate, and finally, stitch together the potential films that might arise from these written works before analysing (literally loosening or untying) them. The French might call such a hypothetical workshop an Ouvroir de Film Potential, or OuFiPo. Those listening carefully might hear in this suggested nomenclature echoes of the Ouvroir de Littérature Potentielle (OuLiPo), a literary movement created by French mathematicians-slash-*hommes de lettres* in the earliest days of informatics. One of the most popular examples of the genre was Raymond Queneau's *Exercices de Style*, in which the same anecdote was recounted ninety-nine times in ninety-nine different styles.[4] (It is indeed possible to imagine the same film remade ninety-nine times in ninety-nine different styles or even genres: leaving pornography to one side, one can envision *The Frankfurt Kabuff* alternatively as a buddy film, claymation action film, animated sci-fi rock opera, spaghetti western, blooper reel, airline safety film, or YouTube unboxing video.) The practitioners of OuLiPo had a particular love of lipograms (an absence made present in the last two syllables of the movement's name), literary texts that lack at least one of the letters of the alphabet (the most illustrious example being Georges Perec's *La Disparition*,[5] a novel written without the letter "e", and brilliantly translated, using the same constraint, as *A Void* by Gilbert Adair[6]). Filmic experiments with omission have been attempted by adherents of the Scandinavian film movement Dogme 95, who made films without artificial lighting, post-synchronous sound, or professional actors.[7] Similar omissions are imagined in the Robert Altman film *The Player*,[8] in which a Hollywood studio executive muses about the advantages of eliminating the screenwriter and the director from the filmmaking process. Experimental films made by Stan Brakhage and others have even done away with the need for movie cameras and projectors by inscribing images directly onto the celluloid film stock. In the digital era, of course, there is no film stock; if we want to eliminate aspects of the filmmaking process, we must find other means. In the spirit of OuFiPo, I therefore offer an extract of a screenplay without a screen, followed by an analysis without an object—in other words, what might be neologistically termed a *lipokine*, a heretofore unused word used here to describe a type of film analysis in which the film itself is absent.

* * *

IRIS FADE IN. . . .

INT. A HOTEL LOBBY. Once-elegant, slightly faded late 1900s décor. On the left side of the lobby, **BEATRICE**, a young Scorpio dressed in fashionable but wrinkled clothes, with silky, lightly mussed hair and a bright red slick of lipstick, sits at a table alone. In the main part of the lobby, several book stalls are set up; people bustle back and forth, carrying books, chatting, etc. At the far edge of the book displays, a lone policeman, tall and broad-shouldered, stands reading a copy of *Das Kapital*, his baton gently swaying from his belt. Standing with his back to the policeman is another man, wearing a trench coat and a pork pie hat, reading a copy of *Mein Kampf*.

Music plays—lush, sweeping.

A **WAITER** arrives at the young woman's table.

WAITER
Guten Abend, Fräulein.

BEATRICE
Guten Abend, Herr—Oh, I'm too tired for this. Just bring me a Negroni, please. Danke schön.

(She pushes her hand through her glossy black mane, letting it cascade over her shoulders.)

(The WAITER nods.)

BEATRICE
Oh, and waiter—where am I?

WAITER
You are at the *Buchmesse*, Madam. In Frankfurt, which is in Deutschland. Otherwise known as Germany.

BEATRICE
The *Buchmesse*? Am I REALLY??

She turns to look towards the main part of the lobby, where suddenly people stop bustling back and forth and burst into song. PUBLISHERS begin spinning revolving book displays, slowly at first.

PUBLISHERS
We have come to make some deals
This is how adventure feels
Audio and ebook sales
'tis the stuff of fairy tales

The spinning speeds up, as does the film editing, which alternates between showing the whole group and focusing on one publisher at a time.

Rights and acquisitions
Agents and submissions
Royalties and licence fees
We must always think of these
When we make a deeeeeaaaaaaal

CHORUS (singing in a whisper)
Kabuff Kabuff Kabuff Kabuff
Kabuff Kabuff Kabuff Kabuff

AGENTS (while scrolling on their phones)
Want a high-performing book?
You'll just have to take a look
At the latest rising star
Who you'll see is not that far
AWAAAAAAAY

CHORUS (whisper growing louder)
Kabuff Kabuff Kabuff Kabuff
Kabuff Kabuff Kabuff Kabuff

ALL
Buying, selling
Lying, telling
It's all happening at the fair
Come and look round if you dare
You'll find books and fun galore
Rights deals, auctions, and much more

CHORUS (pointing to one corner)
Just don't venture over there
In the book fair's secret lair:
(in a louder whisper, culminating in crescendo)
KABUFF! KABUFF! KABUFF! KABUFF!

(OPENING TITLES)

* * *

The film's major themes and motifs (which echo those of the novel) are all encapsulated in the pre-credit sequence—publishing, book fairs, Negronis, red lipstick, storage closets, and both left- and far right-wing politics. Where the film diverges from the novel, however, is in its delay in introducing the chicken shop backstory, which the audience is only made aware of gradually through the use of flashback. This initial lack of context leads the audience to wonder about the origins of Beatrice's insecurities, whereas in the book these origins are at least hinted at in the very beginning. Another departure from the book—the relocation of the book fair to *the very hotel in which Beatrice is staying*—restores the Aristotelian unity of place that is lacking in the novel. What might be called the "re-unification" of place, in deference to the Germanic setting, offsets the elimination of the word "Frankfurt" in the film's title, though the emphasis on the word "Kabuff" retains the Teutonic overtones of the original. The inclusion of an exclamation point can be seen as a nod to musicals such as *Oliver!*, *Oklahoma!*, and *Hello, Dolly!*, alerting viewers that they are in for a whole lot of fun.

The song lyrics alone in this opening musical number raise a number of questions. Is the invitation to "Come and look round if you dare" in the stanza sung by the ensemble cast a solicitation of ~~physical presence~~ (of course, ~~under erasure~~), or is it rather a self-conscious reference to "looking round," or reading around the literal meaning of a word or phrase? Or is "looking round" merely an allusion to the effect of the camera itself, which as we all know adds at least ten pounds? Surely the answers to these questions reside in their unknowability, their endless deferral of meaning, and their ultimate lack of origin (with the exception of the extra ten pounds, which originates in strudel).

The dance numbers in the film are fairly conventional, from "The Dance of the Foreign Rights," which features a succession of co-agents in national dress, to "Slush," in which an editorial intern skis down a mountain of unsolicited manuscripts as they begin to degrade over time. A number of numbers are witty homages to well-known predecessors, such as the rousing *Fiddler-on-the-Roof*-style "Commission" and the thundering rock-musical number "The Chicken Shop of Horrors." As the intricate choreography unfolds, the camera is as much a dance partner as a witness, a dynamic participant-observer that puts the *kino* in cinema and the flash in fiction.

The upbeat tempo of the opening number is matched by rhythmic editing. This stylistic choice evokes an MTV aesthetic in alignment with the late-1900s décor of the hotel in which the book fair takes place. The film's use of rapid editing also engages in Bakhtinian dialogue with André Bazin's famous predilection for the long take, ultimately privileging the montage theory advanced by the Soviet School of the 1920s or, as Bazin would put it, "those directors who put their faith in the image."[9] It might seem somewhat paradoxical that faith in the image is so much in evidence in what is, essentially, an invisible film, but it is precisely this paradox that Hypothetical Film Criticism seeks to explore.

Unusually for a film musical, this non-existent production did not begin life as a Broadway or West End play. There is cinematic precedent for skipping this step (*La La Land*[10] springs to mind) but doing so is a bold choice on the part of Alan Smithee, a director who has no prior musical experience. The fact that Kim Kardashian, who plays Beatrice Deft, has had her songs dubbed by Ozzy Osbourne, recalls the character Lina Lamont in *Singin' in the Rain*,[11] whose grating speaking voice is dubbed by dulcet-toned chorus girl Kathy (Debbie Reynolds). Regé-Jean Page, who plays the policeman in *Kabuff!*, is dubbed by Instagram influencer and K-Pop band member Jungkook. It is only Tom Cruise, who plays the waiter, whose voice has not been suppressed.

Speaking of suppression, we must not neglect to address the sexual politics of *Kabuff!*: is the metaphor of the Kabuff a none-too-subtle allusion to coming out of the closet? A Kabuff is used to store what is excess to requirements, that which cannot be contained within the pre-established boundaries of conformity. It is perhaps no accident that the word "Kabuff" is a neuter noun in German, a non-binary expression of undecidability, neither either/or nor neither/nor, but rather none or all of the above. Then, too, the Kabuff could represent the hidden recesses of the *Unheimlich*, an apparently strange but ultimately all-too-familiar space that, according to Freud, triggers the return of the repressed and transports us back to our ontological origins in our mother's womb (or in Beatrice's case, the chicken shop), literalising the painful trip of nostalgia (*nostos, algos*). We've all been there.

Alternatively, the late-1900s décor of the hotel in the hypothetical film version of *The Frankfurt Kabuff* hints at the possible evocation of fin-de-siècle film theory, which, at least in the transatlantic tradition, revolves around Mulveyan conceptions of visual pleasure and Lacanian phallocentrism.[12] Smithee's rendering of Beatrice Deft does nothing to dispel Mulvey's contention that female characters in Hollywood cinema function primarily in terms of their to-be-looked-atness, harnessing the (presumably heterosexual) male gaze. The augmentation of the waiter role in the cinematic adaptation, to say nothing of the creative licence that allowed Tom Cruise to play the part without a shirt, does provide an alternative model of scopophilia to rival that proposed by Mulvey, but nonetheless the position within the film of Beatrice—with her ever-present slick of bright red lipstick—reminds us that the castration complex is never far behind.

In a nod to the eco-friendly demands of the present climate, the film has the Deft character traveling from Australia to Frankfurt by boat, rather than by plane. The film could have gone further by depicting the book fair as a strictly online event dealing only in ebooks. However, it is important to recognise that progress comes slowly, and to praise any recognition of impending ecological disaster as a step in the right direction. (The fact that the film's premiere was entirely virtual, too, goes some way towards correcting some of the film's diegetic missteps.)

Conclusion

From this brief inaugural contribution to an entirely new field of study, we might draw the following set of conclusions. First, it has become apparent that Hypothetical Film Theory is different from the study of unproduced screenplays, because it is at one more remove from any actual production, adding another layer of distance that is perfectly suited to the virtual era, in which an increasing number of activities are conducted remotely. Second, the well-established field of Adaptation Studies must itself, in the interest of inclusivity, be (hypothetically) adapted to include hypothetical adaptations. Finally, it is pleasing to note that OuLiPo lives on in its filmic (dis-)incarnation, OuFiPo, which, it is to be hoped, will inspire as many potential films, and as many academic analyses of those films, as there are cloud storage devices—or virtual Kabuffs—in which to house the digital offprints.

Notes

1 For defining characteristics and discussions of these film movements, see Elizabeth Ezra, ed., *European Cinema* (New York: Oxford University Press, 2004).

2 André Malraux, *Le Musée Imaginaire* (1947; repr., Paris: Gallimard, 1965).

3 Walter Benjamin, "The Work of Art in the Age of Mechanical Reproduction," in *Illuminations*, ed. Hannah Arendt, trans. Harry Zohn (1935; repr., New York: Schocken Books, 1969), 217–51.

4 Raymond Queneau, *Exercices de Style* (Paris: Gallimard, 1947).

5 Georges Perec, *La Disparition* (Paris: Gallimard, 1969).

6 Georges Perec, *A Void*, trans. Gilbert Adair (London: The Harvill Press, 1995).

7 Among the best-known Dogme 95 films are *Festen*, directed by Thomas Vinterberg (Denmark, 1998; London: Metrodome Video, 2019) and *The Idiots*, directed by Lars von Trier (Denmark, 1999; London: Tartan Video, 2000).

8 *The Player*, directed by Robert Altman (1992; New York, NY: Criterion Collection, 2016), DVD.

9 Andre Bazin, "The Evolution of the Language of Cinema," in *Film Theory and Criticism: Introductory Readings*, ed. Leo Braudy and Marshall Cohen, 5th edition (Oxford: Oxford University Press, 1999), 24.

10 *La La Land*, directed by Damien Chazelle (2016; Santa Monica, CA: Lions Gate Home Entertainment, 2017), DVD.

11 *Singin' in the Rain*, directed by Gene Kelly and Stanley Donen (1952; Burbank, CA: Warner Home Video, 2000), DVD.

12 Laura Mulvey, "Visual Pleasure and Narrative Cinema," *Screen* 16, no. 3 (Autumn 1975): 6–18.

How to Take Over a Book Fair

A Bourdieusian Fiction

ROANNA GONSALVES

FIRST, FILL IN THE ONLINE FORMS AND SAVE YOUR DATA. Remember that marked fields are mandatory fields. Ignore the fact that you are a fish out of water, stuck in a Kabuff, in a kind of field that is in a Dom/Sub relationship with the book fair. The Kabuff is a Sub to the field of the book fair which is a Sub to the field of cultural production which is a Sub to the field of power which is a Sub to the field of class relations. You want to claim your rightful place as a Dom.

Next, provide some information about yourself. Log in and choose your truth. Are you a journalist? Are you a rights manager? Are you an author? Ignore the fact that these practices always contain within them many double truths, often difficult to hold together. Sometimes you are a journalist, sometimes a rights manager, and, when no one's looking, you're writing a comic erotic thriller here in this riverside city.

You must provide a form of verification that can be examined. The invocation of "buzz" will not do. You could claim to be a White saviour, providing proof that you have emancipated people of colour by having published at least one non-White writer, or their neighbour, at some point in the last four centuries. You could claim to give voice to the voiceless, wielding re-orientalised translations full of spicy biryani, deep longings for lullabies sung in the languages of Asia, Africa, and Australia. Such virtue-signalling has always worked for others. But you are unable to ignore the voice in your head any longer. It whispers incessantly, "Shared misrecognition. Shared misrecognition. Shared misrecognition."

Enough is enough. You will not be relegated to the Kabuff any longer, this spidery space where nothing happens. You long for liberty, for the freedom to do as you please, to be a Dom again. You look for the light switch and turn on the light. Suddenly you are a fish out of water no more. You see water all around you and many other fish in it too. They are not voiceless. They are gagged. They do not know the way to the top. In the light, they tear off their gags. They begin to speak again, in Taiwanese, in Santhali, in Pitjantjatjara, in words that you do not understand. You are sure they are not singing lullabies. The multilingual fish at your elbow translates for you: "What is the book fair without international rights? They need us more than we need them."

So you clear your throat and begin to declaim a speech you have prepared, just in case of such emergencies. Your words will galvanise these fish and will break the field. Your words will spur these fish on to first take over Hall 8 where the English-language publishers are revelling in enchanted dependence. Then, who knows, maybe Hall 9 too. You begin to speak. "Let us rise up, fellow fish, against reductionism, against mystique, and against exoticisation. Let us proclaim that all language is euphemistic. Let us take over Hall 8 where the English-language publishers congregate."

But no one budges. The other fish carry on their conversations, clearly disinterested in what you are saying. They seem to have their own agenda. You sense that their conversations are becoming more hectic. Some fish begin to do the Nae Nae and some do the Chicken Dance. Some do the Macarena while a fish on the periphery is doing pilates, working on their core. Then some fish talk over each other in seamless braids of voice and yearning. Maybe they didn't hear you.

Your clear your throat and start again. "Fellow fish, I come before you today to tell you that this is an upside-down world. The book fair is the economic world reversed. But is it really? Rise up, fellow fish and let us take over Hall 8 where…"

The voices around you grow louder, not with applause but with heckling. The light starts to flicker and suddenly it goes out. The darkness seems to embolden the fish. The rise and fall of their voices are unmistakable in their discontent. When you look around in confusion, the multilingual fish is kind enough to translate for you again. "That group of blue fish over there are asking in Igbo, why only Hall 8? The orange fish is shouting in Bengali that they too know that taste classifies and it classifies the classifier. The pair of red fish in the centre are saying in Wiradjuri, 'Why are you dreaming so small?'"

"But what is the little yellow fish saying?" I ask.

"The little yellow fish is saying in Malayalam, 'we don't want to go to Hall 8. We want Hall 8 to come to us. We want the whole book fair to come to us.'"

"What? Here? To the Kabuff?"

"That is what the yellow fish is saying."

"But this is such a messy space of..."

"The yellow fish is saying, 'this is a space of possibilities.'"

Suddenly, as if by the sheer will power of the fish around you, the lights turn on. The walls of the Kabuff melt away. The Kabuff expands outwards and upwards as if swallowing all the other space before it. All obstacles fall away. The barriers between the book fair and the Kabuff, between the autonomous and the heteronomous, between the fish in water and the fish out of water melt into the air of this riverside city.

The fish around you are now one with the book fair.

The fish begin to sing in Swahili, in Konkani, in Arabic, in Warlpiri, in Mandarin, and even in Gaelic. Their songs do not sound like lullabies. Their words are incomprehensible but somehow they all sound like they were made from each other, for each other, by each other.

You can hear the ancient river under their melodies. It is a river connected to all other rivers through the seas.

You realise you have been on the wrong quest.

You lie back as the fair takes over you.

Tagging Beatrice

Fanfic as Reader Response

DANIELLE FULLER

ON 7 SEPTEMBER 2021 COCKTAIL SUPERSTAR JANIELLE Frak interrupted her extensive Zoom tour of mixology symposia to announce her intention to publish a short piece of fan fiction on the social media platform Twitter. Like many a celebrity-turned-author before her, Frak employed her social capital, in particular her friendship with bestselling author Blaire Squiscoll, to attract followers to her new account. As she entered the literary field, albeit via the subcultural practice of writing fan fiction (or "fanfic"), Frak brought with her the cachet of the exclusive cocktail bar and the prestige of a professional at the top of her game. Calling upon lovers of Negronis, Frak's first post also hailed readers of Blaire Squiscoll's *The Frankfurt Kabuff*—a move that attracted a boutique group of followers. Their "likes," occasional comments, and bookish cocktail requests indicated their enthusiasm for both erotic thrillers set against the background of the international publishing industry, and gin-based beverages. Meanwhile, Frak's own fan reader responses to and enthusiasm for Blaire Squiscoll's oeuvre emerged in her adoption of the genre tropes and character traits that have brought her friend's books notoriety and acclaim in multiple formats.

Frak posted three tweets with explicit book reading themes in an effort to obtain followers, before offering her niche audience three teasers for her upcoming fan fiction. Her story was framed as an homage to the publications of her best friend, topically themed to highlight Canada's upcoming role as the Guest of Honour at the 2021 Frankfurt Book Fair. In these teaser posts (reproduced below), Frak cheekily whetted her followers' appetite for Beatrice-oriented adventures, while also blatantly advertising her mixology skills. The enigma of Frak's Twitter profile tagline, "Beatrice Deft is not a wine drinker," thus began to dissolve as rapidly as the cubes of ice in the elaborately decorated Caesar depicted in the third teaser post. After courting some controversy from Canadian followers and vegan readers with regards to the meaty garnish adorning said Caesar, Frak pressed on with her fan fiction, posting daily episodes between 13 and 21 September 2021. Once her story about Beatrice's Canadian adventure was complete, Frak thanked her followers on 22 September, and then…silence.

What Ullapoolist shenanigans could be at work here?

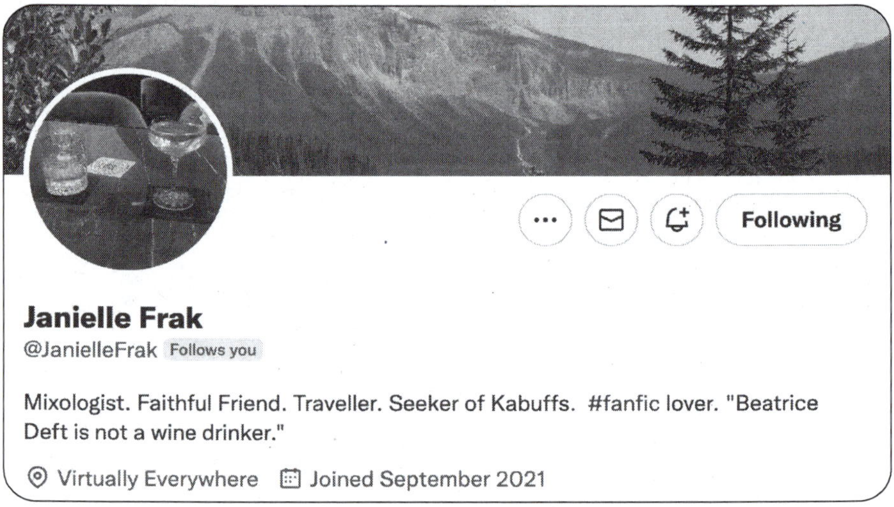

Janielle Frak's Twitter profile. Credit: Danielle Fuller.

Teaser 1

A cancelled #Buchmesse. Lost rights sales. A year of speculation. A second chance as the guest nation suddenly under threat. Only one International Publishing Consultant can save Canada's moment in the spotlight. But where is Beatrice? #FrankfurtKabuff #fanfic @BlaireSquiscoll.

PHOTO: A vintage fountain pen lying on top of two notebooks stacked on top of each other. Alongside the pen is a pile of pink sticky notes. The visible note has handwriting on it which reads "Maple Sugar? Castle."

Teaser 2

It's not easy being an International Publishing Consultant during a pandemic. Traveling is complicated. Access to #Kabuffs is limited. Will Beatrice abandon her watery adventures with Caspian to take on Canada's #Buchmesse mission? Stay tuned…@BlaireSquiscoll and friends.

PHOTO: An archway made of stone jutting out into the ocean from a cliff.

Teaser 3

Beatrice Deft is not a wine drinker. #Negronis are her signature. But maybe a Caesar would tempt her away from her travels so that she can secure Canada's success at the #Frankfurt #Buchmesse 2021? What do you think @BlaireSquiscoll? [2 followers tagged] et al?

PHOTO: A Caesar with a meat-and-olive garnish in a glass with a salted rim.

The fanfic

1. The Call. Beatrice was in the midst of some intense multimodal #reading when her phone buzzed insistently. "Stolen USB drive. Recovery urgent. Tickets & tests booked." A knock at the hotel door confirmed the message: a bulky envelope (Italian stock) on the threshold. A mission.

PHOTO: A headset, e-reader, and hardback book stacked on top of each other on a wooden table.

2. The Journey. After the palaver of tests, checks & questions that had come to characterize pandemic travel, Beatrice was relieved to be #enroute. @AirCanada food was as terrible as ever which was oddly reassuring. She pulled out the ever-excellent magazine. A note fluttered out.

PHOTO: A plastic cup of orange juice, a bag of pretzels, a branded paper serviette and an autographed copy of *The Frankfurt Kabuff* laid out on an airline at-seat table.

3. The Arrival. Beatrice admired the grandeur of her surroundings. Not averse to rough quarters, she was so jetlagged she would happily sleep in a #kabuff. She glanced at the scrap of #Rhodia paper again. "#pandemicbookshelves, 6pm." First a nap: she needed to sharpen her wits.

PHOTO: An ornate chandelier hangs from a decorated plaster ceiling which is painted white.

4. The Puzzle. Beatrice applied her red lipstick & left her room in search of #pandemicbookshelves. A quick glance at the hotel plan confirmed that this gothic labyrinth of a building did not have a library. Hmmmm…maybe a #Negroni would help? Et voilà! A shelf in the bar! 5.55pm.

PHOTO: An arrangement of contemporary Canadian books (spines outward) on a wooden shelf with an owl-shaped wooden bookend on the left-hand side.

5. The Stranger. Beatrice sighed in frustration. She had skimmed all the books, admired their design & snappy blurbs. Why was she sent to these #pandemicbookshelves? A deep voice broke through her musings: "An impressively diverse selection of #Canadian writing, eh?" She looked up.

PHOTO: Two wing-backed upholstered chairs at an angle from each other are facing a large window. The view from the window is of snow-capped mountains and spruce trees. A White human hand rests on the arm of one of the chairs.

6. The mixologist. "Ms Deft?" Beatrice's gaze met eyes as blue as a prairie summer sky. "I see you are not a wine drinker," the tall server continued, placing a fantastical concoction next to her #Negroni. "On the house, or, rather, for the future of the #Buchmesse, Beatrice…"

PHOTO: Two cocktails on a marble table. One is clearly the Negroni, while the other is in a champagne coupe with a pink candy floss garnish.

Screenshot of episode 7 as it appeared on Twitter. Credit: Danielle Fuller.

7. The Clue. Beatrice was feeling a little tipsy. She mustn't lose sight of her mission. Something to do with saving Canada's guest spot at the #FrankfurtBuchmesse? But how? "The Summer Colophon—a classic in sideways thinking," the server murmured as another cocktail appeared.

PHOTO: In the foreground a small wooden side table on top of which lies a copy of *The Frankfurt Kabuff*, an e-reader, and a bookmark. Also on the table, a tall martini-style cocktail glass with a lemon garnish: the Summer Colophon. In the near background a comfortable-looking black leather chair is partially visible.

[various accounts are tagged] Why not join Beatrice? To make a #SummerColophon, pour equal amounts of booze shown below into a shaker, mix and add a dash of orange bitters, plus a lemon garnish.

PHOTO: depicts bottles of gin, sweet vermouth, Lillet, St Germain, and bitters.

8. The Castle. "Not a wine drinker...sideways thinking." Looking into those sky blue eyes, Beatrice finally understood her mission. The object that could save Canada's 2021 #Buchmesse guest spot was hidden nearby. She immediately began her search, moving from room to room...

PHOTO: An empty ballroom with a decorated blue ceiling and stripes of sunlight crossing the wooden floor.
PHOTO: A balcony with three large windows and a series of lit chandeliers.
PHOTO: A darkly lit corridor with an archway visible and illuminated at the far end of it.

..."not a wine drinker...not a wine drinker." Beatrice paused at the top of the corridor and tilted her head. So many rooms and odd signs. So many possibilities... @BlaireSquiscoll and friends. #FrankfurtKabuff #fanfic.

9. The Kabuff. A loud crash startled Beatrice. Her instincts made her run, though her high heels were hardly ideal for a caper. Another crash: breaking glass? Voices coming nearer. She looked around for a place to hide. That's when she saw it: a Weinkabuff. No time to waste! 1/2

PHOTO: A large wooden door flanked by extensive wine racks.

> 2/2. Closing the door behind her, Beatrice found herself inside a space packed with an impressive collection of international wines. A brief memory of #Buchmesses past, of parties & booze, of a coat rack and…a thrilling shudder ran down her spine. She began to study the labels…
>
> PHOTO: A close-up of wrought-iron doors.

10. The Plan. Beatrice studied the wine labels more closely, admiring the different fonts. Aha! Nestling among two #BC wines was a small parcel. Her heart beat wildly. She grabbed the bundle and ripped off the wrapping. Success! The stolen USB! Now what? First, a pick-me-up 1/3

PHOTO: A purple drink in a champagne coupe on a black slate table.

> 2/3. After the excitement of the Weinkabuff, Beatrice was relieved to have a break. Sipping on her Rundle Bar gin-inspired cocktail, she surveyed the room. Two be-suited women were peering at a computer screen. Beatrice decided to take a risk and ask them for help.
>
> 3/3. "Hello, could I?" Beatrice waved the USB, hoping she hadn't made a grave mistake. "Be our guest," the brunette replied. Beatrice opened the file. "Incredible!" gasped the blonde woman, "A plan to banish #manels from the 2021 #Buchmesse." She hit send. Canada's guest spot is saved!
>
> PHOTO: An assemblage of four photos, two mountain landscape scenes, and two photos of food and drinks—one of which is a Negroni.

And so, thanks to a borrowed computer and the quick-thinking actions of our heroine, Beatrice Deft, the emergency email is sent just in time to rescue Canada's pandemic-deferred guest-of-honour spot at the Frankfurt Book Fair. And with a gulp of Deft's signature Negroni cocktail, so too ends Janielle Frak's *Kabuff* fan fiction…

In common with most fanfic, Frak's Twitterfic combined characters and plot tropes from the original with a new setting and situation—as if Deft were moving through an alternative, but parallel, universe. Frak's familiarity with the style and content of her friend Blaire Squiscoll's oeuvre enabled her to play with the text, while the affordances of her publishing platform (Twitter) shaped the short, episodic structure of her fan fiction. Images provided another means of communicating the story's location and, in some cases, offered semiotic complexity. Other features such as hashtags and tagging alerted followers and potential readers, and invited engagement and potential direct interaction with Frak and her story. Frak can be understood to be "Tagging Beatrice" in two senses—through technical actions and through her creative pursuit of the glamorous publishing consultant protagonist made (in)famous by *The Frankfurt Kabuff* and other Beatrice-centric adventure stories.

While Frak's Twitter account remains on the platform, Frak herself appears to have left the literary field as speedily as she entered it. Perhaps she accepted an invitation to Canada's guest night at the Frankfurt Book Fair where no doubt she would have been called upon to produce a signature drink honouring the feature country's literary wares? Or maybe Janielle's talents were required elsewhere, for example, at an emergency meeting of the International Mixologists' Association for Beverage Excellence (IMABE)? Maybe other readers will respond with their own stories of international travel, enticing closets, and complicated cocktails? Whatever the case, let us raise a Summer Colophon in Janielle Frak's name and as a thank you to her for reminding readers everywhere of the important fanfic mantra, "because it's not over until we say it is!"

Kabuff or Wunderkammer?

Review of The Frankfurt Kabuff, *Blaire Squiscoll, 2019*

KELVIN SMITH[1]

FICTIONAL PUBLISHERS OFTEN APPEAR AT INTERNATIONAL book fairs. The setting gives writers the chance to introduce new characters, engineer plot twists, and inject the frisson of drunken conversations and illicit sex. *The Frankfurt Kabuff*, Blaire Squiscoll's recent work, adds a new twist to this, functioning as a mesmerising deconstruction of what it means to be a publisher and what it means to hang out with publishers at such events. It combines many old publishing tropes, sometimes seeming to be more of a *Wunderkammer* than a *Kabuff*.

The central character, Beatrice Deft, is not a publisher but someone who loves books and believes in their power to change lives. She is old school: she smokes, she drinks, she eats meat (there is a flashback subplot of violence against an immigrant at a chicken shop in Australia—don't ask), she flies. Deft enjoys sex (and Sekt) with Caspian, the hunky German cop, of whom we learn little except for his badge number (6969) and the way he wields his impressive baton.

After a violent intervention by the right-wingers surrounding a publishing firm called White Storm—put down with the help of Tante Fran and the knitting book club—the old left-wing publisher Kurt Weidenfeld steps down from his position at Linksphilosophie Verlag in favour of Adriana, Lotte Frankel takes over from the wannabe demagogue Kristoff Weil, and Beatrice begins a new career as an International Publishing Consultant, travelling the world to protect international books from future terrorist attacks. The publishing patriarchy is being overturned.

As Beatrice prepares to jet off on her new mission, the familiar figure of a strapping blond catches her attention. There will be further adventures, but they had better hurry, because this old world of international publishing will soon be brought to a juddering halt, not, as this story suggests, by the threat of right-wing terrorism, but by the surveillance state it has created, the security apparatus it spawned, and—in this time of climate breakdown—the impossibility of sustaining all that smoking, drinking, meat-eating and carbon-fuelled travel that are at the core of the international book fair circuit.

Notes

1. This review was originally published by the author. See Kelvin Smith, "Kabuff or Wunderkammer?" *The Point of Publishing* (blog), July 5, 2019, https://pointofpublishing.com/2019/07/05/kabuff-or-wunderkammer/, and is reproduced with the permission of the author.

Using *The Frankfurt Kabuff* in the Classroom

ALASTAIR HORNE

Introduction

THE FOLLOWING ACTIVITY CAN BE USED TO GENERATE conversation around *The Frankfurt Kabuff*, the Frankfurt Book Fair, and book cultures more generally. It was originally used in Autumn 2020 as an icebreaker at the start of the academic year, forming the basis for an engaging low-stakes activity to build student familiarity with each other and with the systems that would be used for teaching online.

Notes for students

The Frankfurt Kabuff is a (very) short satirical novel set at the Frankfurt Book Fair, written by the mysterious Blaire Squiscoll. Here are some suggested questions that could be used in a classroom context in order.

Discussion questions

1. "'You are going to the Book Fair?" said the cab driver. "I have an idea for a book I've always wanted to write since I arrived here from Turkey. ... It's David Nicholls' *One Day* meets Harry Potter. Two young wizards meet on the same day, July 31st, every year, for 20 years. It will appeal to young adults around the world!'" (page 45 of this edition)
    i. What's the worst "X meets Y" publishing mash-up you can imagine?
    ii. Can you think of any real-life terrible examples?

2. "I know it is old-fashioned ... but I prefer to read on paper." (page 73)
    i. Weidenfeld's preference for reading on paper saves his life. Has a book ever saved your life (metaphorically or literally)? How?
    ii. What's your preferred reading format—print, ebooks, audiobooks, a mixture, or something else?

3. "remembering the technique from a novel, [she] twisted her hand into the minder's pocket, extracted the key without him noticing. She smiled to herself, thinking at last she had something to thank Dickens for..." (page 56)
    i. Have you ever learned something useful from a novel? What was it? How did it come in useful?

4. "'We have book club this afternoon. ... We have a Goodreads page if you want to join us virtually.'" (page 79)
    i. Do you have a Goodreads account, a Bookstagram, BookTube, or Twitter account, a blog, or a Tumblr? Are you willing to share details so that other students can follow you?
    ii. What enjoyment or benefits do you get from these?

5. "Even with its careful paratextual apparatus, she feared the worst from this incendiary volume." (page 61)
    i. "Paratext" is a term coined by French literary critic Gérard Genette and refers to a whole range of elements that transform a text into a book, from the cover and title page to the

font and footnotes. Are there any interesting paratexts in any of your books?

6. "You know, perhaps, that the publishing industry is changing in the twenty-first century. No longer do roles sit in well-defined categories, such as editing, sales, marketing, and production. Increasingly, we have need for people with … diverse skills. Skills such as yours." (page 79)
    i. In Beatrice's case, "diverse skills" does not mean an ability to use XML or WordPress so much as her "ability to chart a moral path between the freedom to publish and the need to support marginalised voices"(!). What special skills do you have that might be useful in publishing?

Note

1. 87 pages.

Assemblages

ORIGINAL PLOT DIAGRAM DRAWN AT THE FRANKFURT HAUPTBAHNHOF, 2019.

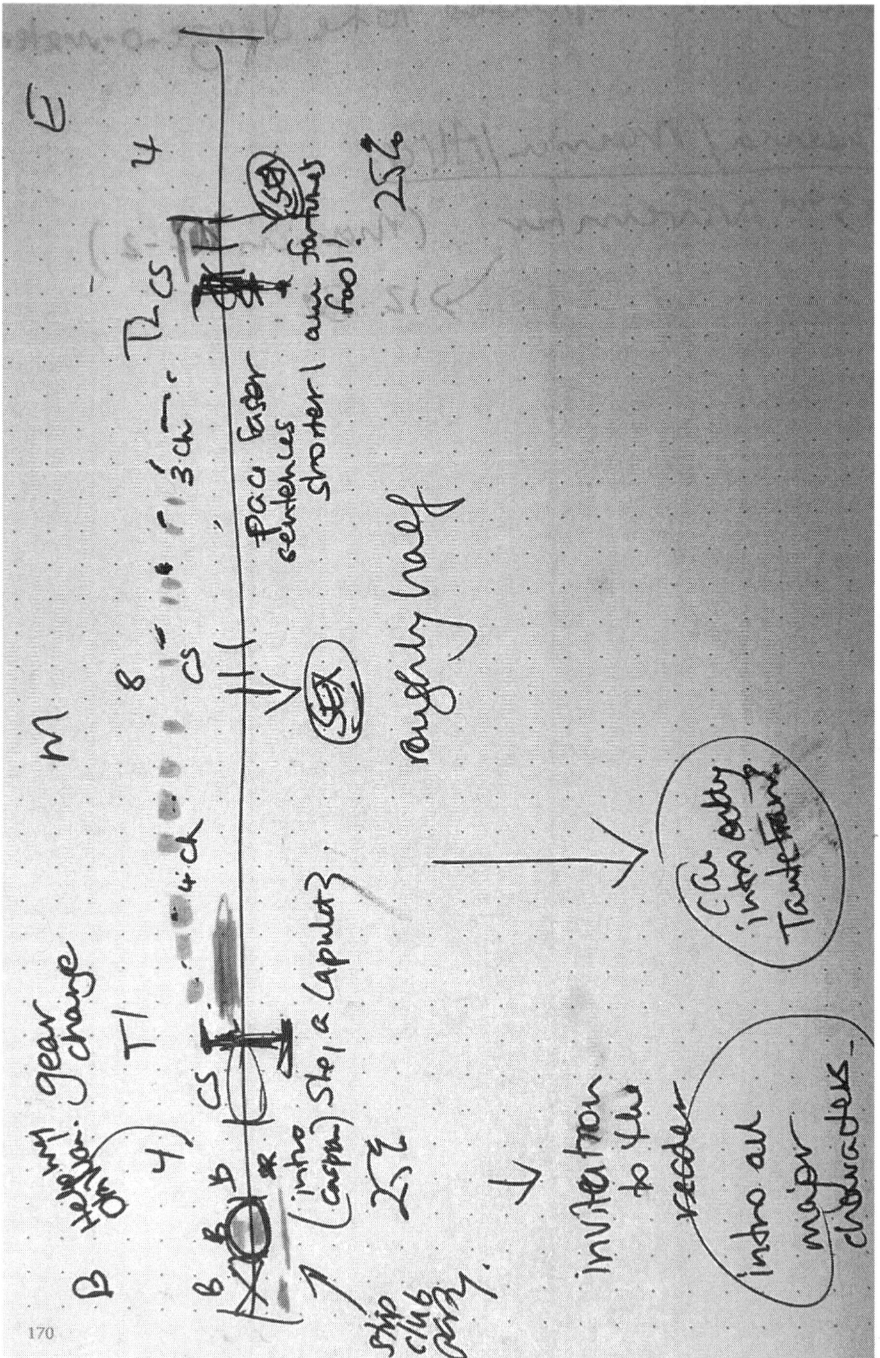

Credit: Kim Wilkins.

Paratextual Elements of *The Frankfurt Kabuff* Print-on-Demand Edition

THE 2019 PRINT-ON-DEMAND EDITION OF *THE FRANKFURT Kabuff* included a number of additional paratextual elements, some of which are included here within the assemblages rather than in the annotated text. These elements include the cover's front and back cover copy, details about the publisher, and the publisher's colophon. The acknowledgements and "ÜBER AUTHOR" have been incorporated into updated biographical information for this critical edition. The "MAP OF FUTURE NOVELS" is included later in the assemblages.

Front cover:

Blaire Squiscoll
The Frankfurt Kabuff
A Beatrice Deft Thriller
Writing and Reading Books Is the Easy Part

Back Cover:

The Frankfurt Kabuff
After a difficult winter, Beatrice Deft is on vacation in Frankfurt during European Autumn, staying at the Hessischer Hof enjoying the quiet of cosmopolitan Germany. When violence breaks out at the stands of the

far-right publishers across the road at the Frankfurt Book Fair, Beatrice tells herself it isn't her problem. But now police patrol the aisles with guns and batons, and queues form at security bag checks, and an old family friend begs for her help. Then she meets Caspian, the very hot policeman with a baton, and finds herself wondering, What is the secret of the Kabuff?

"Stunning in every sense of the word"—Kim Wilkins

From Kabuff Books, first publisher of the Ullapoolism Movement, comes the publishing of a bold new voice

ÜBER KABUFF BOOKS

Kabuff Books was established in 2018, and is an Ullapoolist make-and-do project. For more information, see https://ullapoolism.wordpress.com/

Kabuff Books Colophon

"Dear Diary"

An Account of the Production of the Print-on-Demand Self-Published Edition of The Frankfurt Kabuff

THE FOLLOWING DIARY ENTRIES WERE WRITTEN IN 2019 by Beth Driscoll and Claire Squires to record their autoethnographic experiences as self-publishers and researchers of contemporary publishing. It begins *in media res* as *The Frankfurt Kabuff* is uploaded to digital publishing platforms, and trails off as the distribution process begins. The diary illustrates in kaleidoscopic detail the minutiae involved in the supposedly frictionless process of digital publishing as well as this process's integration with print objects and social relations. Names have been anonymised through the use of initials, which have then been encoded via the key SUPERCALIFRAGILISTICEXPIALIDOCIOUS (which incidentally contains the word ULLAPOOLIST).

Sunday 26 May

Dear Diary,
Following a Facebook comment from S about not being able to see *The Frankfurt Kabuff* on Nielsen PubEasy, I looked back through emails from the Nielsen ISBN store and discovered an extremely helpful message about adding ISBNs to the Nielsen Title Editor, and also information about Legal Deposit in the UK.

I hotfooted it over to Nielsen Title Editor and started to register. Almost immediately I was confused by the "Organisation Type" drop-down box. Is Kabuff Books a Publisher or a Self-Distributing Publisher? Fortunately I then realised there was a "Combination of These Types" category so I plumped for that.

Then it said:

> The Title Editor service is ideally suited to organisations of a certain size. To help us establish if this is the right service for you, please provide estimates for the following:
>
> Approximately how many of your publications are currently available or approximately how many unique ISBNs is your organisation responsible for that are currently on sale?

It does not say what that "certain size" is so I don't know if we'll make the cut. It also asked if we are doing print only or digital only or both. There wasn't a drop-down box for Oh Look a Ferry so I just said both. I then registered, and was informed that it will take five to ten working days to have our registration confirmed and username and password issued. This is nail-biting.

Yours
Claire

Monday 27 May

Dear Diary,
Today I wanted to order several copies of *The Frankfurt Kabuff*, so that I could start distributing it to the Australia-based street team and influencers. I noticed slightly different per unit prices, depending on the number I ordered. For 50 copies, the per unit price was $3.54. For 100 copies, it was $3.34. For 10,000 copies, it was $2.75. Of course then the shipping price increased.

Forgive a meta-textual moment, dear diary, but I wonder if a spreadsheet would be a better format for recording this information, rather than a journal?

The wind howls outside. Its icy blasts tear the last brown leaves from the spindly tree that abuts the John Medley building. The sky is grey, grey, grey. I fear Australian winter has arrived.

Yours
Beth

Monday 27 May

Dear Diary,
Claire here. Self-publishing is TREMENDOUSLY exciting, particularly when you get print copies and not so much per se smell them but more like get the covers a little bit greasy in restaurants and signing copies for friends.

However, there are still challenges ahead. How do books ACTUALLY end up in bookshops?

I am about to take the Ingram Spark "How it Works: Master Print and Digital Self-Publishing" quiz (strapline, "Do you have what it takes to publish like a pro? Take the quiz to find out!" (https://www.ingramspark.com/how-it-works).

As with my previous entry, I have some anxiety about whether the verdict will be that I don't have what it takes. But I have resolved my nerves. Think of me, dear diary.

The first page invites me to "Discover [my] publishing IQ."

- Whether you've been publishing for years or are fresh on the indie scene, this quiz lets you know where you are on the publishing spectrum:
  Professional, Skilled, or Novice
- When all is said and done—regardless of where you fall—you'll receive resources to help you on your way to independent publishing prestige.

"Fresh on the indie scene" sounds a bit dodge, but INDEPENDENT PUBLISHING PRESTIGE! I could do with some of that.

The quiz has asked me what metadata is, and BISAC codes is one of the tick box possibilities. I KNOW THIS ANSWER, yes go me!

These questions are challenging, in a good way:

What do "best-sellers" have in common?

- Strong author platform
- Quality content
- Book reviews
- Great cover design
- Professional editing
- Catchy title
- I'm not sure

What should your BISAC code be?

- Three different main subject headings
- One main subject heading three times
- General category of your book
- Specific category of your book
- Similar to books in your genre
- The same for all formats of your book (eBook, paperback, hardcover)
- I'm not sure

The quiz wants to email me my results which is a bit annoying.

I pretended I knew the answers for the first half of the quiz and didn't know for the second half. And now I have an email from Ingram Spark saying, "Hey there, Novice Publisher." Apparently "Indie publishing stardom is in your future." It has links to some resources for me, including to a "How to Self-Publishing Course".

This sounds quite arduous but I have clicked through the link and there are 9 chapters which apparently take from 2 to 8 minutes to complete, 50 minutes in total.

WOOHOO. They are very encouraging.

Oh, they want my email AGAIN. Crikey.

It is well into the end of the day, so I had best go to sleep. Good night, dear diary. Thank you for being with me during these difficult moments. I still don't really understand about distribution, but I am feeling more confident now I have seen the range of resources that Ingram Spark has available for my self-learning.

Yours thankfully
Claire

Thursday 30 May

Dear Diary,
Beth here. Yesterday several *Kabuff*-related things happened, which I hope to faithfully if belatedly record here.

I worked on the AI Sheet, using a model from Monash University Publishing (a non-fiction book about...states?...politics?...) as well as examples I was able to find from Google. I am happy with the basic look of it, though I think the selling points could be sharper as well as more segmented, and I have struggled MIGHTILY with working in the column format in Word. Am I going to need to learn InDesign—more annoyingly, am I going to need to PURCHASE InDesign? The University has a subscription but it is limited to certain computer labs on campus. Why oh why isn't all software in the cloud these days?

The other aspect of AI Sheet design that I ruminated over yesterday was the ethics of making up blurbs. Not that this is an ethical grey area, really. But it was quite enjoyable to (at least temporarily) imagine what some famous authors might say about *Kabuff*.

This is Claire's news to tell, really, but her first bulk order of *Kabuff*s arrived (sent to a WHISKY SHOP for her to pick up). Also, a Scottish literary journal performed one of the plot points we put in about Callum (the editor wrote an article complaining about funding being withdrawn due to diversity targets...but the literati "only see excellence").[1] Life really does imitate art! Although of course our art is based on life! An ourobookourobos if ever I encountered one.

I feel like there were other *Kabuff* distribution tasks that arose yesterday, but I cannot remember them now. So until next time, adieu!

Yours
Beth

Friday 31 May

Dear Diary,
Today has been a day of highs and lows. It began with the lows. I picked up the box of 50 *Kabuff*s from the reception office of the John Medley Building. My colleague, U, was there, and filmed me "unboxing." My excitement turned to despair as I realised the printing error that had left a white line across the top of each copy. Rewatching the video confirms how little I give away of the true depth of my feelings. I seem quite composed in the face of this calamity.

I went on the Ingram Spark site and engaged in some live chat with "Annie S" (a bot?) who advised me how to report an issue, which I duly did. I hope to receive email correspondence (and some NEW PERFECT BOOKS) within three to five business days.

Trying to make the most of the situation, I took a few of the misprinted books and coloured in the white line with black markers.

I also tried using a guillotine to trim a book. All to no avail but some amusement. P from Research Support assisted with the guillotine.

So much for the lows. But OH the highs!

I successfully set up the ebook on IngramSparks, which involved designing a front cover tile (some fiddling about in Adobe Acrobat and then Preview was required). I then had to pay IngramSparks $25, though I was not sure what that cost covered.

I then set up a KDP account and the book on Amazon and made the book available for pre-order. This was extremely exciting, and quite an easy and enjoyable process. I chose categories and keywords. I filled in tax information (giving my Australian details) and read all about different pricing models. I went with a 35% royalties option so that we could list the title at $0.99 (if I had wanted 70% royalties, the minimum price would have been $2.99). I chose not to set up the print-on-demand option at this time. There was no link to Ingram so again I am unsure of how the Ingram ebook set up works. There was the option to enrol in KDP Select which would have put us in lots of promotions, etc., but it required us not to make the ebook available for sale anywhere else. This is something to discuss with Claire—would we rather put it on Kobo, etc., or explore the options of KDP Select?

Lots of videos, photos and screenshots from today's activities.

Yours in disappointment then resignation then enjoyment,
Beth

Saturday 1 June

Dear Diary,
CLAIRE HERE.

I have much to report, and this in itself demonstrates the challenge of remaining faithful to you, dear diary, and ensuring regular updates. Anyway, I will attempt to record all activities. Unlike those detailed in Beth's account, European Blaire Squiscoll is enjoying only the high life currently and no difficult printing jobs. That said, I remember "pride* before a fall" and will attempt to remain somewhat humble.

*bad print jobs

PART I

As detailed in Beth's previous account, I returned home on Wednesday from UofStirling in the knowledge that I'd missed a UPS delivery from Ingram. This timeline in itself was exciting, because I'd only ordered the books at the weekend and Monday was a bank holiday in the UK (perhaps Ingram doesn't care about bank holidays?) and, moreover, I'd chosen the slowest print option, albeit with paying (not that much) for the courier. Anyway, the books arrived unexpectedly early, and a card awaited me on my return home. I picked it up and—as it was pouring with rain and I wasn't quite sure how heavy the box would be—I drove off to the UPS pick-up point.

I checked the address on Google, which was quite puzzling initially because last time I had a UPS parcel I had got it from the newsagent whereas this was indicating I should pick the parcel up from The Hidden Dram. I assumed the delivery person had got the street number wrong, but as I parked up on Queen Margaret Drive, I could see the newsagent where I'd previously gone, or perhaps it was closed? It was only 7.30pm.

Disappointed, I thought I should walk along the road to the number on the card, i.e., to the fancy off-licence. And LO! It was indeed the UPS pick-up point, as a poster in the window on the door indicated. It looked like a life-size cardboard POS man was actually also the UPS delivery man, which increased my excitement. (Subsequently I realised from studying photographic evidence that Cardboard POS Man was actually advertising some whisky or I think Irish whiskey.)

The same photographic evidence also revealed that The Hidden Dram had a closed sign on the door but thankfully in my excitement I ignored that and went in (the door wasn't locked), but not before, in mounting excitement at the fact that the *Kabuffs* were in an off-licence, taking a photograph.

I went in and handed over my card, and The Hidden Dram man went to get my box. He checked my details and asked to see ID. This was very exciting and I wanted to tell the man and although he was friendly I don't think he was quite ready for this level of Kabuff excitement. He gave the box to me and said to be careful because it was heavy (it wasn't).

I got the box into the car and saw that, pleasingly, someone had written my name and Kabuff Books in black marker pen on the side. I drove off home and then did an unboxing video from the car (nb. it is pretty hard to do unboxing videos yourself).

The books are quite delightful en masse (i.e., 50). This is also VERY EXCITING because they arrived in time for our student showcase at Stirling the next day.

INTERLUDE

Meanwhile, E had brought my attention to the ridiculous statement from the *Scottish Review of Books* and I had a massive Twitter rant about it (see https://twitter.com/ClaireSquires/status/11338212368413352064) and I realised how similar some of it was to Callum's angry comment about not getting funding from the Australia Council. Blaire tweeted something to this effect.

PART 2

On Thursday, it was our annual end-of-year showcase for the MLitt in Publishing Studies at Stirling. We showed their publishing projects, and this year there was the launch of an anthology of creative writing with some readings. There were various speeches from everyone, and I rounded up. I normally say to them that seeing their projects is great because they can all now do what none of the staff can do because they've learned all the different publishing skills. I also showed them a few publications from colleagues (e.g. R's PhD, S's self-publishing booklet, my *Cambridge History of the Book in Britain* Vol 7 i.e., ABSOLUTE UNIT). I also introduced *The Frankfurt Kabuff*, including its tagline "Writing and Reading Books Is the Easy Part," and said actually it seemed that publishing is quite difficult.

I recruited some influencers: C, A, and MLitt students L, I, and F. I promised to send them an AI subsequently, and Beth and I completed it so it was ready on (my) Friday morning.

PART 3

Friday started off well with me sending out the AI to influencers, then got a bit stressful as it seems all trains were being cancelled. Nonetheless I got a slow train to Edinburgh, and picked up my French passport and carte d'identité. Then I went to the bistrot in the French consulate and had lunch with wine to celebrate Being French, and ostentatiously had my passport and *Kabuff* on my table.

After that, I went onto The Printing Press, where I met up with various rabble rousers to rake over the coals of the SRB statement, and to plot a future review. In addition, I drank four Negronis, converted E to them (she had three), and handed out several copies of *Kabuff* with print AI (to R; to A; and to G).

After the end of this, I decided that I was better at doing drinking and book promotion (and possibly social media) rather than global logistics, supply chains, and metadata, but nonetheless was aware of the need to try and actually get *Kabuffs* into stores (see Part 4).

PART 4

The process of recording *Kabuff* activity is weighing heavy, but I have reached today and will conclude my entry before the day itself concludes.

I thought I should spend some time concentrating on global logistics and supply chains, in order to show I was willing.

First, though, I added the AI to the Ullapoolism website.[2]

Next, I had a look at Ingram and discovered that we had to press an Enable button in order to Enable distribution.

I duly Enabled the book. I think I did this for both print and ebooks though now I can't remember. It doesn't mean the book will automatically appear in all stores, as some do make choices apparently.

I then checked in Kobo, and there it was!

I am not sure if the title below it (*Riding with Strangers* (Dogging Adventures) by Blaire Harris) appears as the next title in my search because of metadata or the same first author name.

I decided to preorder *The Frankfurt Kabuff* via Kobo for £1.19, which I duly did. However, I'm confused as it had the wrong publication date and possibly the wrong price on it. Anyway, we'll see if it arrives.

I then checked what Ingram had to say about publishing partners and where *Kabuff* might end up. I was delighted to see that Ingram is pretty much channelling Carmen Sandiego ("Where in the World Are Your Books") and also that we can apparently "Stamp Our Book's Passport!"

Well, that was an exhausting recording of events. I think I'm up to speed. Tomorrow I'm going to delve further into print distribution by packaging up some *Kabuffs* in envelopes.

Dear diary, sleep well, when your time comes.

Yours, multi-facetedly and possibly slightly hungoverly,
Claire

Monday 3 June

Dear Diary,
It's Beth. There is so much to tell you I fear I never shall. So, in the interim, a brief series of dot points:

- Re-did cover file and uploaded to Ingram.
- Commenced destruction of misprints. I ably assisted with this expectedly emotional task.[3]
- Went to pick up guillotine. L offered to let her dogs chew the books as an alternative means of destruction.
- Was interrupted by three colleagues, each of whom claimed a misprint, saving it from the maw of destruction—I, S, and T. T came back for his after S explained the whole thing to him in the corridor (I overheard). S also took an AI Sheet.
- Lined up destroyed books on bookshelf.
- Made a gift hamperesque photo to send as (hopefully sufficient) proof of destruction to Ingram.
- Made art works from covers. I suggested doing the same with the denuded books, also looked great.
- Made paper plane from piece of paper that fell out of one copy post-guillotining.
- I's excellent suggestions/observations:
    - Bare covers make great ebook vouchers, postcards, or things to sign for people who bought the ebook
    - It feels very different destroying a book that you are emotionally attached to. But Beth notes it was also quite fun/creative/interesting

Yours in brevity
Beth

Tuesday 4 June

It's barely 10 a.m., and I've already accomplished two important tasks: approving the proof of the new cover design (with its added black rectangle) and asking for the replacement order to be arranged. So far, so dull.

One bright spark was a conversation with I over Messenger where I asked if he would like a copy of "the rare 'white line' misprint" or a normal edition. He said "the misprint of course!" This cheered me up no end. Despite the drama and tedious tasks, the misprint may perversely end up being a highlight of the whole self-publishing process.

Tweets from the Scottish influencers continue to roll in. These are very pleasing.

Over and out,
Beth

PS Have just realised the association between white line and cocaine which seems apt. Have decided the corrected reprints order shall be dubbed "the rehab edition."

Monday 10 June

Dear Diary,
I am at work today but it is a public holiday—the *Kabuff*s have ARRIVED (at least I strongly suspect so) but I can only GLIMPSE them through the glass door of a LOCKED OFFICE.

Yours in delayed gratification,
Beth

Monday 10 June

Dear Diary,
I realise I have been neglecting you for which my profound apologies. I have been so successful at handing out copies to influencers that I have ordered some additional copies.

The influencers have been busy on the socials which is great; we already have a fantastic gallery of people reading *Kabuff*.

C particularly enjoyed the book and gave us a new quotation, "The Frankfurt Book Fair meets Narnia." I must add it to the AI. She also recognised many of the outfits in the book, including the shapeless but stylish dresses which she feels she may be guilty of having worn. She studied the map at the back carefully and volunteered herself as a research assistant for *The Beijing Kabuff*. She also asked whether she could use the book as a case study in the marketing module next year.

I was also in London last week and while doing a speech to launch the very august, over ten-years-in-the-making *Cambridge History of the Book in Britain Volume 7: The Twentieth Century and Beyond* I managed also to hold up copies of *Kabuff*. I gave one to E, our editor at CUP for the Other Frankfurt Book (OFB), which she read on the train on the way home, and loved, particularly the noticing of gsm etc. I followed up and asked whether she might be interested in a critical edition in due course. She has not replied. I don't think this is a no but we should probably think about approaching other publishers such as X. That said, a bidding war is highly likely shortly to erupt.[4]

I have also sent a copy to my mum; I am sure this will confuse her even more about Ullapoolism.

Meanwhile it does look like it's possible to buy some copies via some outlets online. I need to check with bookseller S if he can see it in his systems.

Finally I would like to apologise to Beth for meanly pointing out her Ingram oversight (the enable distribution button). I must endeavour not to say the first thing that comes out of my mouth just because I think it's amusing, as well as trying harder to keep dear diary up to date.

All best wishes, yours in remissness

Claire

Wednesday 12 June

Dear Diary,

I, Beth, write these notes in brevity and haste. Think of them as a digital cocktail napkin scrawled upon as I am indeed at a bar, The Moat, having just left a soirée and being about to dine with a friend.

At the soirée, a Grattan Street Press function to celebrate if not actually launch colleague P's book as designed, edited etc by the students, a small pile of *Kabuff*s was featured on the book stall. This led to several outrageously fascinating overheard conversations:

- "I didn't think it was an actual book. I thought it was just an experiment, a marketing exercise or something. I'm so glad they actually wrote it" (young man in checked suit to young woman. I recognised neither)
- "Who put this here? What is this? It's certainly not on OUR list"

This latter reflection tempted me mightily to write a sign but I said I definitely couldn't.[5] Fortunately I revel in confusion and discomfort. She noted some of the students would not have liked the thriller look and feel, and also felt a strong sense of ownership over the press and its operations.

I handed out influencer copies to key academics. A bought a copy and I have a picture of her with receipt (I later said I would buy her coffees).

I had a very fruitful chat with a senior academic. Turns out SHE has a secret book she is writing about the workings of academic leadership. It is partly written in the form of unsent emails. I asked if she had a publisher yet. She also has a new playful Twitter account. She got a copy and promised to be an influencer.

Must go. Beth.

17 June, a Monday

DEAR DIARY!

I logged into Ingram Spark and it says that we have POD print sales of 10 copies!!! This is very exciting!!!!
!!!!!!!!!!!!!!!!!!!!!!!!!!

Yours exclamatorily [sp?]
Claire!!!!!!

PS on the other hand today I realised I haven't done the Nielsen title registration thingummy so will endeavour to do that tomorrow.

Monday 24 June

Dear Diary,
Claire and I are meeting right now. Here are some dot points:

- People keep flirting with Blaire
    - Twitter: L and the stock photos
    - Twitter: I and the Russian Doll placement
    - Twitter: D wanting to drink Negronis with Blaire
    - O on the radio with Beth
    - When Claire was in Leicester, conversation about cover model
    - General conversation about cover model (stroking the cover, e.g., C)

- Launch event plans progress apace. We will secure a novelty money box or make one.
- POS for Sam Read Books looks fantastic
- Beth to try local bookshops when she gets back
- Try and get it into the Frankfurt Book Shop
- Send a copy to I and L

Friday 28 June

Dear Diary,
Earlier this week, I (Beth) met with O, our friend from Nielsen BookScan, whomst I first met at Frankfurt 2017 and interviewed in 2018. Since then Melbourne Uni has acquired a package of data from them that includes some consultations, one of which this was. I met with her and U. Interesting discussion ensued. At the end she told us about Book2Look (or Look2Book, I can never remember) as a portable marketing widget to compete with Amazon's Look Inside. She offered us a free set up and I said, ooh for the *Kabuff*, and U did not explicitly disagree.

Warmest best,
Beth

And there the diary ends, with most of the technological challenges of self-publishing resolved, the interpersonal challenges of marketing and distribution continuing apace, and the authors' energy for documenting their research in this form much diminished.

Notes

1 For full details, see Claire Squires, "Patchy and Negligible," *Bella Caledonia*, 4 June 2019, https://bellacaledonia.org.uk/2019/06/04/patchy-and-negligible/.

2 See also page 3 of this edition.

3 The "I" in this sentence is the code name for a person, and not a first-person reference to Beth.

4 *The Frankfurt Kabuff Critical Edition* is fortunate indeed to have found its home through the agency of visionary commissioning editor Siobhan McMenemy, who has an excellent sense of humour in addition to top-notch critical and creative skills. "X" will remain nameless.

5 The SUPERCALIFRAGILISTICEXPIALIDOCIOUS code has produced the very confusion in which Beth revels as per the subsequent sentence.

ADVANCE INFORMATION SHEET
FOR *THE FRANKFURT KABUFF*

NEW BOOK ANNOUNCEMENT

THE FRANKFURT KABUFF

By Blaire Squiscoll

JULY 2019 | ISBN: 978-1-9993676-1-9 | Paperback, 96 pages | AUD$9 UK£5 US$6 EU€6

'Stunning in every sense of the word' - Kim Wilkins

'Hot stuff' - Doris Ruth Eikhof

After a difficult winter, Beatrice Deft is on vacation in Frankfurt during European Autumn, staying at the Hessischer Hof enjoying the quiet of cosmopolitan Germany. When violence breaks out at the stands of far-right publishers across the road at the Frankfurt Book Fair, Beatrice tells herself it isn't her problem. But now police patrol the aisles with guns and batons, and queues form at security bag checks, and an old family friend begs for her help. There she meets Caspian, the very hot policeman with a baton, and finds herself wondering, What is the secret of the Kabuff?

Key Selling Points

- A pacy, pocket-sized political thriller, featuring resurgent Neo Nazis and freedom of speech dilemmas in Europe
- A bold female protagonist whose desire is rekindled in the Kabuff
- Stylish and witty, with jokes about the publishing industry that will appeal to booklovers and sociobookologists
- The relatable tagline 'Writing and Reading Books is the Easy Part' will chime with all publishers and book industry intermediaries
- Based on the author's' first-hand participant observations of the Frankfurt Book Fair in 2017 and 2018

The Frankfurt Kabuff is Blaire Squiscoll's debut novella. Blaire enjoys ferry journeys, drinking Negronis, reading the words of Gerald Murnane, and dancing to Janelle Monáe. Share your Kabuff discoveries with @BlaireSquiscoll and #FrankfurtKabuff on Twitter, and find out more at https://ullapoolism.wordpress.com/blaire-squiscoll-author/

Blaire Squiscoll is the *nom de plume* of Beth Driscoll (University of Melbourne) & Claire Squires (University of Stirling). They are available for media: driscoll@unimelb.edu.au & claire.squires@stir.ac.uk

KABUFF BOOKS First Publisher of the Ullapoolism Movement

Credit: Blaire Squiscoll

Frankfurt Roundup

Linksphilosophie Verlag

Looks Forward and Back in Ali's First List

Following the appointment last year of Adriana Ali to the helm of Linksphilosophie Verlag, her first new list for the left-wing Frankfurt publisher was announced to great acclaim at the Buchmesse last night. Authors, publishers, and intellectual luminaries celebrated the list in an event at the publisher's stand with Sekt and a range of local spreads on toast.

Ali has assembled a list which brings contemporary left-wing thinking to our troubled times, offering an intersectional view across key issues. Key acquisitions include *Palestine Will Be Different*, an account of trans activism in the Occupied Territories, and an anthology of creative responses to climate change by Pacific Island women. In her speech launching the list, Ali stated that "Books are more urgent than ever as means to think through the challenges of our time and bring people together for action." Lotte Frankel, International Rights Agent, Translator, and Vice President for Intellectual Freedom and Inclusion at the Frankfurter Buchmesse, toasted the list, saying "Adriana Ali continues the legacy of this fine publisher with a list that is absolutely of our times."

In addition to its titles on contemporary issues, Linksphilosophie shows itself not to be impervious to a little left-wing nostalgia, with a 50th anniversary anthology of key extracts from across the publisher's history from 1969. Kurt Weidenfeld, erstwhile Publisher and now Editor-at-Large, has produced a beautiful volume which also includes key documentary evidence of the inception of the company during May 1968.

Publishers Weekly *Report on Linksphilosophie Verlag List Launch; Publishers Weekly, Frankfurt Round-Up October 2019*

Conference Abstract Proposal

FOR SHARP (SOCIETY FOR THE HISTORY OF AUTHORSHIP, READING AND PUBLISHING) 2024

Tante Fran's Book Club: Solidarity, Slogans and Knitting Needles

JANIELLE FRAK AND BLAIRE SQUISCOLL,
INDEPENDENT SCHOLARS

THIS PAPER IS A CASE STUDY OF TANTE FRAN'S BOOK Club, a loose but influential grouping of readers established in the 1960s and operational for over fifty years. Initially functioning as a transnational pen pal friendship between the two founding members in Australia and Germany, the book club has flourished over the decades and into the twenty-first century, playing a pivotal, activist role in the saving of the Frankfurter Buchmesse from the neo-Nazi group White Storm in 2018.

Our historiographical research establishes that the early focus of the book club on works by Michèle Bernstein, Guy Debord, and Raoul Vaneigem influenced an in-person meeting in Paris in May 1968. At this point, the membership of the book club extended to include members from Czechoslovakia and the US, but also subsequently developed a key locus in the city of Frankfurt, and a physical location in the back room of a shoe shop.

Through the use of a variety of documentary evidence (letters, philately, oral histories, autofictethnography, Google sheets, conjecture), this paper will present the first definitive list of the rich variety of books read by Tante Fran's Book Club through the ages, ranging from key texts of Marxist theory and intersectional feminist works to mass-market bestsellers. Building on the foundational research on women's reading conducted by Janice Radway (1982) and on book clubs by Elizabeth Long (2003), this paper will advance an understanding of the power of the written word in the lives of the women (inclusive of non-binary, genderfluid, and transgender women) in Tante Fran's Book Club, including analysis of how reading underpinned their political and personal lives, and informed their other activities (slogan-painting, crafts, fashion and general activism).

THIS PAGE
INTENTIONALLY
LEFT BLANK

THE KABUFF JOKE BOOK

Klopf Klopf and Other Jokes

Klopf Klopf Jokes

Knock knock.
Who's there?
Pie.
Pie Who?
Pie-erre Bourdieu.

Knock knock.
Who's there?
Callum.
Callum Who?
Callum down, it's just
an arts grant application.

Knock knock.
Who's there?
The pub.
The pub who?
The publishing industry.

Knock knock.
Who's there?
Kurt.
Kurt Who?
Kurt you fight these neo-Nazis?

Knock knock.
Who's there?
A writer.
A writer who?
A righter of historical wrongs
in the publishing industry.

THE KABUFF JOKEBOOK · 1

Knock knock.
Who's there?
Orange.
Orange who?
Orange you going to invite me to a publishing party?

Knock knock.
Who's there?
Boo.
Boo who?
No need to cry, it's just a trade fair.

Knock knock.
Who's there?
Water.
Water who?
Water you going to acquire rights to this fair?

Knock knock.
Who's there?
To.
To who?
Actually it's ***to whom.***

Other Jokes

How do you get an elephant out of a tree in Frankfurt?
Tell it to stand on a leaf and wait until European autumn.

An agent, an author and a publisher walk into a bar. They order a drink, but the bartender doesn't have a good distribution system

A: Hey, have you got an e-reader?
B: Sure do! I'm hoping they release ones for the other letters of the alphabet soon.

What do you get if you cross a literary prize with a scandal?
Book sales!

THE KABUFF JOKEBOOK · 2

Credit: Blaire Squiscoll

Spotify Playlists

The Frankfurt Kabuff Party 1 (Extremely Legendary)

This playlist pays homage to the atmosphere at an actual publishing party we attended at the Frankfurt Book Fair in 2017 and 2018, one for which tickets are hard to access and much prized (although they cost money) and which people sometimes refer to as "extremely legendary." Based on real and similar-to-real songs from the party, this playlist was described on Twitter as "cursed."

Loaded (Andy Weatherall Mix) · Primal Scream
Gold Digger · Kanye West
I've Got a Woman · Ray Charles
Should I Stay or Should I Go · The Clash
Dancing Queen · ABBA
Babooshka · Kate Bush
Come on Eileen · Dexys Midnight Runners
Girl You Know It's True · Milli Vanilli
Love Will Tear Us Apart · Joy Division
Here I Go Again · Whitesnake
Stagger Lee · Nick Cave
O.P.P. · Naughty By Nature
Fools Gold · The Stone Roses

The Frankfurt Kabuff Party 2 (Literaturhaus)

This playlist is the soundtrack to a fictional party in the novella, which comes after the climax of the plot when the main characters attend an end-of-fair party at the Literaturhaus by the river. The party is a celebration, an extension of Freud's pleasure principle, and exists in the novel purely for the reader's (and writers') enjoyment. As such, these are songs we actually like. These songs celebrate international ideals, multilingualism, Black women, and fun. They are also, in some cases, daggy enough to be plausible picks for a publishing party.

Trans-Europe Express · Kraftwerk
Sous le Soleil de Bodega · Les Négresses Vertes
Nouveau Western · MC Solaar
Milkshake · Kelis
I'm Coming Out · Diana Ross
I Feel Love · Donna Summer
Superstition · Stevie Wonder
Uptown Funk · Bruno Mars
Crazy in Love · Beyonce
Hot in Herre · Nelly
I Got the Juice · Janelle Monáe
Tempo · Lizzo
Intergalactic · Beastie Boys
Push It · Salt-N-Pepa
Work It · Missy Elliot
Big Time Sensuality · Björk
Get Lucky · Pharrell Williams
Kiss · Prince
Young Hearts Run Free · Candi Staton
The Bottle · Gil Scott-Heron
99 Luftballons · Nena
Life on Mars? · Seu Jorge

"The Corona Kabuff" and Other Stories

Want to know what happened after the Literaturhaus party?

The London Book Fair has been cancelled. Coronavirus.

Where does that leave Beatrice Deft, International Publishing Consultant, and the international publishing business?

And how does this question relate to a lover from her past, a luxury Italian hotel, and global supplies of Prosecco?

Read on to find out...

The Corona Kabuff

A Beatrice Deft Short, by Blaire Squiscoll

UNO

Caspian dog-eared the corner of his page, closed the book, drained his coffee cup, and signalled for the bill. The past few weeks had been rough supporting colleagues in the aftermath of the shisha bar attacks. Far-right extremism was on the rise across the world, and not all attempts to thwart it were as successful as when he had headed off White Storm. His superior had given him a fortnight off, to recuperate.

He closed his eyes and remembered the sunny days of the Frankfurter Buchmesse 2018. All those books. Beatrice…

He shook his head, remembering their amicable parting nearly a year and a half ago. He paid the bill and decided to call Tante Fran, to see if she needed any more help putting up shelves in her new cottage in Alsheim. It had been a difficult decision to close her shoe shop, but the time had come for her retirement. No longer would visitors to the Buchmesse acquire elegant footwear from her shop. Too many customers were shopping online, and didn't always care for the careful craftspersonship available from her store. She retired to a small village and bought into a cooperative vineyard.

He pulled his phone out of his pocket just as it trilled in his hand. Beatrice…?

The London Book Fair has been cancelled. Coronavirus.

They'd hardly messaged since the morning they'd parted at the Hessischer Hof. His brow furrowed. Global pandemics were not his speciality. He replied with a "?" while the three dots indicating that she was still writing pulsed on his screen.

I have a layover in Rome. No point heading to London now.

He waited for her suggestion to come through, a smile starting to play on his full lips. He shook his head, simultaneously charmed and concerned by her audacity.

He checked on Google Translate, and messaged back:

Va bene

DUE

Toc toc!

Beatrice leapt from the bed, not noticing her Kindle slithering gently from the silk sheets to clatter on the polished parquet floor. She crossed the several metres to the hotel room door in a few seconds, noting in passing that her signature red lipstick was immaculately in place. She smiled at her reflection, ran her hand through her hair, and put her eye to the spyhole.

Caspian's warm eyes shone back at hers.

She pulled open the door, and pulled him in.

TRE

The curtains shifted gently in the breeze. A familiar old song drifted up to the window. Two suitcases spilled their contents onto the floor, melding together dresses, shoes, and a substantial collection of hardback books.

QUATTRO

Beatrice leaned back on the pillows, leafing through one of Caspian's many hardbacks. She noted with a smile that it had the colophon of Linksphilosophie Verlag. It must be one of first books from the new list. She remembered fondly her final night in Frankfurt over a year ago, when Kurt had handed over the reins of the company to Adriana, his rights director. She had been planning to catch up with Adriana at the London Book Fair, but the cancellation of the event had ruined that plan, among many others.

Still, here she was, in a five-star hotel room in Venice at little over the rate she'd paid for a hostel when backpacking through Italy fifteen years ago. Then, she'd visited the palatial lobby of this hotel to admire its marble columns. Now, she was waiting for Caspian to emerge from the shower.

She loosened the monogrammed bathrobe as she heard the shower pressure clunk off.

CINQUE

The spring sunshine glistened across the lagoon. Gondolas bobbed up and down at their candy stripe posts. Gondoliers sat listlessly on the docks, swiping their phones, barely noticing potential custom as Beatrice and Caspian took in the sights. A large cruise ship was stationery on the horizon, its size dwarfing the church on a neighbouring island. Raised wooden duckboards ran down the sides of the streets, but the stone was dry and the city seemed to be hovering above the water rather than sinking.

The streets were eerily quiet.

Beatrice and Caspian paused to look in the window of a costume shop; the glitter, jewels, and feathers of the carnival masks providing a riot of colour and texture. As they laughingly chose their favourites, a shop assistant entered the window from the inside, placing a plain white medical mask at the centre of the display. A price tag dangled from it. No cheaper than the replica plague doctors' masks and memento moris. Caspian shuddered, and turned to Beatrice.

"Are you sure this is a good idea?" he asked, his eyes downcast.

"No, not really," she replied. She took his hand and squeezed it. "But look, Harry's Bar! Time for cocktails..."

SEI

Beatrice waved over the waiter for another round of Bellinis, before continuing her line of thought.

"Bologna had already been postponed, but it looked for a while as if London might go ahead. But then the conglomerates started to pull out, and they cancelled. All the publishers and others connected with the book supply chain have had to change their plans. Remote working. Virtual canapés."

Caspian nodded. "That does sound disruptive. Do you think the global publishing and hospitality industries can continue without international book fairs?"

Beatrice shrugged. "It's a good question. Some were already asking it because of the climate emergency. Frankfurt last year was full of books about the environment, and publishers jetting in from all around the world to sell them."

"And International Publishing Consultants?"

Beatrice scrutinised Caspian, wondering if she'd misapprehended a slightly mocking tone. "Yes, we are there as well. Not to sell the books, of course, but to ensure the continuance of the international exchange of cultures, languages and stories. And rights, of course, too. Business has to continue."

"Hmm," replied Caspian, his eyes downcast. "Is that what the London Book Fair said?"

"Yes… here. She reached for her phone and scrolled through her feed. "They say they will keep our world moving during this difficult period."

The waiter brought over two glasses and placed them on the table. He coughed, subtly.

"Signori, some food? Carpaccio Cipriani, Risotto Primavera dell'Emisfero Boreale?"

SETTE

Beatrice and Caspian pushed their chairs back from the table, their forks and knives strewn across their plates. "A Negroni for the road?" Beatrice asked.

Caspian shook his head, slowly. "Actually, it was a long journey to get here. Four trains. Let's go back to the hotel."

Beatrice looked at him quizzically, then signed for the bill. They paid and walked out into the street. "Are you OK?"

"A little tired. Work has been… difficult. Our world is a dangerous place."

Beatrice softened, realising that their evening's conversation had mainly focused on the latest publishing industry gossip, mutual acquaintances, the spread of COVID-19, and the concomitant rise in racist attacks, the delay of the new James Bond film and whether the next 007 would finally be a woman, or Black, or both.

Caspian continued. "The world is being turned upside down because of this virus. It's a public health issue, that is for sure. And for those who can work at home with a good social security net and broadband connection, well, they should. We must take care of the old and the ill, and those without steady employment."

Beatrice admired Caspian's grasp of the structural and systemic issues relating to global pandemics. "But…?" she asked.

"I think you know, Beatrice. Perhaps more than anything else this crisis will test whether capitalism can ever work for the good of the people. And what about those who have no choice but to flee their countries because of war or famine? What about the threats of domestic violence, of terrorism?" He paused for a moment, his deep brown eyes clouding. "All those deaths every day from cancer, flu, malnutrition? And look at this city…" He jumped up on one of the duckboards, indicating across the empty square. "This city has been sinking for centuries, but we might finally be in its final days."

"The death of Venice?" Beatrice asked, looking up at Caspian's troubled face.

He pulled her up onto the duckboard, into his arms, and kissed her deeply.

OTTO

Beatrice's hand reached outside the hotel room door and hung the hotel's card from the handle.

NON DISTURBARE

NOVE

Beatrice woke to the sound of the heated voices rapidly arguing underneath the window. As she pulled the curtains back, weak morning sunlight wavered into the room.

A boat laden with household supplies bobbed on the narrow canal below the window. A grey-haired woman wearing a flowered housecoat gesticulated at a valet, smartly dressed in the hotel uniform.

Beatrice leaned her elbows on the windowsill, taking in the atmospheric scene as the voices echoed against the walls surrounding the canal. Beyond the names of cocktails, pasta shapes, and shoe brands, her Italian was rudimentary. But the hand gestures, and vaffanculo, she understood.

Finally a resolution seemed to have been reached. The woman handed up two large shrink-wrapped packages of toilet roll. The valet handed down some bank notes. Beatrice smiled at the authenticity of the scene.

She turned back into the room and noticed a card that had been pushed under the door.

She picked it up, feeling its weight between her fingers. Possibly an even better quality than in Frankfurt? She remembered the note she had received many months ago from Kurt, which had set her off on her career as an International Publishing Consultant. That first meeting in the hotel bar... *Caring can be dangerous*, she whispered to herself, casting her eye back at Caspian. She read the card:

> GENTILISSIMI OSPITI:
>
> The Hotel Management inform our dear guests that due to the current circumstances, we are closing the public bars

> and restaurants. Any further food and drinks orders will be delivered by room service only.
>
> Furthermore, due to restrictions within the city and its wider distribution networks, some crucial items—soap, toilet roll, Prosecco, ice cream and roses—are rationed and we request that such items are used sparingly and with due understanding for the difficult times.
>
> We humbly apologise for the diminished levels of service available, and remain, respectfully,
>
> In bocca al lupo
> La Direzione dell'Hotel

Behind her, from the bed, Caspian coughed, weakly, eyes closed.

DIECI

Beatrice scrutinised the contents of the mini-bar. She leaned back on her stilettos, and sighed.

"Caspian, I'm going out to get some supplies. Will you come?"

Caspian groaned from the bed. "I don't feel well."

"Painkillers?"

"Ja."

UNDICI

As she waited for the lift, Beatrice tapped Caspian's symptoms into her phone.

As she suspected, he had either man flu or COVID-19. The symptoms were remarkably similar, except one was potentially fatal.

She leaned against the heavy brocaded corridor wall. What had she done?

DODICI

The streets all around her were deserted, apart from the occasional masked figure, pulling a wheeled suitcase rapidly behind them.

Beatrice entered several shops. The aisles were empty of essential items.

She returned to the hotel room.

Caspian was breathing heavily. She felt his brow.

Hot. Humid.

* * *

The room hadn't been serviced for a couple of days. Room service was still delivering food, but the portions were becoming more and more meagre. Beatrice never saw the waiter who delivered the food, which was left at the door.

* * *

Their allocation of toilet paper had run out. The mini-bar was long empty. Beatrice looked out of the window. The only humans she could see were police officers, patrolling the canals, their jaws set as they scanned for people attempting to flee the city.

Lockdown.

* * *

She lowered down one of Caspian's books in a basket, in exchange for two black-market beers. She held the icy glass of one against Caspian's forehead, and swigged from the other.

Their paper stock was running low, although at least she had her Kindle. Despite its cracked screen, it still functioned. She ordered the third book in the series she had been keenly awaiting. Political intrigue, centuries old, all too relevant to the turbulent times of today.

* * *

She downloaded the Kobo app to her phone and took advantage of the Mondadori offer of the free Italian translation of the book she had been reading in English.

She saw that the Bologna Book Fair had cancelled its revised dates, after all.

She remembered that cartoon, what was it? Derrida sitting on the toilet. Calling for toilet paper. Text, or paper, what was it? Something about fever, the death drive, emails, archives.

She felt her own forehead. Her head span.

TREDICI

Caspian stirred in the bed beside her.

"Beatrice?" he whispered.

She turned towards him. "I'm sorry. This was a stupid idea."

He shrugged, and smiled. "I feel better. You?"

She paused for a moment, thought through each part of her body.

"Fine," she smiled. "Cabin fever, though."

"This Kabuff—not big enough for the two of us?" Caspian asked, his eyebrows arching.

She laughed, and reached towards him. "What was it you were saying about flattening the curve?"

QUATTORDICI

Beatrice and Caspian stood at the hotel dock. They looked rapidly to the left, right, then left again.

In front of them, the sleek lines of one of the hotel boats was in touching distance.

"Think of it more as requisitioning than stealing," said Caspian.

"Yes, Polizeihauptmeister," replied Beatrice. "You're the law enforcer around here."

Caspian winked at her suggestively, as he jumped into the boat.

She followed him, and turned the keys that had been left hanging in the ignition. The boat purred into life.

"No time to die?" Caspian asked.

"Work to be done…" Beatrice replied. "Quarantine to sail through."

She smiled as she steered the boat into the sunset-lit lagoon, and opened the throttle.

FINE—or is it

This book was originally published on Wattpad, and was accompanied by a Spotify playlist https://open.spotify.com/playlist/2jYus5OWWz4mFZeeh4aavl?si=f911345902644694

Where in the world will Beatrice travel next?

Read more in the ever-expanding world of Beatrice Deft:

THE COP26 KABUFF

The world of international book fairs has ground to a halt for over a year and a half.

But when Beatrice Deft, International Publishing Consultant, receives a summons to Scotland to attend an even bigger and—some might argue—even more urgent event, she rises to the challenge.

Her mission is at COP26, the UN Climate Change Conference, held in Glasgow. The world is facing environmental Katastrophe. There is a planet to save. And a Kabuff. And a hot cop from her past...

Read on to find out more on Wattpad: https://www.wattpad.com/myworks/296999418-the-cop26-kabuff-a-beatrice-deft-short

THE HIGHLAND KABUFFLING

After a reviving spring and a sweltering summer in Continental Europe, Beatrice plans a return trip to Scotland as the first days of European Autumn gently touch the Earth. Travelling slowly—and yet steamily—by boat and rail, she crosses Scotland just in time to intervene in a crucial handover of power. As she once more finds herself at the centre of a struggle between the forces of good and evil, she nonetheless finds some time to read, to immerse herself in local customs, and to taste some of the country's finest offerings.

Forthcoming on Wattpad at https://www.wattpad.com/user/blairesquiscoll

Credit: Blaire Squiscoll

Acknowledgements

The Frankfurt Kabuff Critical Edition is a work of some formal complexity as well as being deeply collaborative. As a result, we have many people to thank. All at Wilfrid Laurier University Press who brought the book to life, especially Siobhan McMenemy, Lisa Quinn, Murray Tong, Lindsey Hunnewell, Clare Hitchens, Maia Desjardins, and the insightful anonymous peer reviewers of the manuscript, as well as designer Michel Vrana. Leslie Howsam for making the initial overtures to WILF. Bonnie Reid for research assistance with referencing and Paula Clarke Bain with indexing. The University of Melbourne and the University of Stirling for funding support towards publication and manuscript preparation costs. The essayists, for embracing the project and adding to it immeasurably with critical thinking, scholarly expertise, and creative brilliance. To these thanks and acknowledgements, we add and reiterate the below, our acknowledgements from the 2019 edition of *The Frankfurt Kabuff*:

The Frankfurt Kabuff owes its improbable, remarkable existence to the gracious assistance of a number of geniuses, to whom we offer our thanks. First, Kim Wilkins, whose guidance, instruction, and enthusiasm (including an impromptu lesson in Freudian plotting conducted using a notebook propped up against a railing at the Frankfurt Hauptbahnhof) has enriched our writing and our lives. To our avant-garde coterie of early readers on Wattpad—including heartclaire (now CillianWendell), fireclaire, SandraDuPrintemps, colounorue, MiriamGrow, SueDriscoll, drdds, skjaldmeyjar, violariveraviolante, LJMaher—thank you for your feedback, encouragement, and the questions that prompted the direction of the manuscript. Thank you to Corinna Norrick-Rühl for expert German language advice, including the right German word for a dusty cobwebby cupboard (all errors remain emphatically our own). Thank you, Alexandra Dane, for sensitive and skilful copyediting—you always knew just how much to query what we were doing. Thanks to Claire Parnell, for providing a critical path and understanding how digital publishing works. Thank you, Will Smith, for securing ISBNs for this book. And thank you to all the publishers at Frankfurt 2018 who let us look into their Kabuffs. Funding support from the Australia Research Council Discovery Project scheme DP160101308 and the AHRC Creativity Without Clusters: Overcoming Fragmentation in the Scottish Creative Economy: Creative Economy Postdoctoral Fellowship AH/R013357/1 is gratefully acknowledged.

And, finally, to all the publishers and publishing-related folk at the Frankfurt Book Fair: this is for you.

Bibliography

2017 Holocaust Memorial Lecture with Professor Philippe Sands. YouTube video. University of Glasgow, 2017. https://www.youtube.com/watch?v=I_f6Y31nDdM.

Abe. "What Is the Name for a 3-d Rectangle?" *What Is Today?* (blog), April 21, 2020. https://www.whatistoday.net/2020/04/cuboid-dilemma.html.

Adams, Thomas R., and Nicolas Barker. "A New Model for the Study of the Book." In *A Potencie of Life: Books in Society*, edited by Nicolas Barker, 5–43. London: British Library, 1993.

Ahmed, Sara. *Living a Feminist Life*. Durham and London: Duke University Press, 2017.

Altman, Robert. *The Player*. DVD. New York, NY: Criterion Collection, 2016.

Anderson, Nicole. "Free-Play? Fair-Play! Defending Derrida." *Social Semiotics* 16, no. 3 (September 2006): 407–20. https://doi.org/10.1080/10350330600823989.

Arendt, Hannah. *Men in Dark Times*. London: Cape, 1970.

Austen, Jane, and Seth Grahame-Smith. *Pride and Prejudice and Zombies*. Philadelphia: Quirk Books, 2009.

Barkin, Noah. "Rethinking German Policy Towards China." *Chatham House*, May 26, 2021. https://www.chathamhouse.org/2021/05/rethinking-german-policy-towards-china/merkels-approach-china.

Bartels, Gerrit. "Leipziger Buchmesse: Diese Bücher sind Angela Merkels 'Lebenselixier.'" *Tagesspiegel*, March 15, 2018. https://www.tagesspiegel.

de/kultur/leipziger-buchmesse-diese-buecher-sind-angela-merkels-lebenselixier/21056562.html.

———. "Schöner Kulissenzauber." *Zeit*, October 14, 2009. https://www.zeit.de/kultur/literatur/2009-10/buchmessen-eroeffnung.

Bazin, Andre. "The Evolution of the Language of Cinema." In *Film Theory and Criticism: Introductory Readings*, edited by Leo Braudy and Marshall Cohen, 5th edition., 23–40. Oxford: Oxford University Press, 1999.

Becker, Howard. *Art Worlds*. Berkeley: University of California Press, 1982.

Benjamin, Ruha. "Racial Fictions, Biological Facts: Expanding the Sociological Imagination through Speculative Methods." *Catalyst: Feminism, Theory, Technoscience* 2, no. 2 (June 2016): 1–28. https://doi.org/10.28968/cftt.v2i2.28798.

Benjamin, Walter. *The Storyteller: Tales Out of Loneliness.* Translated by Sam Dolbear, Esther Leslie, and Sebastian Truskolaski. London: Verso, 2016.

———. "The Work of Art in the Age of Mechanical Reproduction." In *Illuminations*, edited by Hannah Arendt, translated by Harry Zohn, 217–51. 1935. Reprint, New York: Schocken Books, 1969.

Bennett, Toby. "A Post-Critical Theory of Cultural Production? A Review of the Frankfurt Book Fair and Bestseller Business." *Journal of Cultural Analysis and Social Change* 7, no. 1 (July 2022). https://doi.org/10.20897/jcasc/12257.

Bernstein, Michèle. *The Night*. Translated by Clodagh Kinsella. London: Book Works, 2013.

Binelli, Mark. "Is the Next Nobel Laureate in Literature Tending Bar in a Dusty Australian Town?" *The New York Times*, March 27, 2018, sec. Magazine. https://www.nytimes.com/2018/03/27/magazine/gerald-murnane-next-nobel-laureate-literature-australia.html.

Bloch, Ernst. *The Utopian Function of Art and Literature*. Translated by Jack Zipes and Frank Mecklenberg. Cambridge, Mass: MIT Press, 1988.

Bogost, Ian. "Ebooks Are an Abomination." *The Atlantic*, September 15, 2021. https://www.theatlantic.com/books/archive/2021/09/why-are-ebooks-so-terrible/620068/.

Boltanski, Luc. *La Condition Fœtale: Une Sociologie de l'engendrement et l'avortement.* Paris: Gallimard, 2004.

———. *Mysteries and Conspiracies: Detective Stories, Spy Novels and the Making of Modern Societies.* Cambridge: Polity, 2014.

Boltanski, Luc, and Eve Chiapello. *The New Spirit of Capitalism*. London: Verso, 2006.

Bourdieu, Pierre. "A Conservative Revolution in Publishing." *Translation Studies* 1, no. 2 (May 2008): 123–53. https://doi.org/10.1080/14781700802113465.

———. *Anthropologie Économique*. Translated by Richard Nice. Paris: Seuil, 2017.

———. *Distinction*. Translated by Richard Nice. London: RKP, 1984.

———. *The Field of Cultural Production: Essays on Art and Literature*. Translated by Richard Nice. Cambridge: Polity, 1993.

———. "The Field of Cultural Production, or: The Economic World Reversed." *Poetics* 12, no. 4 (November 1983): 311–56. https://doi org/10.1016/0304-422X (83)90012-8.

———. *The Logic of Practice*. Translated by Richard Nice. Cambridge: Polity, 1990.

———. *Masculine Domination*. Translated by Richard Nice. Cambridge: Polity, 2001.

———. *The Rules of Art*. Translated by Susan Emanuel. Cambridge: Polity, 1996.

———. *Sociologie Générale, Vol 2*. Paris: Raisons d'Agir/Seuil, 2016.

———. *Sociology in Question*. Translated by Richard Nice. London: Sage, 1991.

Bowen, Susannah, and Beth Driscoll. "The Australian Publishing Industry Workforce Survey on Diversity and Inclusion." Australian Publishers Association, 2022. https://publishers.asn.au/Web/Member-Resources/ResearchReports/Workforce_Survey_2022.

Bringhurst, Robert. *The Elements of Typographic Style*. 2nd edition. Point Roberts, WA: Hartley & Marks, 1999.

Bristow, Kylee. "Distribution – the Fatal Flaw?" *Publishing Studies*, no. 4 (March 1997): 36–44. https://doi.org/10.3316/informit.762982313828277.

Brouillette, Sarah. "Wattpad, Platform Capitalism, and the Feminization of Publishing Work." *Book History*, Forthcoming.

———. "Wattpad's Fictions of Care." *Post45*, July 13, 2022. https://post45.org/2022/07/wattpads-fictions-of-care/.

Browning, Barbara. *The Gift*. Minneapolis: Coffee House Press, 2017.

Büttner, Urs, and Corinna Norrick-Rühl. "Commerce, Culture – and a Camel: The Re-Establishment of Frankfurt Book Fair as an Institution of Literary Circulation after World War II." In *The Value of Literary Circulation/Der Wert der Literarischen Zirkulation*, edited by Michael Gamper, Jutta Müller-Tamm, David Wachter, and Jasmin Wrobel, 205–22. Berlin: de Gruyter, 2022.

Calvino, Italo. *If on a Winter's Night a Traveller*. Translated by William Weaver. London: Vintage, 1998.

Casanova, Pascale. *The World Republic of Letters*. Translated by M.B. Debevoise. Cambridge, Mass: Harvard University Press, 2004.

Cecchini, Toby. *Cosmopolitan: A Bartender's Life*. Reprint. New York: Crown, 2004.

Chazelle, Damien. *La La Land.* DVD. Santa Monica, CA: Lions Gate Home Entertainment, 2017.

Chowdhury, Radhiah. "It's Hard to Be What You Can't See: Diversity Within Australian Publishing." Australian Publishers Association Beatrice Davis Fellowship Report, 2020. https://web.archive.org/web/20210715215113/https://www.publishers.asn.au/documents/item/799.

Cooper, Britney. *Eloquent Rage. A Black Feminist Discovers Her Superpower.* New York: Picador, 2018.

Copaken Kogan, Deborah. *Shutterbabe: Adventures in Love and War.* Edinburgh: Mainstream Publishing Company, 2002.

Crocombe, Angela. "Allen and Unwin – a Short History." *Publishing Studies*, no. 5 (Spring 1997): 42–46.

Dabiri, Emma. *What White People Can Do Next: From Allyship to Coalition.* Dublin: Penguin Random House, 2021.

Dane, Alexandra. "Cultural Capital as Performance: Tote Bags and Contemporary Literary Festivals." *Mémoires Du Livre / Studies in Book Culture* 11, no. 2 (June 2020): 1–29. https://doi.org/10.7202/1070270ar.

Darnton, Robert. *The Forbidden Best-Sellers of Pre-Revolutionary France.* London: Harper Collins, 1996.

———. *The Kiss of Lamourette: Reflections in Cultural History.* New York: W. W. Norton & Company, 1990.

———. "What Is the History of Books?" *Daedalus* 111, no. 3 (Summer 1982): 65–83.

———. "'What Is the History of Books?' Revisited." *Modern Intellectual History* 4, no. 3 (November 2007): 495–508. https://doi.org/10.1017/S1479244307001370.

Davies, Rosamund. "Collaborative Production and the Transformation of Publishing: The Case of Wattpad." In *Collaborative Production in the Creative Industries*, edited by Alessandro Gandini and James Graham, 51–68. London: University of Westminster Press, 2017.

Debord, Guy. *The Society of the Spectacle.* Translated by Ken Knabb. Berkeley: Bureau of Public Secrets, 2014.

Denning, Michael. *Mechanic Accents.* London: Verso, 1987.

Derrida, Jacques. "Signature, Event, Context." Translated by Alan Bass. In *Margins of Philosophy*, 1–23. Chicago: University of Chicago Press, 1982.

Deutsche Welle. "Frankfurt Book Fair: Violence Follows Calls for 'Active Debate,'" October 14, 2017. https://www.dw.com/en/frankfurt-book-fair-violence-follows-calls-for-active-debate/a-40955476.

Dierig, Carsten. "Der Werbeeffekt ist groß." *Die Welt*, April 2, 2013. https://www.welt.de/print/die_welt/article114925237/Der-Werbeeffekt-ist-gross.html.

Dimitrov, Alex, and Dorothea Lasky. "The Astro Poets: A Field Guide to Scorpios." *Literary Hub*, October 29, 2019. https://lithub.com/the-astro-poets-a-field-guide-to-scorpios/.

Dowding, Geoffrey. *Finer Points in the Spacing & Arrangement of Type*. London: Wace & Company Ltd, 1995.

Driscoll, Beth. *The New Literary Middlebrow*. London: Palgrave Macmillan, 2014.

Driscoll, Beth, and DeNel Rehberg Sedo. "Faraway, So Close: Seeing the Intimacy in Goodreads Reviews." *Qualitative Inquiry* 25, no. 3 (March 2019): 248–59. https://doi.org/10.1177/1077800418801375.

Driscoll, Beth, and Claire Squires. "Blaire Squiscoll's Bookshelves: An Ullapoolist Intertextuality." The Open University, UK (online conference), 2020.

———. "Book Commerce Book Carnival: An Introduction to the Special Issue." *Mémoires Du Livre / Studies in Book Culture* 11, no. 2 (June 2020): 1–17. https://doi.org/10.7202/1070262ar.

———. "'CANAP-YAY or CANAP-NAY?' The Canapé as Environmental Signifier in the Global Book Business," 2021.

———. "The Epistemology of Ullapoolism: Making Mischief from within Contemporary Book Cultures." *Angelaki* 25, no. 5 (September 2020): 137–55. https://doi.org/10.1080/0969725X.2020.1807147.

———. "Experiments with Book Festival People (Real and Imaginary)." *Mémoires Du Livre / Studies in Book Culture* 11, no. 2 (June 2020): 1–40. https://doi.org/10.7202/1070271ar.

———. "Megativity and Miniaturization at the Frankfurt Book Fair." *Post45*, April 8, 2020. https://post45.org/2020/04/megativity-and-miniaturization-at-the-frankfurt-book-fair/.

———. "'Oh Look, a Ferry'; or The Smell of Paper Books." *The Lifted Brow*, October 24, 2018. https://www.theliftedbrow.com/liftedbrow/2018/10/24/oh-look-a-ferry-or-the-smell-of-paper-books-by-beth-driscoll-and-claire-squires.

———. "Serious Fun: Gaming the Book Festival." *Mémoires Du Livre / Studies in Book Culture* 9, no. 2 (May 2018): 1–37. https://doi.org/10.7202/1046988ar.

———. *The Frankfurt Book Fair and Bestseller Business*. Cambridge: Cambridge University Press, 2020.

———. "THE ULLAPOOLISM MANIFESTO." *ASAP/J*, November 1, 2021. https://asapjournal.com/the-ullapoolism-manifesto-beth-driscoll-and-claire-squires/.

———. "The Ullapoolism Time Machine: Travels Through Periodicity in Book History." Panel presented at the SHARP 2021 Moving Texts: From Discovery to Delivery conference, July 28, 2021.

Dubois, Jacques. *L'Institution de La Littérature*. Brussels: Ferdinand Nathan, 1978.

Ellis, Carolyn, Tony E. Adams, and Arthur P. Bochner. "Autoethnography: An Overview." *Historical Social Research / Historische Sozialforschung* 36, no. 4 (138) (2011): 273–90.

Ellwood, Mark. "How The Negroni Became Today's It Cocktail." *Condé Nast Traveler*, August 24, 2015. https://www.cntraveler.com/stories/2015-08-24/how-the-negroni-became-todays-it-cocktail.

Else, Holly. "How to Banish Manels and Manferences from Scientific Meetings." *Nature* 573, no. 7773 (September 2019): 184–86. https://doi.org/10.1038/d41586-019-02658-6.

Ezra, Elizabeth, ed. *European Cinema*. New York: Oxford University Press, 2004.

Febvre, Lucien, and Henri-Jean Martin. *The Coming of the Book: The Impact of Printing, 1450-1800*. Translated by David Gerrard. London: NLB, 1976.

Feyerabend, Paul. *Against Method*. 4th edition. London: Verso, 2010.

Fine, Robert, and Phillip Spencer. *Antisemitism and the Left*. Manchester: Manchester University Press, 2017.

Finkelstein, David, and Alastair McCleery, eds. *The Book History Reader*. 2nd edition. London: Routledge, 2006.

Fišerová, Michaela. "Pragmatical Paradox of Signature." *Signata. Annales Des Sémiotiques / Annals of Semiotics*, no. 9 (December 2018): 485–504. https://doi.org/10.4000/signata.1599.

Flaßpöhler, Svenja. "Wie viel Meinungsfreiheit verträgt die Demokratie?" *Philosophie Magazin*, October 15, 2018. https://www.buchmesse.de/files/media/pdf/PMD_2018_06_72dpi_einzelseiten.pdf.

Fournier, Lauren. *Autotheory as Feminist Practice in Art, Writing, and Criticism*. Cambridge, Mass: The MIT Press, 2021.

Fowler, Bridget. "Figures of Descent from Classical Sociological Theory: Luc Boltanski." In *The Spirit of Luc Boltanski: Essays on 'the Pragmatic Sociology of Critique,'* edited by Simon Susen and Bryan Turner, 67–88. London: Anthem, 2013.

Frankfurter Allgemeine. "Gastland Arabien: Wer zur Buchmesse kommt," July 7, 2004. https://www.faz.net/aktuell/feuilleton/buecher/frankfurter-buchmesse-gastland-arabien-wer-zur-buchmesse-kommt-1178995.html.

Frankfurt Buchmesse. "Politics and Society." Accessed July 15, 2021. https://www.buchmesse.de/en/highlights/reader-delights/politics-society.

———. "Frankfurter Buchmesse." Accessed August 8, 2021. https://www.buchmesse.de/en.

———. "Frankfurter Buchmesse Ends with Significant Increase in Visitors." Accessed March 31, 2021. https://www.buchmesse.de/en/press/press-releases/2019-10-21-frankfurter-buchmesse-ends-significant-increase-visitors.

———. "Prices & Products 2021." Accessed March 31, 2021. https://www.buchmesse.de/files/media/pdf/exhibit-prices-frankfurter-buchmesse-2021.pdf.

Fraser, Nancy. *The Fortunes of Feminism*. London: Verso, 2013.

Frisby, David. *Cityscapes of Modernity: Critical Explorations*. Cambridge: Polity, 2001.

———. *Fragments of Modernity*. Cambridge: Polity, 1985.

Fukuyama, Francis. "The End of History?" *Natural Interest* 16 (1989): 3–18.

Füssel, Stephan, ed. *50 Jahre Frankfurter Buchmesse: 1949–1999*. Frankfurt: Suhrkamp, 2000.

Gadd, Ian. "From Printing Type to Blackboard™: Teaching the History of the Early Modern Book to Literary Undergraduates in a 'New' UK University." In *Teaching Bibliography, Textual Criticism, and Book History*, edited by Ann R. Hawkins, 65–71. London: Pickering & Chatto, 2006.

———. "Ready Reader One: Recovering Reading as an Ambient Practice." In *Ambient Literature: Towards a New Poetics of Situated Writing and Reading Practices*, edited by Tom Abba, Jonathan Dovey, and Kate Pullinger, 27–51. Cham, Switzerland: Palgrave Macmillan, 2021.

Genette, Gérard. *Paratexts: Thresholds of Interpretation*. Translated by Jane E. Lewin. Cambridge: Cambridge University Press, 1997.

Giannakopoulou, Georgia. "Unmasking the Flâneur." In *The Detective of Modernity: Essays on the Work of David Frisby*, edited by Georgia Giannakopoulou and Graeme Gilloch, 208–17. London: Routledge, 2021.

Gilloch, Graeme. "'Hamlet Wird Detektiv': Reflections on Kracauer, Benjamin and (Neo-)Noir." In *The Detective of Modernity: Essays on the Work of David Frisby*, edited by Georgia Giannakopoulou and Graeme Gilloch, 181–95. London: Routledge, 2021.

Goethe, Johann Wolfgang. *Faust. Der Tragödie Erster Teil*. Stuttgart: Reclam, 1986.

Gonsalves, Roanna. "The Survival of the Friendliest: Contemporary Indian Publishing in English at the Frankfurt Book Fair." *Cultural Sociology* 9, no. 3 (September 2015): 425–46. https://doi.org/10.1177/1749975515590244.

Göpfert, Claus-Jürgen. "Direktor der Buchmesse im Interview: 'Der Mythos Buchmesse lebt weiter." *Frankfurter Rundschau*, October 10, 2020. https://

www.fr.de/frankfurt/frankfurter-buchmesse-direktor-juergen-boos-corona-zeiten-digitalisierung-politik-90066043.html.

Grimes, William. *Straight up or on the Rocks: The Story of the American Cocktail.* New York: North Point Press, 2001.

Guillory, John. *Cultural Capital.* Chicago: University of Chicago Press, 1993.

Guinan-Bank, Vanessa, and Maite Fernández Simon. "Authors Pull out of Frankfurt Book Fair over Presence of Far-Right Groups." *Washington Post*, October 20, 2021. https://www.washingtonpost.com/world/2021/10/20/frankfurt-book-fair-far-right/.

Halberstam, Jack. *The Queer Art of Failure.* Durham: Duke University Press, 2011.

Hertwig, Luise. "State-Funded Support of International Trade in Rights and Licenses. Translation Funding Programs of Guests of Honour Argentina and France at the 2010 and 2017 Frankfurt Book Fair." *Mémoires Du Livre / Studies in Book Culture* 11, no. 2 (Spring 2020): 1–38. https://doi.org/doi:10.7202/1070264ar.

Holloway, John. *Crack Capitalism.* London: Pluto Press, 2010.

Houston, Keith. *The Book.* New York: W. W. Norton & Company, 2016.

Howsam, Leslie. *Old Books & New Histories: An Orientation to Studies in Book and Print Culture.* Toronto: University of Toronto Press, 2006.

———. "Thinking Through the History of the Book." *Mémoires Du Livre / Studies in Book Culture* 7, no. 2 (Spring 2016): 1–18. https://doi.org/10.7202/1036851ar.

Hranek, Matt. *The Negroni: A Love Affair with a Classic Cocktail.* New York: Artisan, 2021.

Inckle, Kay. "Telling Tales? Using Ethnographic Fictions to Speak Embodied 'Truth.'" *Qualitative Research* 10, no. 1 (February 2010): 27–47. https://doi.org/10.1177/1468794109348681.

Johns, Adrian. "The Coming of Print to Europe." In *The Cambridge Companion to the History of the Book*, edited by Leslie Howsam, 107–24. Cambridge Companions to Literature. Cambridge: Cambridge University Press, 2014.

Jones, Owen. "Woke-Washing: How Brands Are Cashing in on the Culture Wars." *The Guardian*, May 23, 2019. https://www.theguardian.com/media/2019/may/23woke-washing-brands-cashing-in-on-culture-wars-owen-jones.

Jurt, Joseph. "Le Champ Littéraire Entre Le National et Le Transnational." In *L'Espace Intellectuel En Europe*, edited by Gisèle Sapiro, 213–32. Paris: La Découverte, 2009.

Kelly, Gene, and Stanley Donen. *Singin' in the Rain.* DVD. Burbank, CA: Warner Home Video, 2000.

Kirschenbaum, Matthew. "Bibliologistics: The Nature of Books Now, or A Memorable Fancy." *Post45*, April 8, 2020. https://post45.org/2020/04/bibliologistics-the-nature-of-books-now-or-a-memorable-fancy/.

———. "'Poor Black Squares': Afterimages of the Floppy Disk." In *The Routledge Companion to Media Technology and Obsolescence*, edited by Mark J.P. Wolf, 296–310. Routledge, 2019.

Knabb, Ken. *Situationist International Anthology*. Revised and Expanded edition. Berkeley: Bureau of Public Secrets, 2006.

Kraus, Chris. *I Love Dick*. 1997. Reprint, Cambridge, Mass: Semiotext, 2006.

Kristeva, Julia. "Word, Dialogue and Novel." In *The Kristeva Reader*, edited by Toril Moi. Oxford: Basil Blackwell, 1986.

Lahire, Bernard. *La Condition Littéraire: La Double Vie Des Écrivains*. Paris: La Découverte, 2006.

Lane, Jeremy. "Sociology as Dialogics: Pierre Bourdieu, Mikhail Bakhtin and the Critique of Formalist Aesthetics." In *Face to Face: Bakhtin in Russia and the West*, edited by Carol Adlam, Rachel Falconer, Vitalii Makhlin, and Alastair Renfrew. Sheffield: Sheffield Academic Press, 1997.

Lasky, Dorothea, and Alex Dimitrov. "Astro Poets." Twitter, n.d. https://twitter.com/poetastrologers.

Le Carré, John. *A Legacy of Spies*. London: Penguin, 2017.

———. *The Russia House*. 1989. Reprint, London: Penguin, 2020.

———. *Tinker, Tailor, Soldier, Spy*. London: Hodder and Stoughton, 1974.

Leavy, Patricia. "Fiction and the Feminist Academic Novel." *Qualitative Inquiry* 18, no. 6 (July 2012): 516–22. https://doi.org/10.1177/1077800412442813.

Lenemark, Christian. "Negotiating Value: A Case Study of the Gothenburg Book Fair." *Mémoires Du Livre / Studies in Book Culture* 11, no. 2 (Spring 2020): 1–42. https://doi.org/10.7202/1070266ar.

Levy, Michelle, and Tom Mole, eds. *The Broadview Reader in Book History*. Peterborough: Broadview Press, 2015.

Lewis, Helen. *Difficult Women: A History of Feminism In 11 Fights*. London: Jonathan Cape, 2020.

Long, Elizabeth. *Book Clubs: Women and the Uses of Reading in Everyday Life*. Chicago: Chicago University Press, 2003.

Loveless, Natalie. *How to Make Art at the End of the World: A Manifesto for Research-Creation*. Durham: Duke University Press, 2019.

Lyons, Martyn. "National Histories of the Book in a Transnational Age." *Mémoires Du Livre / Studies in Book Culture* 7, no. 2 (Spring 2016): 1–17. https://doi.org/10.7202/1036855ar.

Mahdawi, Arwa. "Woke-Washing Brands Cash in on Social Justice. It's Lazy and Hypocritical." *The Guardian*, August 10, 2018. https://www.theguardian.com/commentisfree/2018/aug/10/fellow-kids-woke-washing-cynical-alignment-worthy-causes.

Malm, Andreas. *How to Blow Up a Pipeline: Learning to Fight in a World on Fire*. London: Verso, 2021.

Malraux, André. *Le Musée Imaginaire*. 1947. Reprint, Paris: Gallimard, 1965.

Manning, Erin. "Against Method." In *The Minor Gesture*, 26–45. Durham: Duke University Press, 2016.

Marcus, Greil. *Lipstick Traces: A Secret History of the Twentieth Century, Twentieth Anniversary*. 2nd edition. Cambridge, Mass: Belknap Press, 2009.

"'Masterplan 100% Climate Protection' – Frankfurt am Main – General Concept." Frankfurt am Main: City of Frankfurt am Main Municipal Energy Agency, n.d. https://frankfurt.de/-/media/frankfurtde/frankfurt-themen/klima-und-energie/pdf/energiereferat-79a/masterplan-climate-protection---summarised-version.ashx#:~:text=Since%20the%20beginning%20of%202013,95%20%25%20reduction%20of%20carbon%20emissions.

McGrath, Laura B. "Comping White." *Los Angeles Review of Books*, January 21, 2019. https://lareviewofbooks.org/article/comping-white/.

McHenry, Elizabeth. *Forgotten Readers: Recovering the Lost History of African American Literary Societies*. Durham: Duke University Press, 2002.

McKee, Robert. *Story: Substance, Structure, Style, and the Principles of Screenwriting*. London: Methuen, 1999.

McKenzie, D. F. "The Sociology of a Text: Orality, Literacy and Print in Early New Zealand." *The Library* 6th series, 6, no. 4 (December 1984): 333–65. https://doi.org/10.1093/library/s6-VI.4.333.

———. *"What's Past Is Prologue": The Bibliographical Society and History of the Book*. London: Hearthstone Publications, 1993.

Merkel, Angela. "Bulletin 103-2: Rede von Bundeskanzlerin Dr. Angela Merkel zur Eröffnung Der Frankfurter Buchmesse Am 13. Oktober 2009 in Frankfurt am Main." *Bundesregierung*, October 14, 2009. https://www.bundesregierung.de/breg-de/service/bulletin/rede-von-bundeskanzlerin-dr-angela-merkel-799194.

Messe Frankfurt. "Site Map Messe Frankfurt." Accessed September 19, 2021. https://www.sitemap.messefrankfurtlocations.com/.

Miguel, Cristina. "Visual Intimacy on Social Media: From Selfies to the Co-Construction of Intimacies Through Shared Pictures." *Social Media + Society* 2, no. 2 (April 2016): 1–10. https://doi.org/10.1177/2056305116641705.

Miller, Abraham. "'Cuboid' Not the Correct Name for 3d Rectangle?" Mathematics Stack Exchange, December 15, 2019. https://math.stackexchange.com/questions/3476760/cuboid-not-the-correct-name-for-3d-rectangle.

Miller, Laura J. "The Best-Seller List as Marketing Tool and Historical Fiction." *Book History* 3 (2000): 286–304. https://doi.org/10.1353/bh.2000.0012.

Mulvey, Laura. "Visual Pleasure and Narrative Cinema." *Screen* 16, no. 3 (Autumn 1975): 6–18.

Murray, Padmini Ray, and Claire Squires. "The Digital Publishing Communications Circuit." *Book 2.0* 3, no. 1 (June 2013): 3–24. https://doi.org/10.1386/btwo.3.1.3_1.

Nealon, Jeffrey T. "Jokes and the Performative in Austin and Derrida; or, The Truth Is a Joke?" *Cultural Critique* 95 (Winter 2017): 1–24. https://doi.org/10.5749/culturalcritique.95.2017.0001.

Nelson, Maggie. *The Argonauts*. Minneapolis, Minnesota: Graywolf Press, 2015.

Niemeier, Sabine. *Funktionen Der Frankfurter Buchmesse im Wandel*. Wiesbaden: Harrassowitz, 2001.

Noble, Safiya Umoja. *Algorithms of Oppression: How Search Engines Reinforce Racism*. New York: New York University Press, 2018.

Norrick-Rühl, Corinna. "'Die Buchwelt zu Gast in Frankfurt': Understanding the Impact of the Guest of Honour Presentation at Frankfurt Book Fair on the German Literary Marketplace." *Mémoires Du Livre / Studies in Book Culture* 11, no. 2 (Spring 2020): 1–34. https://doi.org/10.7202/1070263ar.

Palmer, Jerry. *Thrillers: Genesis and Structure of a Popular Genre*. London: Edward Arnold, 1978.

Parnell, Claire. "Mapping the Entertainment Ecosystem of Wattpad: Platforms, Publishing and Adaptation." *Convergence* 27, no. 2 (April 2021): 524–38. https://doi.org/10.1177/1354856520970141.

Perec, Georges. *A Void*. Translated by Gilbert Adair. London: The Harvill Press, 1995.

———. *La Disparition*. Paris: Gallimard, 1969.

Piper, Andrew. *Book Was There: Reading in Electronic Times*. Chicago: University of Chicago Press, 2012.

Pressman, Jessica. *Bookishness*. New York: Columbia University Press, 2020.

Queneau, Raymond. *Exercices de Style*. Paris: Gallimard, 1947.

Radway, Janice. *A Feeling for Books: The Book-of-the-Month Club, Literary Taste, and Middle-Class Desire*. Revised edition. Chapel Hill, NC: University of North Carolina Press, 1999.

———. "Zines, Half-Lives, and Afterlives: On the Temporalities of Social and Political Change." *PMLA* 126, no. 1 (2011): 140–50.

@rak_dr. "#sharp19 The Frankfurt Kabuff Is the MOST Serious, Scholarly and Thorough Methodological Experiment at SHARP. Hands-down. @ClaireSquires @Beth_driscoll." *Twitter*, July 18, 2019. https://twitter.com/rak_dr/status/1151920518079098887.

Ramdarshan Bold, Melanie. "The Return of the Social Author: Negotiating Authority and Influence on Wattpad." *Convergence: The International Journal of Research into New Media Technologies* 24, no. 2 (April 2018): 117–36. https://doi.org/10.1177/1354856516654459.

Regan, Gary. *The Negroni: Drinking to La Dolce Vita, with Recipes & Lore*. Illustrated edition. Berkeley: Ten Speed Press, 2015.

Rhodes, Giulia. "Nathan Sawaya: The Artist Making Sculptures from Lego." *The Guardian*, September 22, 2014. https://www.theguardian.com/lifeandstyle/2014/sep/22/nathan-sawaya-artist-sculptures-lego.

Robbins, Derek. *The Bourdieusian Paradigm*. Manchester: Manchester University Press, 2020.

Romero, Shelly, and Adriana M. Martínez Figueroa. "'The Unbearable Whiteness of Publishing' Revisited." *Publishers Weekly*, January 29, 2021. https://www.publishersweekly.com/pw/by-topic/industry-news/publisher-news/article/85450-the-unbearable-whiteness-of-publishing-revisited.html.

Roßbach, Nikola. *Achtung Zensur! Über Meinungsfreiheit und ihre Grenzen*. Berlin: Ullstein, 2018.

Rottenberg, Elizabeth. "The Laughter of Jacques Derrida." *Oxford Literary Review* 36, no. 2 (2014): 296–99. https://doi.org/10.3366/olr.2014.0137.

Rowberry, Simon Peter. *Four Shades of Gray*. Cambridge, Mass: MIT Press, 2022.

Rowland, Bill. "The Negroni: Sophistication in a Glass." *The Cocktail Novice* (blog), July 17, 2014. https://thecocktailnovice.com/negroni-sophistication-in-a-glass/.

Saenger, Paul. "The Impact of the Early Printed Page on the History of Reading." *Bulletin Du Bibliophile*, 1996, 237–300.

Saha, Anamik, and Sandra van Lente. "Rethinking 'Diversity' in Publishing." London: Goldsmiths Press, 2020. https://research.gold.ac.uk/id/eprint/28692/1/Rethinking_diversity_in_publishing_full_booklet_v2.pdf.

Schiffrin, André. *The Business of Books*. London: Verso, 2000.

Scott, Adam. "Farmer's Market." *Parks and Recreation*. NBC, January 23, 2014.

Segall, Marshall H., Donald T. Campbell, and Melville J. Herskovits. "Cultural Differences in the Perception of Geometric Illusions." *Science* 139, no. 3556 (February 1963): 769–71.

Sentance, Nathan Mudyi. "Your Neutral Is Not Our Neutral." *Archival Decolonist* (blog), January 18, 2018. https://archivaldecolonist.com/2018/01/18/your-neutral-is-not-our-neutral/.

Seyer, Ulrike. "Die Frankfurter Buchmesse in den Jahren 1967–1969." In *Die Politisierung des Buchmarkts: 1968 als Branchenereignis*, edited by Stephan Füssel, 159–241. Wiesbaden: Harrassowitz, 2007.

Shakespeare, William. "Romeo and Juliet." In *The Norton Shakespeare*, edited by Stephen Greenblatt, Walter Cohen, Jean E. Howard, and Katherine Eisaman Maus. 1597. Reprint, New York: W. W. Norton & Company, 2008.

Shep, Sydney. "Books in Global Perspectives." In *The Cambridge Companion to the History of the Book*, edited by Leslie Howsam, 53–70. Cambridge Companions to Literature. Cambridge: Cambridge University Press, 2014.

Shep, Sydney J. "Book." In *Literature Now: Key Terms and Methods for Literary History*, edited by Sascha Bru, Ben De Bruyn, and Michel Delville, 36–45. Edinburgh: Edinburgh University Press, 2016.

Simmel, Georg. *The Philosophy of Money*. Edited by David Frisby. London: Routledge, 1978.

———. *The Sociology of Georg Simmel*. Edited by Kurt Wolff. New York: Free Press, 1955.

Sinha, Shamser, and Les Back. "Making Methods Sociable: Dialogue, Ethics and Authorship in Qualitative Research." *Qualitative Research* 14, no. 4 (August 2014): 473–87. https://doi.org/10.1177/1468794113490717.

Smith, Hazel, and Roger T. Dean, eds. *Practice-Led Research, Research-Led Practice in the Creative Arts*. Edinburgh: Edinburgh University Press, 2009.

Smith, Kelvin. "Kabuff or Wunderkammer?" *The Point of Publishing* (blog), July 5, 2019. https://pointofpublishing.com/2019/07/05/kabuff-or-wunderkammer/.

Smithee, Alan. *Kabuff!* DVD. Burbank, CA: Negroni Films, 2021.

So, Richard Jean. *Redlining Culture: A Data History of Racial Inequality and Postwar Fiction*. New York: Columbia University Press, 2020.

Squires, Claire. "Patchy and Negligible." *Bella Caledonia*, June 4, 2019. https://bellacaledonia.org.uk/2019/06/04/patchy-and-negligible/.

———. "Publishing's Diversity Deficit." *CAMEo Cuts* 2 (June 2017): 1–12.

Squires, Claire, and Beth Driscoll. "The Sleaze-O-Meter: Sexual Harassment in the Publishing Industry." *Interscript*, March 8, 2018. https://www.interscriptjournal.com/online-magazine/sleaze-o-meter.

Squiscoll, Blaire. *Tante Fran's May 68 Book Club*. Wattpad, 2019. https://www.wattpad.com/story/202577230-tante-fran%27s-may-%2768-book-club.

———. *The COP26 Kabuff: A Beatrice Deft Short*. Wattpad, 2022. https://www.wattpad.com/story/296999418-the-cop26-kabuff-a-beatrice-deft-short.

———. *The Corona Kabuff: A Beatrice Deft Short*, 2021. https://www.wattpad.com/story/216487145-the-corona-kabuff-a-beatrice-deft-short.

———. *The Frankfurt Kabuff*. Wattpad, 2018. https://www.wattpad.com/myworks/164522893-the-frankfurt-kabuff.

———. *The Frankfurt Kabuff*. Kabuff Books, 2019.

Summers, Chelsea G. "The Politics of Pockets." *Vox*, September 19, 2016. https://www.vox.com/2016/9/19/12865560/politics-of-pockets-suffragettes-women.

Thoburn, Nicholas. *Anti-Book: On the Art and Politics of Radical Publishing*. Minneapolis: University of Minnesota Press, 2016.

Thompson, John. *Merchants of Culture*. Cambridge: Polity, 2010.

Trier, Lars von. *The Idiots*. DVD. London: Tartan Video, 2000.

Tschichold, Jan. *The Form of the Book: Essays on the Morality of Good Design*. Point Roberts, WA: Hartley & Marks, 1991.

Vadde, Aarthi. "Platform or Publisher." *PMLA* 136, no. 3 (2021): 455–62.

Vinterberg, Thomas. *Festen*. DVD. London: Metrodome Video, 2019.

Vulliamy, Ed. "Peter Handke's Nobel Prize Dishonours the Victims of Genocide." *The Guardian*, October 12, 2019, sec. Opinion. https://www.theguardian.com/commentisfree/2019/oct/12/a-nobel-prize-that-dishonours-the-victims-of-genocide-peter-handke.

Walby, Sylvia. *Theorizing Patriarchy*. Oxford: Blackwell, 1990.

Warde, Beatrice. "The Crystal Goblet, or Printing Should Be Invisible." In *The Crystal Goblet: Sixteen Essays on Typography*, edited by Henry Jacob, 11–17. Cleveland and New York: The World Publishing Company, 1956.

Watson, Ash. "Writing Sociological Fiction." *Qualitative Research* 22, no. 3 (January 2021): 337–52. https://doi.org/10.1177/1468794120985677.

Weidhaas, Peter. *Zur Geschichte der Frankfurter Buchmesse*. Frankfurt: Suhrkamp, 2003.

Weiss, Haley. "Performing with Pipilotti." *Interview Magazine*, May 18, 2015. https://www.interviewmagazine.com/art/pipilotti-rist-soluna.

Welle, Deutsche. "Frankfurt Book Fair: Violence Follows Calls for 'Active Debate.'" *DW.COM*, October 14, 2017. https://p.dw.com/p/2lqOC.

Wilkins, Kim, Beth Driscoll, and Lisa Fletcher. *Genre Worlds: Popular Fiction and Twenty-First Century Book Culture*. Amherst: University of Massachusetts Press, 2022.

Wilkins, Kim, Helen Marshall, and Marina Tulic. "Emerging Writers/Established Publishers: A Ten-Year Study of the Hachette Manuscript Development Program." In *Creative Writing Scholars on the Publishing Trade: Practice, Praxis, Print*, edited by Sam Meekings and Marshall Moore, 19–32. Abingdon, Oxon: Routledge, 2021.

Williams, Raymond *The English Novel from Dickens to Lawrence*. London: Chatto and Windus, 1971.

———. *Politics and Letters*. London: NLB, 1979.

Wolff, Janet. "The Invisible Flâneuse. Women and the Literature of Modernity." *Theory, Culture & Society* 2, no. 3 (November 1985): 37–46. https://doi.org/10.1177/026327648500200305.

Woolf, Virginia. *To the Lighthouse*. 1927. Reprint, London: Penguin Books, 1992.

Zeit. "Buchmesse als opportunistisch kritisiert," September 10, 2009. https://www.zeit.de/kultur/literatur/2009-09/frankfurt-china-buchmesse.

Zibrak, Arielle. *Guilty Pleasures*. New York: New York University Press, 2021.

Contributor Biographies

BLAIRE SQUISCOLL is the author of *The Frankfurt Kabuff*, an auto-ethnographic comic-erotic thriller set at the Frankfurt Book Fair. When not exploring cupboards and inequalities at book trade events, Blaire enjoys ferry journeys, reading the works of Gerald Murnane, and dancing to Janelle Monáe.

BETH DRISCOLL, Associate Professor of Publishing and Communication at the University of Melbourne, revels in genre worlds, alongside international and institutional management. She operates under a number of different personae (Penny Power, Esmeralda, etc.), outfits, and epistemologicalisms. She is 50% of Blaire Squiscoll and co-founder of Ullapoolism.

CLAIRE SQUIRES walked down the dimly lit staircase and into the underground speakeasy. "A White Negroni?" the barman called out, "for my favourite Director of the Scottish Graduate School for Arts and Humanities, and Professor of Publishing Studies at the University of Stirling?" Claire grinned. "Don't forget, co-founder of Ullapoolism, 50% of Blaire Squiscoll, and author of some books on publishing studies (etc.). On the rocks."

BAIN, PAULA CLARKE
indexer, freelance
Society of Indexers, Fellow of
writer of book indexes, by the hundreds (but never one quite like this before).

MARK BANKS is an unobtrusive agent who leads an unglamorous life. A deceptively bland middle-aged man, without school, regiment, or trade, he is trusted and respected by subordinates and colleagues. However, he occasionally clashes with the intelligence bureaucracy and sometimes feels that professional duty compromises his personal honour. He is currently on sabbatical from the world of espionage, reading deeply among the lesser cultural theorists at the University of Glasgow.

SARAH BROUILLETTE is Professor of English at Carleton University in Ottawa, Canada. She is the author of three books: *Postcolonial Writers in the Global Literary Marketplace* (2007), *Literature and the Creative Economy* (2014), and *UNESCO and the Fate of the Literary* (2019). She's currently researching young adult fiction publishing and romance genres.

ARPITA DAS runs Yoda Press, an independent publishing house based in New Delhi, India. She is also Senior Writing Instructor and Visiting Faculty at Ashoka University in Haryana, India. In other words, she edits and publishes for the love of words, teaches for the love of her students and a regular income (because indie publishing is not big on that), and returns home to her dog, kids, and husband (in that order) for the love of complexity.

DORIS RUTH EIKHOF is Professor of Cultural Economy & Policy, University of Glasgow. A policy maker once described her work on equality and inclusion as getting people to "behave less sh*t, one day at a time." Which was theoretically and practically 100% accurate. Working across academia, industry and policy, Doris still believes in our potential to understand that structure is agency, agency is structure and walking alone never an option.

ELIZABETH EZRA is Professor of Hypothetical Cinema and Culture at the University of Stirling. She is the author or editor of nine actual books and 814 hypothetical ones.

BRIDGET FOWLER is an Emeritus Professor of Sociology in the University of Glasgow. She is interested in social theory, with particular reference to Marx, Bourdieu, and the sociology of culture. Her books include *The Alienated Reader: Women and Popular Romantic Literature* (1991), *Pierre Bourdieu and Cultural Theory: Critical Investigations* (1997), and *The Obituary as Collective Memory* (2007).

DANIELLE FULLER is a Full Professor in the Department of English and Film Studies, and an Adjunct in Sociology at the University of Alberta, Canada. She is a researcher of readers and contemporary cultures of reading both on- and off-line. Her most recent book, co-authored with DeNel Rehberg Sedo, is *Reading Bestsellers: Recommendation Culture and the Multimodal Reader* (2023). She makes a mean Negroni, and, with the help of Janielle Frak, she has created both fan fiction and original cocktails.

IAN GADD is Professor of English Literature at Bath Spa University, UK, was once President of the Society for the History of Authorship, Reading, and Publishing (SHARP), and never uses the third person.

ROANNA GONSALVES is the award-winning author of the acclaimed collection of short fiction *The Permanent Resident* (UWAP) published in India as *Sunita De Souza Goes To Sydney* (Speaking Tiger). Her four-part radio series *On the tip of a billion tongues,* commissioned and broadcast by ABC RN's *Earshot* program, is an acerbic portrayal of contemporary India through its multilingual writers. She works as a Lecturer in the Creative Writing program at UNSW Sydney.

ALASTAIR HORNE is a lecturer in publishing studies at the University of Stirling; he is also a veteran of many Frankfurt Book Fairs as—variously—a publisher, journalist, and industry commentator. While attending the fair, he has never been locked in a mysterious cupboard by fascists, though he did once get trapped in the bleak concrete depths of the nearby Skyline Plaza.

LESLIE HOWSAM is a Fellow of the Royal Society of Canada, an academic status derived largely from participation in the project of book history. As a historian with a strong sense of disciplinary boundaries, she applies the principles of book history to the genre of history books, an approach best characterised as "material historiography." She has retired from teaching and most leadership roles, but not quite from research and writing.

It's entirely possible that **DR. CORINNA NORRICK-RÜHL** would have never become Professor of Book Studies at WWU Münster (Germany) if she hadn't been dazzled by the Frankfurt Book Fair as a teenager in the early 2000s. Since then, she has published widely on book culture and book history, most recently with the edited volume *Bookshelves in the Age of the COVID-19 Pandemic* (co-edited with Shafquat Towheed).

JULIE RAK, FRSC, holds the Henry Marshall Tory Chair in the Department of English and Film Studies at the University of Alberta, Canada. Her latest book is *False Summit: Gender in Mountaineering Nonfiction* (2021). She researches life writing. In her spare time she jets around the world with celebrity mixologist Janielle Frak, trying brave new cocktails, collecting intriguing fountain pens, and defeating patriarchy and homophobia, one drag show at a time.

KELVIN SMITH was a publisher and publishing educator, with extensive experience of developing innovative postgraduate programmes in higher education institutions in the UK, Africa, and Europe. His publications include *The Publishing Business: A Guide to Starting Out and Getting On*. Frequently seen at the Frankfurt Book Fair, Kelvin also maintained the blog *Point of Publishing*, which included reviews of books with fictional publishers. *The Frankfurt Kabuff* was but one.

KIM WILKINS is a Professor of Writing at the University of Queensland and a widely published novelist of popular fiction. She is less successful than some people she has taught, but more successful than others. She believes Blaire Squiscoll's ultimate impact on the literary world is yet to unfold.

Index

PAULA CLARKE BAIN

50 Jahre Frankfurter Buchmesse: 1949–1999, 154
"99 Luftballons" (Nena), **89**, **89n9**, 163

accents, transliteration of, **37n12**
acquisitions, **30n1**, **36n9**
Adair, Gilbert, *A Void*, 177
Adams, Tony E., 4
Adorno, Prof Dr. Theobald Jürgen Marx-Voss von, **62n9**
Adorno, Theodor, 2
ADRIANA (character). *See* ALI, ADRIANA
Advanced Information (AI) sheets, 208–9, 212, 213, 215, *220*
Ahmed, Sara, 164
alcohol: apfelwein, **33n14**, **90**; autoethnography in parties, 5; beers, **238**; booze-ups, 173; Campari, **36**, **36n10**, **41**, 116; drunken carousing, 4; glamourised model of publishing, 15; off-licences, 211; research ethics, 115; whisk(e)y, 211. *See also* cocktails; Negronis; wine
ALI, ADRIANA (character): in *The Corona Kabuff*, **233**; in *The Frankfurt Kabuff*, **56**, **63**, **87–89**, **92**; in *Publishers Weekly* report, 221; text discussion, 163, 164–65, 167, 174, 195
Allen & Unwin, **32**, **32n8**, **40**, **40n6**, **70**
alphabet, jokes, 227
Alternative für Deutschland, 156
Altman, Robert, *The Player*, 177
Amazon, 6, 15, 148, 210, 218
ambience of absence, 112n16
AMINA (character), **40–41**, **58**, **59**, **71**, 162

Key to index styles: **bold** pp. no. = *Kabuff* novella and fictions · *italic* pp. no. = images · notes format = 35n3 · CHARACTERS · `Screenplay`

Anderson, Benedict, 121
annotated editions, 18, **61n4**[1]
antisemitism, 121, 128, 174
appointment books, 171
artistic autonomy, 22n37
Arts and Humanities Research Council (AHRC), 22n28
art, satire and fictocriticism, 12
arts grants, knock knock joke, 225
assemblages, 2, 18, 19–20, **43n4**, 201–41
asylum seekers, **88**, 163, 164
audiobook fair, 136, 139
Austen, Jane, *Pride and Prejudice and Zombies* (Austen and Grahame-Smith), **45n5**
Australia, **27n4**, **31n4**, **32n8**, **39**, **39n1**, **39n2**, **40n6**, **42n1**, **80n6**, **81**, 104–5
Australia Council, **70**, 212
authorial errors, rare, **42n1**, **52n11**, **61n3**, **81**, 105, 209
authors: authors of colour, **86n6**; and Darnton's communication circuit, 102; rejected, **75n4**
autoethnography, 1, 3, 4–10, 14, 20, **43n3**
autotheory, 7–8, 12, 13, 14

Back, Les, 21n10
bags, tote, **32**, **40**, **40n7**, **74**
Bakhtin, Mikhail, 122, 180
banking, **42n1**
barriers, systemic, **70n6**
Bartels, Gerrit, 156
Bazin, André, 180–81
BEATRICE (character). *See* DEFT, BEATRICE
Becker, Howard, 120, 131n4
beginning, middle and end, 98
The Beijing Kabuff (Squiscoll), 215
Beltz, Matthias, **83n1**
Benjamin, Ruha, 13
Benjamin, Walter, 125, 138, 175–76
Bennett, Toby, 20n3
Bernstein, Michèle, 12, 22n35, 222; *The Night*, 12
bestsellers, 12, 14, **45**, 115, 120, 207
Bibles, **74n1**, 97, 121
bibliography: and book history, 105; Shep model, 104
bibliotherapeutic forms, 150
bidding wars, 216
Binelli, Mark, **81n11**
binge-reading, 100
biographies, **54**, **86**
BISAC (Book Industry Standards and Communications) codes, 207, 208
The Bitch Goddess (cocktail), 117
Black Lives Matter protests, 13
The Black Russian bar, **32n9**
BLONDES, MYSTERIOUS (characters), **47**, **48**, **50**, **53**, **55**, **93**, 110, 193, 196. *See also* ICE QUEEN
Bloomsbury, **40n6**
blue suits, **33**, **33n14**, **36**, **46**, **46n7**, **50**, **55**
blurbs, 190, 209, 220
boats, **91–92**, **91n3**, **92n4**, 166, 182, **233**, **236**, **238**. *See also* ferries
Bochner, Arthur P., 4
Bogost, Ian, **54n3**
Bologna Book Fair, **234**, **238**
Boltanski, Luc, 126, 127–28, 129, 133n50
Bond, James, 114, 162, **235**
Book2Look, 218
book-adjacent products, **46n8**
book clubs. *See* TANTE FRAN: book club
book culture, **36n8**, **80n6**, 150–51
book fairs: audiobooks, 139; Bologna, **234**, **238**; conference paper, 6; *The COP26 Kabuff*, **240**; Edinburgh Book Festival, 115; in Gonsalves's

1 Now with an annotated index.

How to Take Over a Book Fair, 184–86; Gothenburg, 157; history, 120–21; Howsam on, 105; hypothetical film criticism, 176, 180; international, 15, 19, 195–96, **234**, **240**; *Kabuff* and cultural battleground, 142–44; knock knock jokes, 226; Leipzig, 157; London, 116, 231, **232**, **233**, **234**; Moscow, 139; *The Russia House* and *The Frankfurt Kabuff*, 135–36, 137–38, 139–40; virtual era, 182, **234**

book history, 10–11, 17, 18, **72n14**, 101–5

bookishness, **49n4**, 141, 142, 146n3

bookism, 19, 136, 141, 142, 143

book people, **29n8**

books: being good for you, **40n8**; as cultural object and commodity, 154; design, 105, 110; formats, **88**, 108; liking, **29n8**; materiality of, **36n8**, 105, 110; mobility and mutability, 104; portability, 108; readability, 110; rectangularity, 108–9, 110, 111; sales of, 227; saving lives, 198; stopping bullets, **73**, **73–74n1**; tactility, 110; use of, **71**, **71n10**

bookshelves, imaginary, 17

bookshops, 207, 218

Bookstagram and BookTube, 198

Boos, Jürgen, 155, 158

Bösendorfer pianos, **36**, **36n9**

Bourdieu, Pierre: artistic autonomy, 22n37; Bourdieusian fiction, 19; and Darnton's communication circuit, 101, 120; *Distinction*, 122; in *The Frankfurt Kabuff*, **70**, **70n5**; and French publishing, 130; interparatextuality, 17; knock knock joke, 225; and literary field, 122, 123, 131; social space diagram, 161; symbolic capital, 10

Bowen, Susannah, **80n6**

Brakhage, Stan, 177

Brexit, 141

Browning, Barbara, *The Gift*, 8

Buchan, John, 126, 128

Buchmesse. *See* Frankfurt Book Fair

"Buchwelt" ("the world of books"), 156

bullets, stopped by books, **73**, **73–74n1**, 104

buns: man buns, **41**, **41n9**, 145; woman buns, **76**

Busch, Wilhelm, 157

business cards, **52**, **52n11**, **53**, **53n1**, **53n2**, **64**, ***80***, **86**, **91**, 161, 163

Business Club, **48–49n2**, **50n6**

buzz, 3, **34n2**, **50n5**, **86**, **92**, 184

cab drivers, book pitches from, 7, 45, 45n4, 73, 104

CALLUM (character): in *The Frankfurt Kabuff*, **39–41**, **39n3**, **40n4**, **40n5**, **58**, **59**, **69–71**, **69n3**, **70n7**, **70n8**, **71n11**, **86n6**; knock knock joke, 225; man bun, **41**, **41n9**, 145; poetry publishing, 101, 116, 122, 151; red wine as drink of choice, **40**, **58**, 116; symbolic capital, **70**, 101, 122; text discussion, 10, 22n37, 101, 102, 103, 116, 120, 122, 130, 145; thoughts on in "Dear Diary", 209, 212

Calvino, Italo, *If on a Winter's Night a Traveller*, 112n14

Canada, **40n6**, 187–94

canapés, 5, **65n7**, **84**, **88**, **234**

capital, symbolic, 10, **70**, 101, 122, 163

capitalism, 12, 15, 127, 128, 129–30, 133n50, 165, **235**

cardboard models, **51–52**, **51n8**, 107

Key to index styles: **bold** pp. no. = *Kabuff* novella and fictions · *italic* pp. no. = images · notes format = 35n3 · CHARACTERS · `Screenplay`

carnivalesque, 3, 122
carpentered world hypothesis, 111n6
Carter, Angela, 17, **59**, **59n5**, **71**, 145
Casanova, Pascale, **28n5**
CASPIAN (character). *See* SCHORLE, CASPIAN
The Castle (film), **81n10**
Cecchini, Toby, 116
censorship, 15, **51**, **51n9**, 155, 156
Chandler, Raymond, 122, 124, 133n38
Chase, Sky, *Saving Everest*, 152n5
Chiapello, Eve, 133n50
chicken shop incident: in *The Frankfurt Kabuff*, **27**, **28**, **31**, **31n2**, **40–41**, **58–59**, **62**, **70–72**, **73**, **79**; text discussion, 101, 105, 180, 195
"The Chicken Shop of Horrors" (hypothetical song), 180
China, 155, 156
chocolate, **35**, **35n4**
Chowdhury, Radhiah, **80n6**
Christie, Agatha, 129
classics, **40**, **56n12**, 157
classroom work, 19, 197–99
clichés, **59n5**
climate change, **27n3**, **65n7**, **234**, **240**
cloakrooms, **86**
clothes: blue suits, **33**, **33n14**, **36**, **46**, **46n7**, **50**, **55**; dresses, 5, **31**, **42n2**, **64**, **80**, 163–66, 215; male publishers, **55n6**. *See also* shoes
cocktails: Bellini, 116, **234**; The Bitch Goddess, 117; Caesar, 188; in *The Corona Kabuff*, **234**; Cosmopolitan, 116; Frak as mixologist, 187, 191–92, 193; in *The Frankfurt Kabuff*, **92–93**, **92n5**; invention, 116; Martini, 114, 116; recipes, 117, 192; The Summer Colophon, 117, 191, *191*, 192, 194. *See also* alcohol; Negronis; wine
codices, 108, 112n10
colophon, 203, 204, 233
comic strip, 12, 19, *228*
"Commission" (hypothetical song), 180
communication, non-book forms of, **76**
communication circuit (Darnton), 10, **70**, 101–3, 104, 106n4, 120
conceptual high art, 12
Condé, Maryse, **92**
conferences, 6, 23n48, **76**, 105, 222–23
confidentiality, 6, 114
consent, **63n10**
Cooper, Britney, 166, 167
The COP26 Kabuff (Squiscoll), **37n13**, **240**
Copaken Kogan, Deborah, 107
co-published editions, **76**
copyeditor, of this critical edition, **61n6**[2]
copyright, **54n5**
The Corona Kabuff (Squiscoll), 116, **231–39**
cover design, 203–4, 214–15, 217, *220*
COVID-19 (coronavirus) pandemic, 3, **51n7**, 116, 161, 231, **232**, **235**, **237**
C— Party, **32n9**, **33n16**
creative writing, 5, 6, 9, 18, 97–100, 149, 212
critical theory, 2, 20
cubicles, 111n4
cultural capital, 123
cultural interchange, **88**
culture jamming, 12
"culture wars", 142
cupboards, cobwebby, 8–9, **40n4**, **47**, **48**, **52**. *See also* Kabuffs
curiosity, 156

Dabri, Emma, 166, 167
Dada, 11
"The Dance of the Foreign Rights" (hypothetical song), 180
Dane, Alexandra, **40n7**

2 A salute to a fellow editorial freelancer.

Darnton, Robert, 10, 17, **70**, **70n5**, 101, 102–3, 104, 106n2, 106n4, 120
"Dear Diary", 11, 15, 19–20, 205–19
death drive, 98, **238**
Debord, Guy, 12, 223
decolonisation, 165
DEFT, BEATRICE (character): birth of and inspiration for, 7–8; being Australian, **27**, **28**, **31n4**, **34**, **39**, **42**, **70**, **81**; book fair as cultural battleground, 143, 144, 145; Callum relationship, 10, **39–41**, **58–59**, **69–71**, 101, 122, 145, 151; Caspian first look, **33**; Caspian first meeting, **34–35**; Caspian attraction, **43**, **44–45**, **53–54**; Caspian messages, **48–49**, **93**, **232**; Caspian sex scenes, **62–63**, **86–87**, 151; Caspian as hero, **62n8**, **74**, **82**; Caspian future, **90–91**, **92**; chicken shop incident, **27**, **28**, **31**, **40–41**, **58–59**, **62**, **70–72**, **73**, **79**, **87**, 162, 181; choice of reading matter, **59n5**, **92n5**, 132n21; in *The COP26 Kabuff*, **240**; in *The Corona Kabuff*, 116, 231, **232–39**; Darnton and Bourdieu, 10, **70**, **70n5**, 101, 102, 120; and detective genre, 119–20; diverse skills, **79**, 199; dresses, **31**, **42**, **64**, **80**, 163, 165, **233**; FBF excess, 2; FBF politics, 153, 156; Ferrero Rocher advert appearance, **35n4**; in Frak's fan fiction, 188–94; at Frankfurt Book Fair, 2, **45–47**, **48–52**, **53–57**, **60–63**, **64–65**, **73–82**; in *The Frankfurt Kabuff*, **27–93**; future adventures, **92n3**, 231, 240, *241*; hair and hairstyles, 7, **31**, **53**, **74**, **76**, 177; in *The Highland Kabuffling*, **240**; in hypothetical film, 177–78, 180, 181–82; and Ice Queen, **59**, **61**; as international publishing consultant, **80–81**, **91–92**, 151, 163, 164, 195, **231**, **234**, **236**, **240**; in the Kabuff, **56–57**, **60–63**; `Kabuff! musical screenplay`, 177–78; lipstick, **27**, **28**, **50**, **66**, **90**, 113, 165, 166, 190, **233**; on manboats and manels, **91–92**; Negroni drinking, **27**, **28**, **33**, **37**, **89**, **92–93**, 98, 161, 190; Negroni refusal and regret, **51**, **53**, 113; Negronis as method, 18, 102, 113–17; not a wine drinker, 188, 189, 191, 192; print on demand paratext, 203–4; at publisher parties, **32–33**, **83–89**, **90**; and rectangularity, 107, 110; in review of *The Frankfurt Kabuff*, 195–96; shoes, **31**, **36**, **42–43**, **75**, **78**, **83**, **87**, 98, 113, 165; smoking, **27**, **28**, **29**, **32**, **53**, **69**, **70**, **72**, 162, 195; and social change, 161–67; The Summer Colophon cocktail, 117, 191, *191*, 192, 194; as typical Scorpio, **28**, **80**, **90**, 177, **233**
dérive, 12
Derrida, Jacques, 113, 114, **238**
detective genre, 19, 119–34
détournement, 12
diary. *See* "Dear Diary"
Dickens, Charles, **56**, **91n2**, 131; *Oliver Twist*, **56n11**; *The Pickwick Papers*, **91n2**
digital publishing, 11, 14, **73n1**, **77**, **79**, **88**, 111, 205, 207
digital technologies, **79**, **79n5**, **79n6**
direct action, sideways thinking, **77**
distribution, 11, **40n6**, 206, 208, 209, 213, 216, 227
diversity in publishing, 10, **80n6**, 148, 164, 166, 209
DJs, **33n10**, **33n16**, **85**

Key to index styles: **bold** pp. no. = *Kabuff* novella and fictions · *italic* pp. no. = images · notes format = 35n3 · CHARACTERS · `Screenplay`

Dogme 95, 177, 183n7
Doyle, Arthur Conan, 127
dresses: autoethnography, 5; need for pockets, **42n2**; shapeless yet stylish, **31**, **80**, 163–64, 165, 215; and social change, 163, 164, 165, 166; somewhat crumpled, **64**, 177
Driscoll, Beth: on Australian publishing, **80n6**; boats and ferries, **91n3**; "Dear Diary" entries, 205, 206, 208–10, 214–15, 216–17, 218; "The Epistemology of Ullapoolism", 113; FBF as site for research, 114, 155; *The Frankfurt Book Fair and Bestseller Business* (Driscoll and Squires), 3, 9, 20n3, **38n16**, **40n7**, **45n6**, **46n8**, **46n9**, **51n8**; *The Frankfurt Kabuff Critical Edition* (Driscoll and Squires), 18–20, 216, 219n4; on literary legitimation, 123. *See also* Squiscoll, Blaire
Dubois, Jacques, 123
Durkheim, Émile, *Suicide*, 127

ebooks, 11, **54n3**, 148, 182, 210, 213
Edinburgh International Book Festival, 115
Ellis, Carolyn, 4
embodied methodologies, 5, 6
emergency vehicle sounds, **28n5**, **71**, **71n12**
envelopes, mysterious, **36**, **69**, **79**, **93**, 189
environment, 15, **31n4**, **47n10**, 182
ephemera, **72n14**
~~erasure, 180~~
e-readers, 110, 227
erotic scenes, 13, **32**, 173–74
erotic thriller genre, 13, 16, **40n4**, 173–74
errorrs: printing errors, 105, 209, 210; rare authorial errors, **42n1**, **52n11**, **61n3**, **81**, 105, 209
ethics, 3–6, 21n10, 20n5, 115, 209
excess, 2, 122
exchange of ideas, **38**, **51**, **76**, **92**, 105, 144, 163, **234**
exclamation points! 180!
Executive Club, **48**, **48n2**, **50–54**, 165

Facebook, 170, 205
fan fiction (fanfic), 19, 149, 187–94
far-right publishers, 6, 8, 9, **37**, **51n9**, 157
FBF. *See* Frankfurt Book Fair
FBM (Frankfurter Buchmesse). *See* Frankfurt Book Fair
Febvre, Lucien, 121
Federation homes, **39**, **39n3**
femininity, and detective genre, 119, 129
feminism: academic fiction writing, 14; and autotheory, 7, 8; and capitalism, 129–30; dresses with pockets, **42n2**; feminist icon publisher, 173; Kelis's "Milkshake", **85n4**; solidarity, **56n9**, **77**, 163. *See also* gender relations; women
Ferrero Rocher, **35**, **35n4**
ferries, **37n12**, **84**, **84n3**, 105, 165
Festhalle, 111n6
FFS. *See* Frankfurt School of Critical Theory
fictionalisation, 5, 6, 13, 20
fictional publishers, **23n43**, 195
fiction writing, 5–6, 97–98
fictocriticism, 7, 13
fieldwork, 4, **40n7**
film criticism, hypothetical, 175–83
financial remuneration, in publishing, **81**
fingerspitzengefühl ("finger-tips feeling"), 107
fish: FBF takeover, 19, 185–86; fortune-telling miracle, 3
flâneur, 125
flashbacks, 10, **39–41**, **58–59**, **69–72**, 180

Flaßpöhler, Svenja, 157–58
floppy disk, **64–65n2**
fonts, **39n1**, **55**, **55n7**, 105, 110, 199[3]
footnotes, as paratext, 199[4]
forbidden literature, 138
foreign rights, 171–72, 180
foreshadowing, heavy-handed, **67n12**
"Fortress Hachette", **46n6**
Fournier, Lauren, 7–8, 12, 13, 14
Frak, Janielle, 19, 117, 118n26, 187–88, 194, 222–23
Fraktur typeface, **55n7**
FRANKEL, LOTTE (character): in *The Frankfurt Kabuff*, **64**, **66**, **67**, **78–82**, **87–88**, **91**, **93**; text discussion, 158, 163, 165, 195, 221; as Vice President for Intellectual Freedom and Inclusion, **78**, **87**, 163, 221
Frankfurt: banking, **42n1**; climate change, **27n3**; history, 120–21; *Kabuff* settings, 104
Frankfurt Book Fair (FBF) (Frankfurter Buchmesse): Ambassadors program, **49n2**; autoethnography, 4, 5, 7; books about, 154; Business Club, **48–49n2**, **50n6**; cardboard model, **51n8**; as carnival, 3; Das's *A Frankfurt Memoir*, 169–74; digital event, 158; fieldwork, 2; *The Frankfurt Kabuff* origins, 6; Guest of Honour programme, **60n2**, 155, 156, 187, 194; history, 2–3, **38n16**, 120–21, 154–55; ideology, **38n16**; infrastructure, **74**, **74n3**; interparatextuality, 17; Invitation Programme, 170, 171, 174; Kabuff! musical screenplay, 177–79; need for comfortable shoes, **43n3**; NUNU OTOT comic strip, *228*; opening ceremony, 155, 156; Peace Prize, **65**, **65n3**, **66–67**, **87**, 155, 163; politics of, 153, 154, 157–58; protests, 155; public-facing image, 9; rectangularity, 107–8, 109, 111n4; size of, 3, 171; and social change, 161; Spotify playlists, 229–30; Squiscoll method, 115; stand sizes, **45**, **45–46n6**; using *Kabuff* in the classroom, 197–99; violence at 2017 FBF, **51n9**; virtual era, 154, 234; website, 154
The Frankfurt Book Fair and Bestseller Business (Driscoll and Squires), 3, 9, 20n3, **38n16**, **40n7**, **45n6**, **46n8**, **46n9**, **51n8**
Frankfurter Buchmesse (FBM). *See* Frankfurt Book Fair
The Frankfurt Kabuff (Squiscoll), **25–93**; Advanced Information (AI) sheets, *220*; annotations, 18; art, satire and fictocriticism, 12–16; autoethnography, autotheory and creative work, 4–10; and autotheory, 12; book fair as cultural battleground, 142–46; book history, 10, 11; centrality of Kabuffs, **40n4**; cover design, *220*; as creative critique, 1–20; Das's *A Frankfurt Memoir*, 169, 174; "Dear Diary", 205–19; detective genre, 119, 130, 131; and Frak's fan fiction, 187; Howsam on, 101; hypothetical film criticism, 175, 176;

3 *See also* fonts and style use in this index.
4 Now including index annotations.

Key to index styles: **bold** pp. no. = *Kabuff* novella and fictions · *italic* pp. no. = images · notes format = 35n3 · CHARACTERS · Screenplay

interparatextuality, 17; *Kabuff! musical screenplay*, 177–79; Kelvin Smith review, 195–96; launch at FBF, 2; lightning speed of creation, 4; map of future novels, *241*; Negronis as method, 113; novella as situation, 10–12, 16; origins, 3–4, 6–7; paratext in print on demand edition, 203–4; plotting diagram, *202*; politics of FBF, 153, 156, 158; publication history, 104; rectangularity, 107–9, 110; romancing book culture, 150, 151; and *The Russia House*, 135, 143–46; and social change, 161–64; Spotify playlists, 229–30; strapline, **70n1**, 102; thriller genre, 8, 15; using *Kabuff* in the classroom, 197–99; Wilkins on, 99; writing of, 6–7
The Frankfurt Kabuff Critical Edition (Driscoll and Squires), 18–20, 216, 219n4
Frankfurt Literaturhaus, **82**, **83**, **83n1**, 90, 105, 230
Frankfurt School of Critical Theory, 2, 20n3, 123
Fraser, Nancy, 129, 130
freedom of speech, 9, 14, **38n15**, **51**, **78n1**, 144, 151, 156
freedom to publish, **80**, 199
freelance behaviour, **81**
French publishing, 120, 130
Freud, Sigmund, 181, 230
Friedenspreis des Deutschen Buchhandels. *See* Peace Prize of the German Book Trade
Frisby, David, 124
from from [*sic*], **61**, **61n3**
front cover, 203, *220*
Fukuyama, Francis, 144
fun, having, 114, 115
funding, 151, 209, 212
furphy, **33n15**
gatecrashers, **66**, **66n8**
gender relations: detective genre, 131; equality in publishing, **81n9**; at FBF, 5, 7; FBF Business Club, **50n6**, **51n7**; FBF interchanges, **56n10**; non-inclusive speech openings, **66n11**; and Sleaze-O-Meter, 5, **56n10**, 115
Genesis, 97
Genette, Gérard, 17, 198
genocide, **81n11**
genre fiction, 16, 19, 99, 123
George Allen and Co., **32n8**
German language, **64n1**, 162, 171
Germany, **89**, **89n9**, 105, 120, 155, 156
Gibson-Graham, J. K., 13
Gilbert and George, 13
Gilloch, Graeme, 128, 129
Global South, 144, 170
Goethe, Johann Wolfgang von, 157, 162
Gollancz, Victor, **67**
gondolas, **233**
Gonsalves, Roanna, 155; *How to Take Over a Book Fair*, 184–86
Goodreads, **79**, 198
Google, 208, 211; Google Docs, 13; Google Maps, **43**, **75**; Google Play, **46**, **46n9**, **57**, 145; Google Translate, **57n13**, **232**
Gothenburg Book Fair, 157
Grahame-Smith, Seth, *Pride and Prejudice and Zombies* (Austen and Grahame-Smith), **45n5**
grammar, not entirely perfect, **61n6**
grant applications, as joke, 225
green room, 115
gsm (grams per square metre), **36**, **36n8**, **93**, 161, 216
Guerrilla Girls, 13
Guest of Honour programme, **60n2**, 155, 156, 187, 194
"guilty pleasure", 152

Guinan-Bank, Vanessa, **51n9**
Gutenberg printing press, 105, 120

Habermas, Jürgen, **67, 67n13**[5]
Hachette, **86n6**; "Fortress Hachette", **46n6**
hairstyles: of Beatrice, 7, **31, 53, 74, 76,** 177; of Callum, **41, 41n9, 70,** 145
Halberstam, Jack, 2
Hammett, Dashiell, 124, 125
Handke, Peter, **81n11**
handshakes, **50–51, 51n7**
handsiness, 5
hardboiled detectives, 124, 125, 129
HarperCollins, **32n8, 46n6**
Harris, Blaire, *Riding with Strangers* (Dogging Adventures), 213
Harry Potter novels, **40n6, 45**
hashtags, 194
heroes, **62n8, 82n12, 82n13,** 125
Hertwig, Luise, **60n2,** 155
Hessischer Hof, **33n10, 83, 90**
The Hidden Dram, 211
high art, 13
The Highland Kabuffling (Squiscoll), **240**
hipsters, and man buns, **41n9**
Hitler, Adolf, **55n7**; *Mein Kampf* (*My Struggle*), 14, **60, 61, 61n4,** 104, 121
Holmes, Sherlock, 124, 127–28
honeytrap methods, 5
Horatian satire, 16
Houston, Keith, 111n10
Howsam, Leslie, 106n2
How to Take Over a Book Fair (Gonsalves), 184–86
humour, 8, 13, 16, **77n10,** 114, 219n4; *The Kabuff Joke Book*, 225–27
Hypothetical Film Criticism, 175–83

ICE QUEEN (character), **59, 61.** See also BLONDES, MYSTERIOUS
images: intentionally overexplained, **70n9**; in storytelling, 194
imaginary communities, 121
immersion, in Frankfurt parties, 5
Inckle, Kay, 5–6
inclusion, **75n4, 78n1, 80n6,** 148, 150, 164, 165
independent publishers, **40n6, 86n6,** 207
InDesign, 209
indexer, of this critical edition, 262[6]
indexing unmet needs, 152
India, 170, 171
inequality, **32, 43,** 144, 151
informal buzz, **50n5**
infrastructure, **74, 74n3**
Ingram, 15, 210, 211, 213, 214, 216; IngramSpark, 207, 208, 209, 210, 217
Instagram, **85n5,** 166, 198
intellectual freedom, 9, **52,** 64, **78n1**
interdisciplinarity, 101, 106n2
international book fairs, 15, 19, 195–96, **234, 240.** *See also* book fairs
interparatextuality, 2, 17, 20
intertext, 17
Invitation Programme (FBF), 170, 171, 174
Ireland, 173
Irish pub, **90**
ISBNs, 205, 206

5 An index footnote of appreciation for this text footnote.
6 This indexer also enjoys having a play.

Key to index styles: **bold** pp. no. = *Kabuff* novella and fictions · *italic* pp. no. = images · notes format = 35n3 · CHARACTERS · `Screenplay`

Italian language, **236**, **238**
Italy, **232**, **233–36**, **238**

Jackson, Jenny, **30n1**
James Bond films, 114, 162, **235**
Jenny the Horse, **30n1**
jokes, 13, **77n10**, 114; *The Kabuff Joke Book*, 225–27
juice (Schorle), **35n5**
Jurt, Joseph, 123
Juvenalian satire, 16

Kabuff! (the film musical), 175, 177–81; screenplay, 177–79
Kabuff Books, 204, 206, 211
The Kabuff Joke Book, 225–27
Kabuffs: cardboard model, **52**; in *The COP26 Kabuff*, **240**; in *The Corona Kabuff*, **238**; "Dear Diary" entries, 214; definition, 8–9, 21n26, **52**; in *The Frankfurt Kabuff*, **40n4**, **47**, **48**, **52**, **54–57**, **60–62**, **87**; Gadd on rectangularity, 107, 108, 111; in Gonsalves's *How to Take Over a Book Fair*, 184, 185, 186; guided tours, **60n1**; Howsam on, 105, 106; in *Kabuff!* the musical, 181; politics of FBF, 156; sex scene in, **62–63**
Kafka, Franz, 122; *The Trial*, 127
Kant, Immanuel, 122
Kästner, Erich, 157
KDP. *See* Kindle Direct Publishing
Kelis, "Milkshake", **84**, **84–85n4**, **85n5**, 113
Kindle, **35**, **35n6**, **233**, **238**
Kindle Direct Publishing (KDP), 148, 210
Kirschenbaum, Matthew, **41n10**
klopf, **30n1**
Klopf Klopf jokes, 225–26
Knausgaard, Karl Ove, *My Struggle*, **60–61**, **60n2**, 121
knitting needles, **74**, **76**, **87**, 119, 162, 164
knock knock jokes, 225–26
Knopf publishing company, **30n1**
Kobo, 210, 213, **238**
Kollontai, Alexandra, 129
Kracauer, Siegfried, 123, 124
Kraftwerk, "Trans-Europe Express", **84**, **84n2**, 146n3
Kraus, Chris, *I Love Dick*, 7
Kristeva, Julia, 17
Kuhnke, Jasmina, **51n9**
KURT (character). *See* WEIDENFELD, KURT

Laclos, Pierre Ambroise Choderlos de, *Les Liaisons Dangereuses*, 12
Lahire, Bernard, 123
La La Land (film), 181
laser measurers, 3
launch events, 218
Leavy, Patricia, 14
le Carré, John, 19, 135–42, 144, 145; *A Legacy of Spies*, 141–42; *The Russia House*, 19, 135, 136, 137–40; *The Spy Who Came in From the Cold*, 141; *Tinker, Tailor, Soldier, Spy*, 141
leering, a tally of, 5
leftists, **58n1**
left-wing publishers, 116, 143, 153, 162, 221
Legal Deposit, 205
Leipzig Book Fair, 157
Lenemark, Christian, 157
letters, mysterious, **36**, **69**, **79**, **79n2**, **93**, 189
Lettrists, 11
Lewis, Helen, 166
LGBTQ+ writing, 173
liberalism, 144
licences, **54n5**
lifesavers, books as symbolic and actual, **73–74n1**
lighting, mood, **62n9**
Lindgren, Astrid, **67**

Linksphilosophie Verlag, **51**, **54**, **54n4**, **62**, **67**, **88**, **89**, **92**, 221–22, **233**
lipograms, and *lipokine*, 177
lipstick: in *The Frankfurt Kabuff*, **27**, **28**, **50**, **66**, **66n9**, **90**; text discussion, 5, 113, 116, 161–63, 165–66, 177, 179, 182, 190, **233**
lire au coeur (reading by heart), 110
literal, literally correct use of, **74**
literary agents, 171–72
literary fiction, **59n5**, **61**, 122
Literature Train, **60n2**
Literaturhaus, **82**, **83**, **83n1**, **90**, 105, 230
lived experience, 5, 131
logistics, **41**, **41n10**, 213
London Book Fair, 116, 231, **232**, **233**, **234**
Long, Elizabeth, **43n4**, 223
looking round, 180
Look Inside (Amazon feature), 218
LOTTE (character). *See* FRANKEL, LOTTE
low theory, 2, 13, 17
Luxemburg, Rosa, 163; *The Accumulation of Capital*, **79**
lyrics, hypothetical, 178, 179, 180

Maigret novels, 128
makeup, 165, 166. *See also* lipstick
male apologies, welcomeness of, **44n2**
male gaze, 181
male publishers, **33n14**, **55n6**
male readers, **54n3**
Malm, Andreas, *How to Blow Up a Pipeline*, **34n2**
Malraux, André, 175
manboats, **91–92**, **91n3**, **92n4**, 166
Man Booker Prize, 123
man buns, **41**, **41n9**, 145
manels, **92**, **92n4**, 105, 192
man flu, **237**
Mann, Heinrich, 9, 17, **52**, **52n10**
Manning, Erin, 116
mansplaining, 5
maps: future novels, 203, 215, *241*; Messe complex, **74n3**
Marcus, Greil, 12
Marcuse, Herbert, **43**, 163
marginalised voices, **80**, 145, 199
Martin, Henri-Jean, 121
mash-ups, 12, **45n5**, 198
mass-market books, 109, 222–23
materiality: of the book, **36n8**, 105, 110; of business cards, **52n11**
May 1968 protests, Paris, **32n7**, 221, 222
McGrath, Laura B., **80n6**
McHenry, Elizabeth, **43n4**
McKee, Robert, *Story*, 99
McKenzie, D.F., 103
McMenemy, Siobhan, 219n4
measurers, laser, 3
mechanical reproduction, age of, 176
media archaeology, **64n2**
Melbourne, **31n5**, **31n6**, **39n1**, **39n2**, **42**, **42n1**, 100, 104
memes, **58n1**
memoirs, **86**
memory institutions, pseudo-neutrality of, 160n31
men: in blue suits, **46**; boring men, 5; instantly walking away from, 5; male apologies, **44n2**; male gaze, 181; male publishers, **33n14**, **55n6**; male readers, **54n3**; manboats, **91–92**, **91n3**, **92n4**, 166; man buns, **41**, **41n9**, 145; manels, **92**, **92n4**, 105, 192; man flu, **237**; mansplaining, 5; with power tools, **81**, **81n9**

Key to index styles: **bold** pp. no. = *Kabuff* novella and fictions · *italic* pp. no. = images · notes format = 35n3 · CHARACTERS · `Screenplay`

Menippean satire, 16
Mercier, Louis-Sébastien, *L'An 2440*, 120
mergers, **30n1**, **36n9**
Merkel, Angela, 155, 156, 157
Messe complex, 3, 111n6, 171
metacommentary, 10
metadata, 207, 213
#MeToo movement, **81n11**
Miguel, Cristina, **49n4**
misprints, 214, 215
mixology, 187, 188, 191
mockery, 16
modernism, 22n37
Monáe, Janelle, **81n11**; "I Got the Juice", **87**, **87n7**; similarities to Gerald Murnane, **81n11**
Monash University Publishing, 208
mood lighting, **62n9**
Moscow Book Fair, 139
movies. *See* Hypothetical Film Criticism; musicals
msiprints. *See* misprints
Mulvey, Laura, 181
Murnane, Gerald, **81n11**
musée imaginaire, 175–76
music: Janelle Monáe's "I Got the Juice", **87**, **87n7**; Kanye West's "Gold Digger", **32n10**; Kelis's "Milkshake", **84**, **84–85n4**, **85n5**, 113; Kraftwerk's "Trans-Europe Express", **84**, **84n2**, 146n3; music business, **85n5**; Music and Guinness evening, 173; Nelly's "Hot in Herre", **85**, **85n5**; Nena's "99 Luftballons", **89**, **89n9**, 163; pianos, **36**, **36n9**; Primal Scream's "Loaded", **32**, **32n10**; Spotify, **85n5**; Spotify playlists, **32n10**, 229–30, **239**
musicals, 19, 175, 177–79, 180
My Struggle (Knausgaard), **60**, **61**, 121
My Struggle (*Mein Kampf*) (Hitler), 14, **60**, **61**, **61n4**, 104, 121
NAFF (Not Actually Fungible Film), 176
narrative structure, 97, 98, 99–100
Nazism, **37**, **37n14**, **55**, **55n7**, **55n8**, **67**
Negronis: at airport bars, **92–93**; and Campari, **36n10**; in *The Corona Kabuff*, **235**; "Dear Diary" entries, 212–13, 217; in Frak's fan fiction, 187, 189–94; glamourised model of publishing, 15; Howsam on, 102, 105; invention of, **30n1**, **32n8**; magically appearing, **37**; origin of, **27n1**; refused, **51**, 113; regret at refusal, **53**, 113; as signature cocktail and method, 18, 113–18; and social change, 161; Squiscoll penchant for, 98; superlative nature of, **93n6**; time for another, **89**; waiting for, **33**; wanting more, **93**; without capitals, **33n13**. *See also* alcohol; cocktails; wine
Nelly, "Hot in Herre", **85**, **85n5**
Nelson, Maggie, *The Argonauts*, 7
Nena, "99 Luftballons", **89**, **89n9**, 163
neoliberalism, 15, 129, 130
neo-Nazis, 8, 14, **37n14**, **55n7**, **61n5**, **75n4**, 116, 121
Netflix, 100
New Academy prize in literature, **92**, **92n5**
newspapers, **55**, 157
Nicholls, David, *One Day*, **45**
Nielsen: BookScan, 218; PubEasy, 205; Title Editor, 205–6, 217
Niemeier, Sabine, *Funktionen der Frankfurter Buchmesse im Wandel*, 154
Nobel Prize in Literature, **81**, **81n11**, **92n5**
"No Insight Without Inside, No Inside Without Outside", 4, *228*
non-book forms, **46n8**, **76**
non-fiction, **54n3**, **92n5**
Norrick-Rühl, Corinna, **60n2**

notes. *See* footnotes[7]
novella as situation, 10–12
novels, 6, 7, 110, 198
novice publishers, 207, 208
NUNU OTOT: comic strip, *228*; principle, 4, 19
Nya Tider (newspaper), 157

Obama, Michelle, 17, **86**
Ocasio-Cortez, Alexandria, 165
off-licences, 211
OLAF ("Oh Look, a Ferry"), **37n12, 84n3, 91n3**, 206
Oprah Book Club, 123
orientation, unusual, *241*
Orwell, George, 16, 126; *Animal Farm*, 16
Other Frankfurt Book (OFB), 216
OTOT. *See* NUNU OTOT
Otto, Hans-Joachim, 155
OuFiPo (Ouvroir de Film Potential), 19, 176, 177, 182
OuLiPo (Ouvroir de Littérature Potentielle), 176, 177, 182
ourobookourobos, 209
over-explaining, intentional, **70n9**

Page, Regé-Jean, 181
Palmer, Jerry, 125
paper formats, **88**, 198
paper planes, 214
paper weights, **36, 52n11, 236**
paratext, 17, 19, 198–99, 203–4
Paris protests, May 1968, **32n7**, 221, 222
participant observation, 5, 7, 116, 180
parties: autoethnography and immersion in, 4–5; C— Party, **32n9, 33n16**; "extremely legendary", 229; in *The Frankfurt Kabuff*, **32, 66, 83–85**; gatecrashers, **66, 66n8**; hot parties with heroes, **82n13**; knock knock joke, 226; Literaturhaus, **83–84, 83n1**; music at, **84–85, 84n4**; party frocks, 5; and The Predicament, 4; *Kabuff* and *The Russia House*, 143; as site of situatedness, 4; Spotify playlists, 229–30; thriller genre, 8
partnerships, mischievous, 13
pastiches, bad: of criminal talk, **59n4**; of neo-Nazi talk, **61n5**
Peace Prize of the German Book Trade, **65, 65n3, 66–67, 87**, 155, 163
Penguin Random House, **30n1, 46n6, 86n6**
Penny and Polly (journalists), **60n2**
Perec, Georges, *La Disparition*, 177
phallocentrism, 181
photography, 175–76
pianos, **36, 36n9**
Pinkerton Rules, 125
Piper, Andrew, 109
pitching, 7, **45, 45n4**, 73, 104
placeography, *103*, 104
place, unity of, 180
planes, 182, 214
The Player (film), 177
playfulism, 15, 104

7 *See also* down here.

Key to index styles: **bold** pp. no. = *Kabuff* novella and fictions · *italic* pp. no. = images · notes format = 35n3 · CHARACTERS · Screenplay

playlists. *See* Spotify: playlists
pleasure principle, 98, 230
plot structure, 7, 99
plotting diagram, 19, 98, *202*
podcasts, **69**, **69n2**
poetry, **58**, **58n2**, **69**, 122, 151
police, 6, **33**, **33n12**, **34**, **35n7**, **53n2**
politics, 13, 15, 16, 19, **33n15**, 153–60, 165
popular culture, 120, 122, 123, 131
populism, 141
pornography, 173, 176
posters, **72n14**
power relations, 3, 15, **28n5**
power tools, **81**, **81n9**
practice-led research, 9, 12
The Predicament, 4, 5
preorders, 213
~~presence, under erasure, 180~~
pricing models, 210
Primal Scream, "Loaded", **32**, **32n10**
print: books, 11, **73**, **73n1**, 108, 207, 213; ephemera, **72n14**; and rectangularity, 110
printer's errors, 105, 209, 210
printing press, 105, 120
The Printing Press, 212
print on demand, 11, 203–4, 210, 217
prizes: literary prizes, 227; Man Booker Prize, 123; New Academy prize in literature, **92**, **92n5**; Nobel Prize in Literature, **81**, **81n11**, **92n5**; Peace Prize of the German Book Trade, **65**, **65n3**, **66–67**, **87**, 155, 163
production relations, 125
prophylactics, **63n10**
prosopography, *103*, 104
protests, **32n7**, 155, 156, 221, 222
psychiatry, 127
Publishers Weekly report, 221–22
publishing industry: and creative writing pedagogy, 98; Darnton's communication circuit, 102; difficulty compared to reading and writing, **70**, 101, 102, 106; diversity and inclusion, **80n6**; future vision of, **88**; getting into, 149; glamourised model, 15; interparatextuality, 17; knock knock jokes, 225–26; need for diverse skillsets, **79**, **79n5**, 199; niceness of, **33n11**; and politics, **33n15**; power relations, 3; publishing IQ, 207; publishing rights agents, 171; publishing studies, 10, 18; shrinkage of, **47**, **47n10**; supply-chain logistics, **41n10**; technology, **48n1**; uncoolness, **49n2**; using *Kabuff* in the classroom, 199; Whiteness in, 149, 150, 151

Queneau, Raymond, *Exercices de Style*, 176
"Question of England" novels, 127

racial fictions, 13
Radway, Janice, **37n13**, 223
Random House, **30n1**
readers: agency and change, **76**, **76n9**; comments, 11, **70n5**, 149, 187, 194; Darnton's communications circuit, 102
reading: ambience of absence, 112n16; in the bath, **84**; ease compared to publishing, **70**, 101, 102, 106; on ferries, **84**; formats, 198; by heart, 110; rectangularity, 108, 110; silent reading, 110
reading the room, 170
rectangularity, 18, 107–12
red-light district, **32n9**
refugees, **40**, 120, 144
relationships, economic aspects of, **69**
remuneration, **81**
research: methods and ethics, 3–6, 21n10, 20n5, 115, 209; practice-led research, 9, 12; research-creation, 9–10, 22n28; researcher and researched, 5; research-led fiction, 13

reviews, 195–96, 220
rights, **34n2**, **38**, **54**, **54n5**, 171–72, 176, **234**
right-wing publishers, 6, 8, 9, **37**, **51n9**, 153, 156, 157
Rio de Janeiro, probably a Scorpio, **80n7**
Roberts, Nora, **92**
romance fiction, 19, **63n10**, **92n5**, 120, 149–51
Rowberry, Simon Peter, *Four Shades of Gray*, **35n6**
royalties, 210
Rudolf Molzberger Schuh Krolla, **43n3**
The Russia House (le Carré), 19, 135, 136, 137–40

safe sex, **63n10**
Saha, Anamik, **80n6**
Sam Read Books, 218
Sandiego, Carmen, 213
Sands, Philippe, 121
satire, 2, 3, 16, 142
Scandi-noir, 129
Schiffrin, André, 130
schnitzel, **33n14**, **90**, **90–91n1**
scholarly critique, need to invigorate, 3
SCHORLE, CASPIAN (character): Beatrice first meeting, **34–35**; Beatrice attraction, **43**, **44–45**, **53–54**; Beatrice messages, **48–49**, **93**, **232**; Beatrice sex scenes, **62–63**, **86–87**, 151; Beatrice future, **90–91**, **92**; books of choice, **54**, **54n3**, **86**, **86n6**, 116; character origins, 6; in *The Corona Kabuff*, 116, **232–39**; at FBF, **45–46**, **52–54**, **64–68**, **74**, **75**, **82**; in Frak's fan fiction, 189; as hero, **62n8**, **74**, **82**, **82n12**, **82n13**; hotness of, **62n8**, **63**, **82**, **92**, 163, 204, 237; impressive baton, **33**, **52**, 177, 195, 204; inconsistent Germanification of dialogue, **64n1**; ***Kabuff!*** **musical screenplay**, 177; at Literaturhaus party, **83–88**; mood lighting value, **62n9**; police badge number 6969, **35**, **84**, 162, 195; promotion to Polizeihauptmeister, **84**, 163; in review of *The Frankfurt Kabuff*, 195; Schorle surname, **35n5**, **87n7**; and Tante Fran relation, **36**, **43**, 163, **232**; text discussion, 6, 113, 116, 119, 129, 143, 163
Scorpios, **28**, **28n6**, **80**, **80n7**, **90**
Scotland, 129, **240**
Scottish Review of Books, **70n6**, 212
screenplays, 177–79, 182
screen reading, **49n4**, 108, 110
secrecy, 124
security, 6, 157, 174, 196
Sedo, DeNel Rehberg, **49n4**
Segall, Marshall H., 111n5
self-publishing: "Dear Diary" entries, 205–19. *See also* Wattpad
self-referentiality, 13, 279
Senghor, Léopold Sédar, 155
Sentance, Nathan Mudyi, 160n31
serial publication, 6, 11
sex scenes, 7, 13, **62–63**, **63n10**, **86–87**, 151
sexual politics, 115, 181
Seyer, Ulrike, 154–55
Shakespeare, William, 98–99; *A Midsummer Night's Dream*, 137; *Romeo and Juliet*, 99
SHARP (Society for the History of Authorship, Reading and Publishing), 21n17, 102–3, 104, 106n7, 114, 222–23

Key to index styles: **bold** pp. no. = *Kabuff* novella and fictions · *italic* pp. no. = images · notes format = 35n3 · CHARACTERS · Screenplay

Shep, Sydney, 103, 104, 105, 110
Sherlock Holmes series, 124, 127–28
shoes: in *The Corona Kabuff*, **237**; in Das's *A Frankfurt Memoir*, 173; in Frak's fan fiction, 193; in *The Frankfurt Kabuff*, **31**, **36**, **42**, **43**, **43n3**, **75**, **78**, **83**, **87**; and social change, 165; Squiscoll penchant for, 98
signature cocktail, 18, 19, 113–18
signatures, 114
silent reading, 110
Simenon, Georges, 128
Simmel, Georg, 124
Simon, Maite Fernández, **51n9**
Singin' in the Rain (film), 181
Sinha, Shamser, 21n10
siren noises, **28n5**, **71**, **71n12**
situated knowledges, *103*, 104
situation, *The Frankfurt Kabuff* as, 2, 4, 10–12
situationists, 11–12
size, not being dazzled by, 3, **45n6**
skills, in publishing, **79**, **79n5**, 169–70, 199
skyscrapers, **42**, **42n1**
Sleaze-O-Meter, 5, **56n10**, 115
"Slush" (hypothetical song), 180
small publishers, **86n6**, 130
smartphones, **48n1**, 108, 151
Smith, Kelvin, 15, 19, 23n43, 195–96
Smithee, Alan, 181
smoking, 15, **27**, **27n2**, **28**, **29**, **32**, **53**, **69**, **70**, **72**, 162, 171, 195, 196
snobbishness, literary, 14
social capital, 187
social change, 19, 161–68
social justice, **65n7**, 165
social media, 11, **79**, 148, 165, 166, 170, 213, 215. *See also* Twitter
society of the spectacle, 11
software issues, 208–9, 210
"So much for the tolerant left" meme, **58**, **58n1**
songs (hypothetical), 178, 179, 180
South Asian publishers, 169, 170, 172, 174
Spotify, **85n5**; playlists, **32n10**, 229–30, **239**
spreadsheets, 206
spy novels, 126
Squires, Claire: boats and ferries, **91n3**; *The Cambridge History of the Book in Britain: Volume 7* (Nash, Squires and Willison, eds), 212, 216; cocktail suggestion, 118n26; "Dear Diary" entries, 205–6, 207–8, 210–13, 217; on diversity deficit, **80n6**; "The Epistemology of Ullapoolism", 113; *The Frankfurt Book Fair and Bestseller Business* (Driscoll and Squires), 3, 9, 20n3, **38n16**, **40n7**, **45n6**, **46n8**, **46n9**, **51n8**; *The Frankfurt Kabuff Critical Edition* (Driscoll and Squires), 18–20, 216, 219n4; politics of FBF, 155; on *Scottish Review of Books*, **70n6**, 212. *See also* Squiscoll, Blaire
Squiscoll, Blaire: birth of, 6; *The Beijing Kabuff*, 215; boats and ferries, **91n3**; coining of name, 6; *The COP26 Kabuff*, **37n13**, **240**; *The Corona Kabuff*, 116, **231–39**; "Dear Diary" entries, 210, 212, 217; and Frak's fan fiction, 19, 187, 194; *The Frankfurt Kabuff*, **25–93**; *The Frankfurt Kabuff* Advanced Information sheets, 220; *The Highland Kabuffling*, **240**; imaginary bookshelves, 17; interparatext, 17; Kelvin Smith *Kabuff* review, 195; map of future novels, *241*; NUNU OTOT comic strip, *228*; penchant for shoes and Negronis, 98; and satire, 16; SHARP conference abstract proposal, 222–23; signature cocktail, 114; *Tante Fran's May 1968 Book Club*, **44n3**; using *Kabuff* in the

classroom, 197; Wilkins tutorial, 97. *See also The Frankfurt Kabuff* (Squiscoll)
SSHRC (Social Sciences and Humanities Research Council), 22n28
stands, at FBF, **45**, **45–46n6**, **46n9**, **48n2**, **49n2**, **51–52**, **65n6**, 157
Stein, Philip, **51n9**
stereotypes, 16
Stirling, University of, 211, 212
story writing, 98–100
straplines, **70n1**, 102
structure of narratives, 97, 98, 99–100
strudel, 180
students, 155, 197–99, 212, 217
style, and substance, 164–66
submissions policies, **88**
subsidiary rights, 172
suits, blue, **33**, **33n14**, **36**, **46**, **46n7**, **50**, **55**
Summer, Chelsea G., **42n2**
The Summer Colophon (cocktail), 117, 191, *191*, 192, 194
SUPERCALIFRAGILISTICEXPIA-LIDOCIOUS key, 205, 219n5
supply-chain logistics, **41**, **41n10**, 213
Surrealists, 11
sustainability, 15, **47n10**
Swaya, Nathan, 108
Sweden, 157
Sydney, **42n1**, **91n3**
symbolic capital, 10, **70**, 101, 122, 163
systems theory, 154

tagging, 194
taglines, 102, 188, 212
TANTE FRAN (character): Beatrice meets, **43**; blessing of union, **63n11**; book club, **43**, **43n4**, **44**, **44n3**, **53**, **66**, **67**, **74**, **76–79**, **83**, 104, 162–65, 195, 222–23; and Caspian relation, **36**, **43**, 163, **232**; in *The Corona Kabuff*, **232**; feminist solidarity and hugs, **77**, **79**; knitting needles, **67**, **74**; and Kurt Weidenfeld, **44**, **44n3**, **88**, 162; letter to Beatrice, **79**; retirement, **232**; in SHARP conference abstract proposal, 222–23; shoe shop, **36**, **43**, **43n3**, **56**, **63n11**, **75**, 165; telephonic communication, **44n1**; text discussion, 104, 162–65, 195, 222–23
Tante Fran's May 1968 Book Club (Squiscoll), **44n3**
tartan-noir, 129
tastes, **35n4**, 122, 123, 164, 166
taxi drivers, book pitches from, 7, **45**, **45n4**, **73**, 104
teaching, 19, 197–99
technology, **48n1**, **70n9**, **77**
telephones, **44n1**, **64n2**
theorists (white, male), 11
theory, niche appeal of, 14
Thoburn, Nicholas, 12
Thompson, John, 130
thriller genre, 8, 15, 19, **48n1**, **59n5**, **65n5**, 125, 126, 135, 217
tinny (small metal boat), **91n3**
Title Editor. *See* Nielsen: Title Editor
Todd, Anna, *After*, 149
toilet paper, **236**, **237**, **238**
toilets, **46**, **46n9**, **47**, **47n10**, **50**, **50n5**
Tokarczuk, Olga, **81n11**
tolerant left meme, **58**, **58n1**
Tolkien, J. R. R., **32n8**
Tories, dressing like, **33n14**
tote bags, **32**, **40**, **40n7**, **74**
trade fairs: knock knock joke, 226. *See also* book fairs
tragedies, 99

Key to index styles: **bold** pp. no. = *Kabuff* novella and fictions · *italic* pp. no. = images · notes format = 35n3 · CHARACTERS · Screenplay

translation rights, 8, **92**, 172
translations, **76**, **232**, **238**
transliteration of accents, **37n12**
tropes, old-fashioned, **62n8**
trumpets, unlikely, **66n10**

Twitter: Author Yurt account, 115; "Dear Diary" entries, 212, 217; Frak's fan fiction, 187–92, 194; inspiration for Das's *A Frankfurt Memoir*, 170; Spotify playlists, 229; tolerant left meme, **58n1**; using *Kabuff* in the classroom, 198

typefaces and typography, **39n1**, **55**, **55n7**, 105, 110, 199[8]

"ÜBER AUTHOR", 203
Ullapoolism: autoethnography, 4, 5; context of conceptual school, 1, 3, 11, 20n4; "Dear Diary" entries, 213; "The Epistemology of Ullapoolism", 113; ferries importance, **37n12**; Frak's fan fiction, 188; fun and ethics, 115; Kabuff Books, 204; Monáe or Murnane quiz, **81n11**; mum confusion, 216; NUNU OTOT, 4, 19, *228*; role of humour, 16; slogans, **77n11**; time machine, 155; THE ULLAPOOLISM MANIFESTO, **77n11**
unboxing, 209, 211
uncoolness, **49n2**
Unheimlich, 181
unity of place, 180
University of Stirling, 211, 212
unsolicited manuscripts, 180
Unwin, Stanley, **32n8**
UPS, 211

vaffanculo, **236**
Vaneigem, Raoul, 222
van Lente, Sandra, **80n6**
Venice, 116, 233–36
vibe of the thing, **81**, **81n10**
vice, **65n4**
Vice President for Intellectual Freedom. *See* WIEL, KRISTOFF
Vinterberg, Thomas, *Festen*, 183n7
violence, 6, 9, **33**, **34**, **35n3**, **51n9**, **52**
visual pleasure, 101
von Trier, Lars, *The Idiots*, 100n7

Walby, Sylvia, 134n63
Warde, Beatrice, 110
water, and bookishness, **84**, **84n3**
"Water Rats" (New South Wales police), **91n3**
Watson, Ash, 6
Watson, Jo, *Big Boned*, 152n5
Watson, Natalie, *Revenge of the Sluts*, 152n5
Wattpad: and chicken shop incident, **31n2**; *The COP26 Kabuff*, **240**; *The Corona Kabuff*, **239**; *The Frankfurt Kabuff* history, 6, 7, 11, 15, **31n2**, 104, 148–50, 152n3; *The Highland Kabuffling*, **240**; and narrative structure, 99–100; rejected authors, **75n4**; romancing book culture, 148–50, 152n3
Wattpad Books, 148, 152n5
weather, **39**, **39n1**
Weidenfeld, George, **37n11**, 104, 121, 132n17
WEIDENFELD, KURT (character): in *The Corona Kabuff*, **233**, **236**; in *The Frankfurt Kabuff*, **36–38**, **36n10**, **37n11**, **42**, **44**, **44n3**, **45**, **46**, **50–52**, **53–56**, **65–68**, **73–74**, **75**, **82**, **87–89**; joke, 226; name of, **37n11**, 121; *Publishers Weekly* report, 222; text

8 *See also* key for other typeface and style use in this index.

discussion, 9, 104, 116, 120, 121, 143, 144, 153, 162–65, 195, 198
Weidhaas, Peter, 154
weight: of fair goers, 180; of paper, **36**, **36n8**, **52n11**, **93**, 161, 216, **236**
West, Kanye, "Gold Digger", **32n10**
Whiteness in publishing, 149, 150, 151
White Storm: in *The Corona Kabuff*, **232**; in *The Frankfurt Kabuff*, **37**, **37n14**, **44**, **51**, **52**, **55**, **57**, **61**, **62**, **64**, **65**, **67**, **78**; in SHARP conference abstract proposal, 222; text discussion, 104, 147n36, 153, 161, 163
widows (typesetting), 105
WIEL, KRISTOFF (Vice President for Intellectual Freedom) (character): in *The Frankfurt Kabuff*, **51–52**, **53**, **66–68**, **75–76**, **78**; text discussion, 8–9, 107, 144
Wikipedia, 16, **67n13**
Wilkins, Kim, 6, 7, 18, 19, 204; plotting diagram, *202*
Williams, Pharrell, **85n4**
Williams, Raymond, 119, 127, 133n31
wine: and Being French, 212; dodgy, 174; not being a wine drinker, 188, 189, 191, 192; Prosecco, 231, **237**; red, **40**, **41**, **58**, 116; Sekt, **84**, 113, 143, 161, 195, 221; sparkling (general), **84**, 117; warm white, 136; Weinkabuff, 193. *See also* alcohol; cocktails; Negronis
"woke washing", 166
women: authors of colour, **86n6**; book clubs, **43n4**, **76**; exclusion of, 14; FBF Business Club staff, **49n2**; feeling of danger, **34n1**; female detectives, 129; guilty pleasures, 152; and Kelis's "Milkshake", **85n4**; loving a hero, **82n12**, **82n13**; in publishing, 5, 121, 219n4; readers, 149, 150, 223; status of, 129[9]
Woolf, Virginia, 21n19
Word documents, 209
WordPress, **79**, 199
workmen, and workwomen, **81**, **81n9**
writing books, ease compared to publishing, **70**, 101, 102, 106

XML, **79**, 199

young adult (YA) fiction, **45**, 149
young women readers, 150
Yousafzai, Malala, **86**

Zibrak, Arielle, 152
zines, **37**, **37n13**

9 This book was indexed with pleasure by Paula Clarke Bain, another woman in publishing.

Key to index styles: **bold** pp. no. = *Kabuff* novella and fictions · *italic* pp. no. = images · notes format = 35n3 · CHARACTERS · `Screenplay`